George Haven Putnam

Representative Essays

George Haven Putnam

Representative Essays

ISBN/EAN: 9783744685740

Printed in Europe, USA, Canada, Australia, Japan

Cover: Foto ©Thomas Meinert / pixelio.de

More available books at **www.hansebooks.com**

REPRESENTATIVE ESSAYS

SELECTED FROM THE SERIES OF "PROSE MASTER-
PIECES FROM THE MODERN ESSAYISTS."

COMPRISING

TWELVE UNABRIDGED ESSAYS BY IRVING, LAMB, DE QUINCEY,
EMERSON, ARNOLD, MORLEY, LOWELL, CARLYLE,
MACAULAY, FROUDE, FREEMAN AND
GLADSTONE.

———————

NEW YORK AND LONDON

G. P. PUTNAM'S SONS

The Knickerbocker Press

1886

PREFACE.

THE present volume has been prepared for the purpose more particularly of meeting the requirements of students and teachers who were not in a position to use advantageously the full series of Essays presented in the set of "Prose Masterpieces from the Modern Essayists."

The purpose of the "Prose Masterpieces" was stated by the editor to be, to bring together such productions of the great modern writers of English prose as should not only present good specimens of English style, but should also be fairly characteristic of the methods of thought and manner of expression of the several writers.

The present selection comprises twelve out of the twenty papers given in the original set, those contributions having been omitted which seemed less likely to prove of interest for younger readers.

As in the larger series, only complete essays are given, in which the thoughts and arguments of the writers on the several subjects considered, find their full expression.

The editor believes that the selections presented, can safely be recommended to students as specimens of effective literary expression and of finished literary style.

G. H. P.

CONTENTS.

THE MUTABILITY OF LITERATURE.

A COLLOQUY IN WESTMINSTER ABBEY.

BY WASHINGTON IRVING.

(BORN 1783, DIED 1859.)

> I know that all beneath the moon decays,
> And what by mortals in this world is brought,
> In time's great period shall return to naught.
> I know that all the muse's heavenly lays,
> With toil of sprite which are so dearly bought,
> As idle sounds, of few or none are sought;
> That there is nothing lighter than mere praise.
>
> DRUMMOND OF HAWTHORNDEN.

HERE are certain half-dreaming moods of mind, in which we naturally steal away from noise and glare, and seek some quiet haunt, where we may indulge our reveries and build our air-castles undisturbed. In such a mood I was loitering about the old gray cloisters of Westminster Abbey, enjoying that luxury of wandering thought which one is apt to dignify with the name of reflection; when suddenly an interruption of madcap boys from Westminster School, playing at football, broke in upon the monastic stillness of the place, making the vaulted passages and mouldering tombs echo with their merriment. I sought to take refuge from their noise by penetrating still deeper into the solitudes of the pile, and applied to one of the vergers for admission to the library. He conducted me through a portal rich with the crumbling sculpture of former ages, which opened upon a gloomy passage leading to the chapter-house and the chamber in which dooms-day-book is deposited. Just within the passage is a small door on the left. To this the verger applied a key; it was double-locked, and opened with some difficulty, as if seldom used. We now ascended a dark, narrow staircase, and, passing through a second door, entered the library.

I found myself in a lofty antique hall, the roof supported by massive joists of old English oak. It was soberly lighted by a row of Gothic windows at a considerable height from the floor, and which apparently opened upon the roofs of the cloisters. An ancient picture of some reverend dignitary of the church in his robes hung over the fireplace. Around the hall and in a small gallery were the books, arranged in carved oaken cases. They consisted principally of old polemical writers, and were much more worn by time than use. In the centre of the library was a solitary table with two or three books on it, an inkstand without ink, and a few pens parched by long disuse. The place seemed fitted for quiet study and profound medita-tion. It was buried deep among the massive walls of the abbey, and shut up from the tumult of the world. I could only hear now and then the shouts of the schoolboys faintly swelling from the cloisters, and the sound of a bell tolling for prayers, echoing soberly along the roofs of the abbey. By degrees the shouts of merriment grew fainter and fainter, and at length died away; the bell ceased to toll, and a profound silence reigned through the dusky hall.

I had taken down a little thick quarto, curiously bound in parchment, with brass clasps, and seated myself at the table in a venerable elbow-chair. Instead of reading, however, I was beguiled by the solemn monastic air, and lifeless quiet of the place, into a train of musing. As I looked around upon the old volumes in their mouldering covers, thus ranged on the shelves, and apparently never disturbed in their repose, I could not but consider the library a kind of literary catacomb, where authors, like mummies, are piously entombed, and left to blacken and moulder in dusty oblivion.

How much, thought I, has each of these volumes, now thrust aside with such indifference, cost some aching head! how many weary days! how many sleepless nights! How have their authors buried themselves in the solitude of cells and cloisters; shut themselves up from the face of man, and the still more blessed face of nature; and devoted themselves to painful research and intense reflection! And all for what? to occupy an inch of dusty shelf, — to have the title of their works read now and then in a future age, by some drowsy churchman or casual straggler like myself; and in another age to be lost, even to remembrance. Such is the amount of this boasted immortality. A mere temporary rumor, a local sound; like the tone of that bell which has just tolled among these towers, filling the ear for a moment — lingering transiently in echo — and then passing away like a thing that was not!

While I sat half murmuring, half meditating these unprofitable speculations, with my head resting on my hand, I was thrumming with the other hand upon the quarto, until I accidentally loosened the clasps; when, to my utter astonishment, the little book gave two or three yawns, like one awaking from a deep sleep; then a husky hem; and at length began to talk. At first its voice was very hoarse and broken, being much troubled by a cobweb which some studious spider had woven across it; and having probably contracted a cold from long exposure to the chills and damps of the abbey. In a short time, however, it became more distinct, and I soon found it an exceedingly fluent, conversable little tome. Its language, to be sure, was rather quaint and obsolete, and its pronunciation, what, in the present day, would be deemed barbarous; but I shall endeavor, as far as I am able, to render it in modern parlance.

It began with railings about the neglect of the world — about merit being suffered to languish in obscurity, and other such commonplace topics of literary repining, and complained bitterly that it had not been opened for more than two centuries. That the dean only looked now and then into the library, sometimes took down a volume or two, trifled with them for a few moments, and then returned them to their shelves. "What a plague do they mean," said the little quarto, which I began to perceive was somewhat choleric, — "what a plague do they mean by keeping several thousand volumes of us shut up here, and watched by a set of old vergers, like so many beauties in a harem, merely to be looked at now and then by the dean? Books were written to give pleasure and to be enjoyed; and I would have a rule passed that the dean should pay each of us a visit at least once a year; or, if he is not equal to the task, let them once in a while turn loose the whole School of Westminster among us, that at any rate we may now and then have an airing."

"Softly, my worthy friend," replied I; "you are not aware how much better you are off than most books of your generation. By being stored away in this ancient library, you are like the treasured remains of those saints and monarchs which lie enshrined in the adjoining chapels; while the remains of your contemporary mortals, left to the ordinary course of nature, have long since returned to dust."

"Sir," said the little tome, ruffling his leaves and looking big, "I was written for all the world, not for the bookworms of an abbey. I was intended to circulate from hand to hand, like other great contemporary works; but here have I been clasped up for more than two centuries, and might have silently fallen a prey to these worms that are playing the very vengeance with my intestines, if you had not by chance given me an opportunity of uttering a few last words before I go to pieces."

"My good friend," rejoined I, "had you been left to the circulation of which you speak, you would long ere this have been no more. To judge from your physiognomy, you are now well stricken in years: very few of your contemporaries can be at present in existence; and those few owe their longevity to being immured like yourself in old libraries; which, suffer me to add, instead of likening to harems, you might more properly and gratefully have compared to those infirmaries attached to religious establishments, for the benefit of the old and decrepit, and where, by quiet fostering and no employment, they often endure to an amazingly good-for-nothing old age. You talk of your contemporaries as if in circulation, — where do we meet with their works? What do we hear of Robert Groteste, of Lincoln? No one could have toiled harder than he for immortality. He is said to have written nearly two hundred volumes. He built, as it were, a pyramid of books to perpetuate his name; but, alas! the pyramid has long since fallen, and only a few fragments are scattered in various libraries, where they are scarcely disturbed even by the antiquarian. What do we hear of Giraldus Cambrensis, the historian, antiquary, philosopher, theologian, and poet? He declined two bishoprics, that he might shut himself up and write for posterity : but posterity never inquires after his labors. What of Henry of Huntingdon, who, besides a learned history of England, wrote a treatise on the contempt of the world, which the world has revenged by forgetting him? What is quoted of Joseph of Exeter, styled the miracle of his age in classical composition? Of his three great heroic poems one is lost forever, excepting a mere fragment; the others are known only to a few of the curious in literature; and as to his love-verses and epigrams, they have entirely disappeared. What is in current use of John Wallis, the Franciscan, who acquired the name of the tree of life? Of William of Malmsbury; of Simeon of Durham; of Benedict of Peterborough; of John Hanvill of St. Albans; of———"

"Prithee, friend," cried the quarto, in a testy tone, "how old do you think me? You are talking of authors that lived long before my time, and wrote either in Latin or French, so that they in a manner expatriated themselves, and deserved to be forgotten[1]; but I, sir, was ushered into the world from the press

---

[1] In Latin and French hath many soueraine wittes had great delyte to endite, and have many noble thinges fulfilde, but certes there ben some that speaken their poisye in French, of whith speche the Frenchmen have as good a fantasye as we have in hearying of Frenchmen's Englishe. — *Chaucer's Testament of Love.*

of the renowned Wynkyn de Worde. .I was written in my own native tongue, at a time when the language had become fixed ; and, indeed, I was considered a model of pure and elegant English."

(I should observe that these remarks were couched in such intolerably antiquated terms, that I have had infinite difficulty in rendering them into modern phraseology.)

" I cry your mercy," said I, " for mistaking your age ; but it matters little : almost all the writers of your time have likewise passed into forgetfulness ; and De Worde's publications are mere literary rarities among book-collectors. The purity and stability of language, too, on which you found your claims to perpetuity, have been the fallacious dependence of authors of every age, even back to the times of the worthy Robert of Glou-cester, who wrote his history in rhymes of mongrel Saxon.[1] Even now many talk of Spenser's ' Well of pure English unde-filed ' as if the language ever sprang from a well or fountain-head, and was not rather a mere confluence of various tongues, perpetually subject to changes and intermixtures. It is this which has made English literature so extremely mutable, and the reputation built upon it so fleeting. Unless thought can be committed to something more permanent and unchangeable than such a medium, even thought must share the fate of everything

---

· 1 Holinshed, in his Chronicle, observes : " Afterwards, also, by deligent travell of Geffry Chaucer and of John Gowre, in the time of Richard the Second, and after them of John Scogan and John Lydgate, monke of Berrie, our said toong was brought to an excellent passe, notwithstanding that it never came unto the type of perfection until the time of Queen Elizabeth, wherein John Jewell, Bishop of Sarum, John Fox, and sundrie learned and excellent writers, have fully accomplished the ornature of the same, to their great praise and immortal commendation.

else, and fall into decay. This should serve as a check upon the vanity and exultation of the most popular writer. He finds the language in which he has embarked his fame gradually altering, and subject to the dilapidations of time and the caprice of fashion. He looks back and beholds the early authors of his country, once the favorites of their day, supplanted by modern writers. A few short ages have covered them with obscurity, and their merits can only be relished by the quaint taste of the bookworm. And such, he anticipates, will be the fate of his own work, which, however it may be admired in its day, and held up as a model of purity, will in the course of years grow antiquated and obsolete ; until it shall become almost as unintelligible in its native land as an Egyptian obelisk, or one of those Runic inscriptions said to exist in the deserts of Tartary. I declare," added I, with some emotion, " when I contemplate a modern library, filled with new works, in all the bravery of rich gilding and binding, I feel disposed to sit down and weep ; like the good Xerxes, when he surveyed his army, pranked out in all the splendor of military array, and reflected that in one hundred years not one of them would be in existence ! "

" Ah," said the little quarto, with a heavy sigh, " I see how it is ; these modern scribblers have superseded all the good old authors. I suppose nothing is read nowadays but Sir Philip Sydney's ' Arcadia,' Sackville's stately plays, and ' Mirror for Magistrates,' or the fine-spun euphuisms of the ' unparalleled John Lyly.' "

" There you are again mistaken," said I ; " the writers whom you suppose in vogue, because they happened to be so when you were last in circulation, have long since had their day. Sir

Philip Sydney's 'Arcadia,' the immortality of which was so fondly predicted by his admirers,[1] and which, in truth, is full of noble thoughts, delicate images, and graceful turns of language, is now scarcely ever mentioned. Sackville has strutted into obscurity; and even Lyly, though his writings were once the delight of a court, and apparently perpetuated by a proverb, is now scarcely known even by name. A whole crowd of authors who wrote and wrangled at the time, have likewise gone down, with all their writings and their controversies. Wave after wave of succeeding literature has rolled over them, until they are buried so deep, that it is only now and then that some industrious diver after fragments of antiquity brings up a specimen for the gratification of the curious.

"For my part," I continued, "I consider this mutability of language a wise precaution of Providence for the benefit of the world at large, and of authors in particular. To reason from analogy, we daily behold the varied and beautiful tribes of vegetables springing up, flourishing, adorning the fields for a short time, and then fading into dust, to make way for their successors. Were not this the case, the fecundity of nature would be a grievance instead of a blessing. The earth would groan with rank and excessive vegetation, and its surface become a tangled wilderness. In like manner the works of genius and learning decline, and make way for subsequent productions. Language

---

1 Live ever sweete booke; the simple image of his gentle witt, and the golden-pillar of his noble courage; and ever notify unto the world that thy writer was the secretary of eloquence, the breath of the muses, the honey-bee of the daintyest flowers of witt and arte, the pith of morale and intellectual virtues, the arme of Bellona in the field, the tonge of Suada in the chamber, the sprite of Practise in *esse*, and the paragon of excellency in print. — *Harvey Pierce's Supererogation.*

gradually varies, and with it fade away the writings of authors who have flourished their allotted time; otherwise, the creative powers of genius would overstock the world, and the mind would be completely bewildered in the endless mazes of literature. Formerly there were some restraints on this excessive multiplication. Works had to be transcribed by hand, which was a slow and laborious operation; they were written either on parchment, which was expensive, so that one work was often erased to make way for another; or on papyrus, which was fragile and extremely perishable. Authorship was a limited and unprofitable craft, pursued chiefly by monks in the leisure and solitude of their cloisters. The accumulation of manuscripts was slow and costly, and confined almost entirely to monasteries. To these circumstances it may, in some measure, be owing that we have not been inundated by the intellect of antiquity; that the fountains of thought have not been broken up, and modern genius drowned in the deluge. But the inventions of paper and the press have put an end to all these restraints. They have made everyone a writer, and enabled every mind to pour itself into print, and diffuse itself over the whole intellectual world. The consequences are alarming. The stream of literature has swollen into a torrent — augmented into a river — expanded into a sea. A few centuries since, five or six hundred manuscripts constituted a great library; but what would you say to libraries such as actually exist, containing three or four hundred thousand volumes; legions of authors at the same time busy; and the press going on with activity, to double and quadruple the number. Unless some unforeseen mortality should break out among the progeny of the Muse, now that she has become so prolific, I tremble for posterity. I fear the mere fluctuation of language will not be sufficient. Criticism may do much. It increases with the increase of literature, and resembles one of those salutary checks on population spoken of by economists. All possible encouragement, therefore, should be given to the growth of critics, good or bad. But I fear all will be in vain; let criticism do what it may, writers will write, printers will print, and the world will inevitably be overstocked with good books. It will soon be the employment of a lifetime merely to learn their names. Many a man of passable information, at the present day, reads scarcely anything but reviews; and before long a man of erudition will be little better than a mere walking catalogue."

"My very good sir," said the little quarto, yawning most drearily in my face, "excuse my interrupting you, but I perceive you are rather given to prose. I would ask the fate of an author who was making some noise just as I left the world. His reputation, however, was considered quite temporary. The learned shook their heads at him, for he was a poor, half-educated varlet, that knew little of Latin, and nothing of Greek, and had been obliged to run the country for deer-stealing. I think his name was Shakespeare. I presume he soon sunk into oblivion."

"On the contrary," said I, "it is owing to that very man that the literature of his period has experienced a duration beyond the ordinary term of English literature. There rise authors now and then, who seem proof against the mutability of language, because they have rooted themselves in the unchanging principles of human nature. They are like gigantic trees that we sometimes see on the banks of a stream; which, by their vast and deep roots, penetrating through the mere surface, and laying hold on the very foundations of the earth, preserve the soil around them from being swept away by the ever-flowing current, and hold up many a neighboring plant, and, perhaps, worthless weed, to perpetuity. Such is the case with Shakespeare, whom we behold defying the encroachments of time, retaining in modern use the language and literature of his day, and giving duration to many an indifferent author, merely from having flourished in his vicinity. But even he, I grieve to say, is gradually assuming the tint of age, and his whole form is overrun by a profusion of commentators, who, like clambering vines and creepers, almost bury the noble plant that upholds them."

Here the little quarto began to heave his sides and chuckle, until at length he broke out in a plethoric fit of laughter that had well-nigh choked him, by reason of his excessive corpulency. "Mighty well!" cried he, as soon as he could recover breath; "mighty well! and so you would persuade me that the literature of an age is to be perpetuated by a vagabond deer-stealer! by a man without learning! by a poet, forsooth — a poet!" And here he wheezed forth another fit of laughter.

I confess that I felt somewhat nettled at this rudeness, which, however, I pardoned on account of his having flourished in a less polished age. I determined, nevertheless, not to give up my point.

"Yes," resumed I, positively, "a poet; for of all writers he has the best chance for immortality. Others may write from the head, but he writes from the heart, and the heart will always understand him. He is the faithful portrayer of nature, whose features are always the same, and always interesting. Prose-writers are voluminous and unwieldy; their pages are crowded with commonplaces, and their thoughts expanded into tedious-ness. But with the true poet every thing is terse, touching, or brilliant. He gives the choicest thoughts in the choicest lan-guage. He illustrates them by everything that he sees most striking in nature and art. He enriches them by pictures of human life, such as it is passing before him. His writings, therefore, contain the spirit, the aroma, if I may use the phrase, of the age in which he lives. They are caskets which enclose within a small compass the wealth of the language, — its family jewels, which are thus transmitted in a portable form to poster-ity. The setting may occasionally be antiquated, and require now and then to be renewed, as in the case of Chaucer; but the brilliancy and intrinsic value of the gems continue unaltered. Cast a look back over the long reach of literary history. What vast valleys of dulness, filled with monkish legends and acade-mical controversies ! what bogs of theological speculations ! what dreary wastes of metaphysics ! Here and there only do we behold the heaven-illuminated bards, elevated like beacons on their widely separate heights, to transmit the pure light of poeti-cal intelligence from age to age." [1]

---

1 Thorow earth and waters deepe,
   The pen by skill doth passe ;
And featly nyps the worldes abuse,
   And shoes us in a glasse
The vertu and the vice
   Of every wight alyve :
The honey comb that bee doth make
   Is not so sweet in hyve,

I was just about to launch forth into eulogiums upon the poets of the day, when the sudden opening of the door caused me to turn my head. It was the verger who came to inform me that it was time to close the library. I sought to have a parting word with the quarto, but the worthy little tome was silent; the clasps were closed; and it looked perfectly unconscious of all that had passed. I have been to the library two or three times since, and have endeavored to draw it into further conversation, but in vain; and whether all this rambling colloquy actually took place, or whether it was another of those odd day-dreams to which I am subject, I have never to this moment been able to discover.

As are the golden leves
  That drop from poet's head!
Which doth surmount our common talke
  As farre as dross doth lead.

Churchyard.

IMPERFECT SYMPATHIES.

BY CHARLES LAMB.
(BORN 1775, DIED 1834.)

" I am of a constitution so general, that it consorts and sympathizeth with all things; I have no antipathy, or rather idiosyncrasy in anything. Those natural repugnancies do not touch me, nor do I behold with prejudice the French, Italian, Spaniard, or Dutch." — *Religio Medici.*

HAT the author of the " Religio Medici," mounted upon the airy stilts of abstraction, conversant about notional and conjectural essences — in whose categories of Being the possible took the upper hand of the actual — should have overlooked the impertinent individualities of such poor concretions as mankind, is not much to be admired. It is rather to be wondered at, that in the genus of animals he should have condescended to distinguish that species at all. For myself — earth-bound and fettered to the scene of my activities —

Standing on earth, nor rapt above the sky,

I confess that I do feel the differences of mankind, national or individual, to an unhealthy excess. I can look with no indifferent eye upon things or persons. Whatever is, is to me a matter of taste or distaste; or when once it becomes indifferent, it begins to be disrelishing. I am, in plainer words, a bundle of prejudices — made up of likings and dislikings — the veriest thrall to sympathies, apathies, antipathies. In a certain sense, I hope it may be said of me that I am a lover of my species. I can feel for all indifferently, but I cannot feel toward all equally. The more purely-English word that expresses sympathy, will better explain my meaning. I can be a friend to a worthy man, who upon another account, cannot be my mate or *fellow*. I cannot *like* all people alike.[1]

I have been trying all my life to like Scotchmen, and am obliged to desist from the experiment in despair. They cannot like me — and, in truth, I never knew one of that nation who attempted to do it. There is something more plain and ingenuous in their mode of proceeding. We know one another at first sight. There is an order of imperfect intellects (under which

---

1 I would be understood as confining myself to the subject of *imperfect sympathies*. To nations or classes of men there can be no direct antipathy. There may be individuals born and constellated so opposite to another individual nature, that the same sphere cannot hold them. I have met with my moral antipodes, and can believe the story of two persons meeting (who never saw one another before in their lives) and instantly fighting.

> We by proof find there should be
> 'Twixt man and man such an antipathy,
> That though he can show no just reason why
> For any former wrong or injury,
> Can neither find a blemish in his fame,
> Nor aught in face or feature justly blame,
> Can challenge or accuse him of no evil,
> Yet notwithstanding, hates him as a devil.

The lines are from old Heywood's " Hierarchie of Angels," and he subjoins a curious story in confirmation, of a Spaniard who attempted to assassinate a King Ferdinand of Spain, and being put to the rack could give no other reason for the deed but an inveterate antipathy which he had taken to the first sight of the king.

> The cause which to that act compell'd him
> Was, he ne'er loved him since he first beheld him.

mine must be content to rank) which in its constitution is essentially anti-Caledonian. The owners of the sort of faculties I allude to, have minds rather suggestive than comprehensive. They have no pretences to much clearness or precision in their ideas, or in their manner of expressing them. Their intellectual wardrobe (to confess fairly) has few whole pieces in it. They are content with fragments and scattered pieces of Truth. She presents no full front to them — a feature of side-face at the most. Hints and glimpses, germs and crude essays at a system, is the utmost they pretend to. They beat up a little game peradventure — and leave it to knottier heads, more robust constitutions, to run it down. The light that lights them is not steady and polar, but mutable and shifting: waxing, and again waning. Their conversation is accordingly. They will throw out a random word in or out of season, and be content to let it pass for what it is worth. They cannot speak always as if they were upon their oath — but must be understood, speaking or writing, with some abatement. They seldom wait to mature a proposition, but e'en bring it to market in the green ear. They delight to impart their defective discoveries as they arise, without waiting for their full development. They are no systematizers, and would but err more by attempting it. Their minds, as I said before, are suggestive merely. The brain of a true Caledonian (if I am not mistaken) is constituted upon quite a different plan. His Minerva is born in panoply. You are never admitted to see his ideas in their growth — if, indeed, they do grow, and are not rather put together upon principles of clock-work. You never catch his mind in an undress. He never hints or suggests anything, but unlades his stock of ideas in perfect order and completeness. He brings his total wealth into company, and gravely unpacks it. His riches are always about him. He never stoops to catch a glittering something in your presence to share it with you, before he quite knows whether it be true touch or not. You cannot cry *halves* to anything that he finds. He does not find, but bring. You never witness his first apprehension of a thing. His understanding is always at its meridian — you never see the first dawn, the early streaks. He has no falterings of self-suspicion. Surmises, guesses, misgivings, half-intuitions, semi-consciousnesses, partial illuminations, dim instincts, embryo conceptions, have no place in his brain or vocabulary. The twilight of dubiety never falls upon him. Is he orthodox — he has no doubts. Is he an infidel — he has none either. Between the affirmative and the negative there is no border-land with him. You cannot hover with him upon the confines of truth, or wander in the maze of a probable argument. He always keeps the path. You cannot make excursions with him — for he sets you right. His taste never fluctuates. His morality never abates. He cannot compromise, or understand middle actions. There can be but a right and a wrong. His conversation is as a book. His affirmations have the sanctity of an oath. You must speak upon the square with him. He stops a metaphor like a suspected person in an enemy's country. " A healthy book ? " said one of his countrymen to me, who had ventured to give that appellation to " John Buncle," — "did I catch rightly what you said ? I have heard of a man in health, and of a healthy state of body, but I do not see how that epithet can be properly applied to a book." Above all, you must beware of indirect expressions before a Cale-

donian. Clap an extinguisher upon your irony, if you are unhappily blessed with a vein of it. Remember you are upon
your oath. I have a print of a graceful female after Leonardo
da Vinci, which I was showing off to Mr. ——. After he had
examined it minutely, I ventured to ask him how he liked MY
BEAUTY (a foolish name it goes by among my friends) — when he
very gravely assured me, that "he had considerable respect for
my character and talents" (so he was pleased to say), "but had
not, given himself much thought about the degree of my personal pretensions." The misconception staggered me, but did
not seem much to disconcert him. Persons of this nation are
particularly fond of affirming a truth — which nobody doubts.
They do not so properly affirm, as annunciate it. They do indeed appear to have such a love for truth (as if, like virtue, it
were valuable for itself) that all truth becomes equally valuable,
whether the proposition that contains it be new or old, disputed,
or such as is impossible to become a subject of disputation. I
was present not long since at a party of North Britons, where a
son of Burns was expected; and happened to drop a silly expression (in my South British way), that I wished it were the
father instead of the son — when four of them started up at
once to inform me, that "that was impossible, because he was
dead." An impracticable wish, it seems, was more than they
could conceive. Swift has hit off this part of their character,
namely, their love of truth, in his biting way, but with an illi-
berality that necessarily confines the passage to the margin.[1]

---

[1] There are some people who think they sufficiently acquit themselves, and entertain their company, with relating facts of no consequence, not at all out of the road of
such common incidents as happen every day; and this I have observed more fre-

The tediousness of these people is certainly provoking. I wonder if they ever tire one another? In my early life I had a passionate fondness for the poetry of Burns. I have sometimes foolishly hoped to ingratiate myself with his countrymen by expressing it. But I have always found that a true Scot resents your admiration of his compatriot, even more than he would your contempt of him. The latter he imputes to your "imperfect acquaintance with many of the words which he uses;" and the same objection makes it a presumption in you to suppose that you can admire him. Thompson they seem to have forgotten. Smollett they have neither forgotten nor forgiven, for his delineation of Rory and his companion, upon their first introduction to our metropolis. Speak of Smollett as a great genius, and they will retort upon you Hume's History compared with *his* continuation of it. What if the historian had continued Humphrey Clinker?

I have, in the abstract, no disrespect for Jews. They are a piece of stubborn antiquity, compared with which Stonehenge is in its nonage. They date beyond the pyramids. But I should not care to be in habits of familiar intercourse with any of that nation. I confess that I have not the nerves to enter their synagogues. Old prejudices cling about me. I cannot shake off the story of Hugh of Lincoln. Centuries of injury, contempt, and hate, on the one side, — of cloaked revenge, dissimulation, and hate, on the other, between our and their fathers,

---

quently among the Scotch than any other nation, who are very careful not to omit the minutest circumstances of time or place; which kind of discourse, if it were not a little relieved by the uncouth terms and phrases, as well as accent and gestures peculiar to that country, would be hardly tolerable. — *Hints Toward an Essay on Conversation.*

must and ought to affect the blood of the children. I cannot believe it can run clear and kindly yet; or that a few fine words, such as candor, liberality, the light of a nineteenth century, can close up the breaches of so deadly a disunion. A Hebrew is nowhere congenial to me. He is least distasteful on 'Change — for the mercantile spirit levels all distinctions, as all are beauties in the dark. I boldly confess that I do not relish the approximation of Jew and Christian, which has become so fashionable. The reciprocal endearments have, to me, something hypocritical and unnatural in them. I do not like to see the Church and Synagogue kissing and congeeing in awkward postures of an affected civility. If *they* are converted, why do they not come over to us altogether? Why keep up a form of separation when the life of it is fled? If they can sit with us at table, why do they kick at our cookery? I do not understand these half-convertites. Jews christianizing — Christians judaizing — puzzle me. I like fish or flesh. A moderate Jew is a more confounding piece of anomaly than a wet Quaker. The spirit of the synagogue is essentially *separative.* B—— would have been more in keeping if he had abided by the faith of his forefathers. There is a fine scorn in his face which nature meant to be of —— Christians. The Hebrew spirit is strong in him, in spite of his proselytism. He cannot conquer the shibboleth. How it breaks out when he sings, "The children of Israel passed through the Red Sea!" The auditors, for the moment, are as Egyptians to him, and he rides over our necks in triumph. There is no mistaking him. B—— has a strong expression of sense in his countenance, and it is confirmed by his singing. The foundation of his vocal excellence is sense.

He sings with understanding, as Kemble delivered dialogue. He would sing the Commandments, and give an appropriate character to each prohibition. His nation in general have not over-sensible countenances. How should they? — but you seldom see a silly expression among them. Gain, and the pursuit of gain, sharpen a man's visage. I never heard of an idiot being born among them. Some admire the Jewish female physiognomy. I admire it but with trembling. Jael had those full, dark, inscrutable eyes.

In the negro countenance you will often meet with strong traits of benignity. I have felt yearnings of tenderness toward some of these faces — or rather masks — that have looked out kindly upon one in casual encounters in the streets and highways. I love what Fuller beautifully calls — these "images of God cut in ebony." But I should not like to associate with them, to share my meals and my good nights with them — because they are black.

I love Quaker ways, and Quaker worship. I venerate the Quaker principles. It does me good for the rest of the day when I meet any of their people in my path. When I am ruffled or disturbed by any occurrence, the sight, or quiet voice of a Quaker, acts upon me as a ventilator, lightening the air, and taking off a load from the bosom. But I cannot like the Quakers (as Desdemona would say) "to live with them." I am all over sophisticated — with humors, fancies, craving hourly sympathy. I must have books, pictures, theatres, chit-chat, scandal, jokes, ambiguities, and a thousand whimwhams, which their simpler taste can do without. I should starve at their primitive banquet. My appetites are too high for the salads

which (according to Evelyn) Eve dressed for the angel; my
gusto too excited

> To sit a guest with Daniel at his pulse.

The indirect answers which Quakers are often found to return
to a question put to them may be explained, I think, without the
vulgar assumption that they are more given to evasion and
equivocating than other people. They naturally look to their
words more carefully, and are more cautious of committing
themselves. They have a peculiar character to keep up on this
head. They stand in a manner upon their veracity. A Quaker
is by law exempted from taking an oath. The custom of resort-
ing to an oath in extreme cases, sanctified as it is by all religious
antiquity, is apt (it must be confessed) to introduce into the
laxer sort of minds the notion of two kinds of truth, — the one
applicable to the solemn affairs of justice, and the other to the
common proceedings of daily intercourse. As truth bound upon
the conscience by an oath can be but truth, so in the common
affirmations of the shop and the market-place a latitude is expected and conceded upon questions wanting this solemn coven-
ant. Something less than truth satisfies. It is common to hear
a person say, " You do not expect me to speak as if I were upon
my oath." Hence a great deal of incorrectness and inadvertency,
short of falsehood, creeps into ordinary conversation; and a kind
of secondary or laic-truth is tolerated, where clergy-truth — oath-
truth — by the nature of the circumstances, is not required. A
Quaker knows none of this distinction. His simple affirmation
being received, upon the most sacred occasions, without any further test, stamps a value upon the words which he is to use upon
the most indifferent topics of life. He looks to them naturally

with more severity. You can have of him no more than his word. He knows if he is caught tripping in a casual expression, he forfeits, for himself at least, his claim to the invidious exemption. He knows that his syllables are weighed — and how far a consciousness of this particular watchfulness, exerted against a person, has a tendency to produce indirect answers, and a diverting of the question by honest means, might be illustrated, and the practice justified, by a more sacred example than is proper to be adduced upon this occasion. The admirable presence of mind, which is notorious in Quakers upon all contingencies, might be traced to this imposed self-watchfulness — if it did not seem rather an humble and secular scion of that old stock of religious constancy, which never bent or faltered, in the Primitive Friends, or gave way to the winds of persecution, to the violence of judge or accuser, under trials and racking examinations. "You will never be the wiser, if I sit here answering your questions till midnight," said one of those upright justicers to Penn, who had been putting law cases with a puzzling subtlety. "Thereafter as the answers may be," retorted the Quaker. The astonishing composure of this people is sometimes ludicrously displayed in lighter instances. I was travelling in a stage-coach with three male Quakers, buttoned up in the straitest nonconformity of their sect. We stopped to bait at Andover, where a meal, partly tea apparatus, partly supper, was set before us. My friends confined themselves to the tea-table. I in my way took supper. When the landlady brought in the bill, the eldest of my companions discovered that she had charged for both meals. This was resisted. Mine hostess was very clamorous and positive. Some mild arguments were used on the part of the Quakers, for which the heated mind of the good lady seemed by no means a fit recipient. The guard came in with his usual peremptory notice. The Quakers pulled out their money and formally tendered it—so much for tea—I, in humble imitation, tendering mine—for the supper which I had taken. She would not relax in her demand. So they all three quietly put up their silver, as did myself, and marched out of the room, the eldest and gravest going first, with myself closing up the rear, who thought I could not do better than follow the example of such grave and warrantable personages. We got in. The steps went up. The coach drove off. The murmurs of mine hostess, not very indistinctly or ambiguously pronounced, became after a time inaudible—and now my conscience, which the whimsical scene had for a while suspended, beginning to give some twitches, I waited in the hope that some justification would be offered by these serious persons for the seeming injustice of their conduct. To my great surprise, not a syllable was dropped on the subject. They sat as mute as at a meeting. At length the eldest of them broke silence, by inquiring of his next neighbor, "Hast thee heard how indigos go at the India House?" and the question operated as a soporific on my moral feeling as far as Exeter.

CONVERSATION.

BY THOMAS DE QUINCEY.

(BORN 1785, DIED 1859.)

MONGST the arts connected with the *elegancies* of social life, in a degree which nobody denies, is the art of conversation; but in a degree which almost everybody denies, if one may judge by their neglect of its simplest rules, this same art is not less connected with the *uses* of social life. Neither the luxury of conversation, nor the possible benefit of conversation, is to be under that rude administration of it which generally prevails. Without an art, without some simple system of rules, gathered from experience of such contingencies as are most likely to mislead the practice, when left to its own guidance, no act of man nor effort accomplishes its purposes in perfection. The sagacious Greek would not so much as drink a glass of wine amongst a few friends without a systematic art to guide him, and a regular form of polity to control him, which art and which polity (begging Plato's pardon) were better than any of more ambitious aim in his "Republic." Every *symposium* had its set of rules, and vigorous they were; had its own *symposiarch* to govern it, and a tyrant he was. Elected democratically, he became, when once installed, an autocrat not less despotic that the king of Persia. Purposes still more slight and fugitive have been organized into arts. Taking soup gracefully, under the difficulties opposed to it by a dinner dress at that time fashionable, was reared into an art about forty-five years ago by a Frenchman, who lectured upon it to ladies in London; and the most brilliant duchess of that day was amongst his best pupils. Spitting — if the reader will pardon the mention of so gross a fact — was shown to be a very difficult art, and 'publicly prelected upon about the same time, in the same great capital. The professors in this faculty were the hackney-coachmen; the pupils were gentlemen who paid a guinea each for three lessons ; the chief problem in this system of hydraulics being to throw the salivating column in a parabolic curve from the centre of Parliament Street, when driving four-in-hand, to the foot pavements, right and left, so as to alarm the consciences of guilty peripatetics on either side. The ultimate problem, which closed the *curriculum* of study, was held to lie in spitting round a corner; when *that* was mastered, the pupil was entitled to his doctor's degree. Endless are the purposes of man, merely festal or merely comic, and aiming but at the momentary life of a cloud, which have earned for themselves the distinction and apparatus of a separate art. Yet for conversation, the great paramount purpose of social meetings, no art exists or has been attempted.

That seems strange, but is not really so. A limited process submits readily to the limits of a technical system; but a process so unlimited as the interchange of thought, seems to reject them. And even, if an art of conversation were less unlimited,

the means of carrying such an art into practical effect, amongst
so vast a variety of minds, seem wanting. Yet again, perhaps,
after all, this may rest on a mistake. What we begin by mis-
judging is the particular phasis of conversation which brings it
under the control of art and discipline. It is not in its relation
to the intellect that conversation ever has been improved or *will*
be improved primarily, but in its relation to manners. Has
a man ever mixed with what in technical phrase is called "good
company," meaning company in the highest degree polished,
company which (being or *not* being aristocratic as respects its
composition) is aristocratic as respects the standard of its
manners and usages? If he really *has*, and does not deceive
himself from vanity or from pure inacquaintance with the world,
in that case he must have remarked the large effect impressed
upon the grace and upon the freedom of conversation by a few
simple instincts of real good-breeding. Good-breeding — what
is it? There is no need in this place to answer that question
comprehensively; it is sufficient to say, that it is made up
chiefly of *negative* elements ; that it shows itself far less in what
it prescribes, than in what it forbids. Now, even under this
limitation of the idea, the truth is, that more will be done for the
benefit of conversation by the simple magic of good-manners
(that is, chiefly by a system of forbearances), applied to the
besetting vices of social intercourse, than ever *was* or *can* be
done by all varieties of intellectual power assembled upon the
same arena.   Intellectual graces of the highest order may
perish and confound each other when exercised in a spirit of
ill-temper, or under the license of bad manners : whereas, very
humble powers, when allowed to expand themselves colloquially

in that genial freedom which is possible only under the most absolute confidence in the self-restraint of your collocutors, accomplish their purpose to a certainty, if it be the ordinary purpose of liberal amusement, and have a chance of accomplishing it even when this purpose is the more ambitous one of communicating knowledge, or exchanging new views upon truth.

In my own early years, having been formed by nature too exclusively and morbidly for solitary thinking, I observed nothing. Seeming to have eyes, in reality I saw nothing. But it is a matter of no very uncommon experience, that, whilst the mere observers never become meditators, the mere meditators, on the other hand, may finally ripen into close observers. Strength of thinking, through long years, upon innumerable themes, will have the effect of disclosing a vast variety of questions, to which it soon becomes apparent that answers are lurking up and down the whole field of daily experience ; and thus an external experience which was slighted in youth, because it was a dark cipher that could be read into no meaning, a key that answered to no lock, gradually becomes interesting as it is found to yield one solution after another to problems that have independently matured in the mind. Thus, for instance, upon the special functions of conversation, upon its powers, its laws, its ordinary diseases, and their appropriate remedies, in youth I never bestowed a thought or a care. I viewed it, not as one amongst the gay ornamental arts of the intellect, but as one amongst the dull necessities of business. Loving solitude too much, I understood too little the capacities of colloquial intercourse. And thus it is, though not for *my* reason, that most people estimate the intellectual relations of conversation. Let these, however, be what they may, one thing seemed undeniable — that this world talked a great deal too much. It would be better for all parties, if nine in every ten of the *winged words* flying about in this world (Homer's *epea pteroenta*) had their feathers clipped amongst men, or even amongst women, who have a right to a larger allowance of words. Yet, as it was quite out of my power to persuade the world into any such self-denying reformation, it seemed equally out of the line of my duties to nourish any moral anxiety in that direction. *To talk* seemed then in the same category as *to sleep;* not an accomplishment, but a base physical infirmity. As a moralist, I really was culpably careless upon the whole subject. I cared as little what absurdities men practised in their vast tennis-courts of conversation, where the ball is flying backward and forward to no purpose forever, as what tricks Englishmen might play with their monstrous national debt. Yet at length what I disregarded on any principle of moral usefulness, I came to make an object of the profoundest interest on principles of art. *Betting*, in like manner, and *wagering*, which apparently had no moral value, and for that reason had been always slighted as inconsiderable arts (though, by the way, they always had one valuable use, namely, that of evading quarrels, since a bet summarily intercepts an altercation), rose suddenly into a philosophic rank, when successively Huyghens, the Bernoullis, and De Moivre, were led, by the suggestion of these trivial practices amongst men, to throw the light of a high mathematical analysis upon the whole doctrine of chances. Lord Bacon had been led to remark the capacities of conversation as an organ for sharpening one particular mode of intellectual power. Circumstances, on the other hand, led me into remarking the special capacities of conversation, as an organ for absolutely creating another mode of power. Let a man have read, thought, studied, as much as he may, rarely will he reach his possible advantages as a *ready* man, unless he has exercised his powers much in conversation — that was Lord Bacon's idea. Now, this wise and useful remark points in a direction not objective, but subjective — that is, it does not promise any absolute extension to truth itself, but only some greater facilities to the man who expounds or diffuses the truth. Nothing will be done for truth objectively that would not at any rate be done, but subjectively it will be done with more fluency, and at less cost of exertion to the doer. On the contrary, my own growing reveries on the latent powers of conversation (which, though a thing that then I hated, yet challenged at times unavoidably my attention) pointed to an absolute birth of new insight into the truth itself, as inseparable from the finer and more scientific exercise of the talking art. It would not be the brilliancy, the ease, or the adroitness of the expounder that would benefit, but the absolute interests of the thing expounded. A feeling dawned on me of a secret magic lurking in the peculiar life, velocities, and contagious ardor of conversation, quite separate from any which belonged to books; arming a man with new forces, and not merely with a new dexterity in wielding the old ones. I felt, and in this I could not be mistaken, as too certainly it was a fact of my own experience, that in the electric kindling of life between two minds, and far less from the kindling natural to conflict (though *that* also is something) than from the kindling through sympathy with the object discussed, in its momentary coruscation of shifting phases, there sometimes arise glimpses and shy revelations of affinity, suggestion, relation, analogy, that could not have been approached through any avenues of methodical study. Great organists find the same effect of inspiration, the same result of power creative and revealing, in the mere movement and velocity of their own voluntaries, like the heavenly wheels of Milton, throwing off fiery flakes and bickering flames; these *impromptu* torrents of music create rapturous *fioriture*, beyond all capacity in the artist to register, or afterward to imitate. The reader must be well aware that many philosophic instances exist where a change in the degree makes a change in the kind. Usually this is otherwise; the prevailing rule is, that the principle subsists unaffected by any possible variation in the amount or degree of the force. But a large class of exceptions must have met the reader, though from want of a pencil he has improperly omitted to write them down in his pocket-book — cases, namely, where, upon passing beyond a certain point in the graduation, an alteration takes place suddenly in the *kind* of effect, a new direction is given to the power. Some illustration of this truth occurs in conversation, where a velocity in the movement of thought is made possible (and often natural), greater than ever can arise in methodical books; and where, secondly, approximations are more obvious and easily effected between things too remote for a steadier contemplation. One remarkable evidence of a *specific* power lying hid in conversation may be seen in such writings as have moved by impulses most nearly resembling those of conversation; for instance, in those of Edmund Burke. For one moment, reader, pause upon the spectacle of two contrasted intellects, Burke's and Johnson's: one, an intellect essentially going forward, governed by the very necessity of growth — by the law of motion in advance; the latter, essentially an intellect retrogressive, retrospective, and throwing itself back on its own steps. This original difference was aided accidentally in Burke by the tendencies of political partisanship, which, both from moving amongst moving things and uncertainties, as compared with the more stationary aspects of moral philosophy, and also from its more fluctuating and fiery passions, must unavoidably reflect in greater life the tumultuary character of conversation. The result from these original differences of intellectual constitution, aided by these secondary differences of pursuit, is, that Dr. Johnson never, in any instance, GROWS a truth before your eyes, whilst in the act of delivering it, or moving toward it. All that he offers, up to the end of the chapter he had when he began. But to Burke, such was the prodigious elasticity of his thinking, equally in his conversation and in his writings, the mere act of movement became the principle or cause of movement. Motion propagated motion, and life threw off life. The very violence of a projectile, as thrown by *him*, caused it to rebound in fresh forms, fresh angles, splintering, coruscating, which gave out thoughts as new (and that would at the beginning have been as startling) to himself as they are to his reader. In this power, which might be illustrated largely from the writings of Burke, is seen something allied to the powers of a prophetic seer, who is compelled oftentimes into seeing things as unexpected by himself as by others. Now, in conversation, considered as to its *tendencies* and capacities, there sleeps an intermitting spring of such sudden revelation, showing much of

the same general character; a power putting on a character
essentially differing from the character worn by the power of
books. •

 If, then, in the *colloquial* commerce of thought, there lurked a
power not shared by other modes of that great commerce,
a power separate and *sui generis*, next it was apparent that a
great art must exist somewhere, applicable to this power; not in
the pyramids, or in the tombs of Thebes, but in the unwrought
quarries of men's minds, so many and so dark. There was an
art missing. If an art, then an artist missing. If the art (as we
say of foreign mails) were "due," then the artist was "due."
How happened it that this great man never made his appearance? But perhaps he *had*. Many people think Dr. Johnson
the *exemplar* of conversational power. I think otherwise, for
reasons which I shall soon explain, and far sooner I should
look for such an *exemplar* in Burke. But neither Johnson nor
Burke, however they might rank as *powers*, was the *artist* that I
demanded. Burke valued not at all the reputation of a great
performer in conversation; he scarcely contemplated the skill
as having a real existence; and a man will never be an artist
who does not value his art, or even recognize it as an object
distinctly defined. Johnson, again, relied sturdily upon his
natural powers for carrying him aggressively through all conversational occasions or difficulties that English society, from its
known character and composition, could be supposed likely to
bring forward, without caring for any art or system of rules that
might give further effect to that power. If a man is strong
enough to knock down ninety-nine in a hundred of all antago-
nists, in spite of any advantages as to pugilistic science which

they may possess over himself, he is not likely to care for the improbable case of a hundredth man appearing with strength equal to his own, superadded to the utmost excess of that artificial skill which is wanting in himself. Against such a contingency it is not worth while going to the cost of a regular pugilistic training. Half a century might not bring up a case of actual call for its application. Or, if it did, for a single *extra* case of that nature, there would always be a resource in the *extra* (and, strictly speaking, foul) arts of kicking, scratching, pinching, and tearing hair.

The conversational powers of Johnson were narrow in compass, however strong within their own essential limits. As a *conditio sine quâ non*, he did not absolutely demand a *personal* contradictor by way of "stoker" to supply fuel and keep up his steam, but he demanded at least a *subject* teeming with elements of known contradictory opinion, whether linked to partisanship or not. His views of all things tended to negation, never to the positive and the creative. Hence may be explained a fact, which cannot have escaped any keen observer of those huge Johnsonian *memorabilia* which we possess, namely, that the gyration of his flight upon any one question that ever came before him was so exceedingly brief. There was no process, no evolution, no movements of self-conflict or preparation; a word, a distinction, a pointed antithesis, and, above all, a new abstraction of the logic involved in some popular fallacy, or doubt, or prejudice, or problem, formed the utmost of his efforts. He dissipated some casual perplexity that had gathered in the eddies of conversation, but he contributed nothing to any weightier interest; he unchoked a strangulated sewer in some blind alley, but what river is there that felt his cleansing power? There is no man that can cite any single error which Dr. Johnson unmasked, or any important truth which he expanded. Nor is this extraordinary. Dr. Johnson had not within himself the fountain of such power, having not a brooding or naturally philosophic intellect. Philosophy in any acquired sense he had none. How else could it have happened that upon David Hartley, upon David Hume, upon Voltaire, upon Rousseau, the true or the false philosophy of his own day, beyond a personal sneer, founded upon some popular slander, he had nothing to say and said nothing? A new world was moulding itself in Dr. Johnson's meridian hours, new generations were ascending, and "other palms were won." Yet of all this the Doctor suspected nothing. Countrymen and contemporaries of the Doctor's, brilliant men, but (as many think) trifling men, such as Horace Walpole and Lord Chesterfield, already in the middle of that eighteenth century, could read the signs of the great changes advancing, already started in horror from the portents which rose before them in Paris, like the procession of regal phantoms before Macbeth, and have left in their letters records undeniable (such as now read like Cassandra prophecies) that already they had noticed tremors in the ground below their feet, and sounds in the air, running before the great convulsions under which Europe was destined to rock full thirty years later. Many instances, during the last war, showed us that in the frivolous dandy might often lurk the most fiery and accomplished of *aides-de-camp;* and these cases show that men, in whom the world sees only elegant *roués,* sometimes from carelessness, sometimes from want of opening for display, conceal qualities of penetrating sagacity, and a learned spirit of observation, such as may be looked for vainly in persons of more solemn and academic pretension. But there was a greater defect in Dr. Johnson, for purposes of conversation, than merely want of eye for the social phenomena rising around him. He had no eye for such phenomena, because he had a somnolent want of interest in them; and why? because he had little interest in man. Having no sympathy with human nature in its struggles, or faith in the progress of man, he could not be supposed to regard with much interest any forerunning symptoms of changes that to him were themselves indifferent. And the reason that he felt thus careless was the desponding taint in his blood. It is good to be of a melancholic temperament, as all the ancient physiologists held, but only if the melancholy is balanced by fiery aspiring qualities, not when it gravitates essentially to the earth. Hence the drooping, desponding character, and the monotony of the estimate which Dr. Johnson applied to life. We were all, in *his* view, miserable, scrofulous wretches; the "strumous diathesis" was developed in our flesh, or soon would be; and, but for his piety, which was the best indication of some greatness latent within him, he would have suggested to all mankind a nobler use for garters than any which regarded knees. In fact, I believe that, but for his piety, he would not only have counselled hanging in general, but hanged himself in particular. Now, this gloomy temperament, not as an occasional but as a permanent state, is fatal to the power of brilliant conversation, in so far as that power rests upon raising a continual succession of topics, and not merely of using with lifeless talent the topics offered by

others. Man is the central interest about which revolve all the
fleeting phenomena of life; these secondary interests demand
the first; and with the little knowledge about them which must
follow from little care about them, there can be no salient
fountain of conversational themes. *Pectus —id est quod disertum*
facit. From the heart, from an interest of love or hatred, of
hope or care, springs all permanent eloquence; and the elastic
spring of conversation is gone, if the talker is a mere showy
man of talent, pulling at an oar which he detests.

What an index might be drawn up of subjects interesting to
human nature, and suggested by the events of the Johnsonian
period, upon which the Doctor ought to have talked, and must
have talked if his interest in man had been catholic, but on
which the Doctor is not recorded to have uttered one word!
Visiting Paris once in his life, he applied himself diligently to
the measuring — of what? Of gilt mouldings and diapered
panels! Yet books, it will be said, suggest topics as well as
life, and the moving sceneries of life. And surely Dr. Johnson
had *this* fund to draw upon? No; for though he had read
much in a desultory way, he had studied nothing [1]; and,
without that sort of systematic reading, it is but a rare chance
that books can be brought to bear effectually, and yet indirectly

---

[1] *"Had studied nothing."* — It may be doubted whether Dr. Johnson understood
any one thing thoroughly, except Latin; not that he understood even *that* with the
elaborate and circumstantial accuracy required for the editing critically of a Latin
classic. But if he had less than *that*, he also had more; he *possessed* that language in
a way that no extent of mere critical knowledge could confer. He wrote it genially,
not as one translating into it painfully from English, but as one using it for his
original organ of thinking. And in Latin verse he expressed himself at times with the
energy and freedom of a Roman. With Greek his acquaintance was far more slender.

upon conversation; while to make them directly and formally
the subjects of discussion, presupposes either a learned audience, or, if the audience is not so, much pedantry and much
arrogance in the talker.

CONVERSATION.

(*Second Paper*).

The flight of our human hours, not really more rapid at any
one moment than another, yet oftentimes to our feelings *seems*
more rapid, and this flight startles us like guilty things with a
more affecting *sense* of its rapidity, when a distant church-clock
strikes in the night-time; or when, upon some solemn summer
evening, the sun's disk, after settling for a minute with farewell
horizontal rays, suddenly drops out of sight. The record of our
loss in such a case seems to us the first intimation of its
possibility; as if we could not be made sensible that the hours
were perishable until it is announced to us that already they
have perished. We feel a perplexity of distress when that
which seems to us the cruelest of injuries, a robbery committed
upon our dearest possession by the conspiracy of the world
outside, seems also as in part a robbery sanctioned by our own
collusion. The world, and the customs of the world, never
cease to levy taxes upon our time; that is true, and so far the
blame is not ours; but the particular *degree* in which we suffer
by this robbery depends much upon the weakness with which
we ourselves become parties to the wrong, or the energy with
which we resist it. Resisting or not, however, we are doomed

to suffer a bitter pang as often as the irrecoverable flight of our time is brought home with keenness to our hearts. The spectacle of a lady floating over the sea in a boat, and waking suddenly from sleep to find her magnificent ropes of pearl-necklace by some accident detached at one end from its fastenings, the loose string hanging down into the water, and pearl after pearl slipping off forever into the abyss, brings before us the sadness of the case. That particular pearl, which at the very moment is rolling off into the unsearchable deeps, carries its own separate reproach to the lady's heart. But it is more deeply reproachful as the representative of so many others, uncounted pearls, that have already been swallowed up irrecoverably while she was yet sleeping, and of many besides that must follow before any remedy can be applied to what we may call this jewelly hemorrhage. A constant hemorrhage of the same kind is wasting our jewelly hours. A day has perished from our brief calendar of days, and *that* we could endure; but this day is no more than the reiteration of many other days, days counted by thousands, that have perished to the same extent and by the same unhappy means — namely, the evil usages of the world made effectual and ratified by our own *lacheté.* Bitter is the upbraiding which we seem to hear from a secret monitor: "My friend, you make very free with your days; pray, how many do you expect to have? What is your rental, as regards the total harvest of days which this life is likely to yield?" Let us consider. Threescore years and ten produce a total sum of twenty-five thousand five hundred and fifty days; to say nothing of some seventeen or eighteen more that will be payable to you as a *bonus* on account of leap-years. Now, out of this total, one third must be deducted at a blow for a single item — namely, sleep. Next; on account of illness, of recreation, and the serious occupations spread over the surface of life, it will be little enough to deduct another third. Recollect also that twenty years will have gone from the earlier end of your life (namely, above seven thousand days) before you can have attained any skill or system, or any definite purpose, in the distribution of your time. Lastly, for that single item, which, among the Roman armies, was indicated by the technical phrase "*corpus curare*," tendance on the animal necessities — namely, eating, drinking, washing, bathing, and exercise, deduct the smallest allowance consistent with propriety, and, upon summing up all these appropriations, you will not find so much as four thousand days left disposable for direct intellectual culture. Four thousand, or forty hundreds, will be a hundred forties; that is, according to the lax Hebrew method of indicating six weeks by the phrase of "forty days," you will have a hundred bills or drafts on Father Time, value six weeks each, as the whole period available for intellectual labor. A solid block of about eleven and a half continuous years is all that a long life will furnish for the development of what is most august in man's nature. After *that*, the night comes when no man can work; brain and arm will be alike unserviceable; or, if the life should be unusually extended, the vital powers will be drooping as regards all motions in advance.

Limited thus severely in his *direct* approaches to knowledge, and in his approaches to that which is a thousand times more important than knowledge, namely, the conduct and discipline of the knowing faculty, the more clamorous is the necessity that a wise man should turn to account any INDIRECT and supplementary means toward the same ends ; and amongst these means a chief one by right and potentially is CONVERSATION.   Even the primary means, books, study, and meditation, through errors from without and errors from within, are not *that* which they might be made.   Too constantly, when reviewing his own efforts for improvement, a man has reason to say (indignantly, as one injured by others ; penitentially, as contributing to this injury himself) : "Much of my studies have been thrown away ; many books which were useless, or worse than useless, I have read ; many books which ought to have been read, I have left unread ; such is the sad necessity under the absence of all preconceived plan ; and the proper road is first ascertained when the journey is drawing to its close."   In a wilderness so vast as that of books, to go astray often and widely is pardonable, because it is inevitable ; and in proportion as the errors on this primary field of study have been great, it is important to have reaped some compensatory benefits on the secondary field of conversation. Books teach by one machinery, conversation by another ; and, if these resources were trained into correspondence to their own separate ideals, they might become reciprocally the complements of each other.   The false selection of books, for instance, might often be rectified at once by the frank collation of experiences which takes place in miscellaneous colloquial intercourse.   But other and greater advantages belong to conversation for the effectual promotion of intellectual culture.   Social discussion supplies the natural integration for the deficiencies of private and sequestered study.   Simply to rehearse, simply to express in words amongst familiar friends, one's own intellectual perplexities, is oftentimes to clear them up. It is well known that the best means of learning is by teaching; the effort that is made for others is made eventually for ourselves; and the readiest method of illuminating obscure conceptions, or maturing such as are crude, lies in an earnest effort to make them apprehensible by others. Even this is but one among the functions filled by conversation. Each separate individual in a company is likely to see any problem or idea under some difference of angle. Each may have some difference of views to contribute, derived either from a different course of reading, or a different tenor of reflection, or perhaps a different train of experience. The advantages of colloquial discussion are not only often commensurate in *degree* to those of study, but they recommend themselves also as being different in *kind;* they are special and *sui generis.* It must, therefore, be important that so great an organ of intellectual development should not be neutralized by mismanagement, as generally it is, or neglected through insensibility to its latent capacities. The importance of the subject should be measured by its relation to the interests of the intellect; and on this principle we do not scruple to think that, in reviewing our own experience of the causes most commonly at war with the free movement of conversation as it ought to be, we are in effect contributing hints for a new chapter in any future " Essay on the Improvement of the Mind." Watts' book under that title is really of little practical use, nor would it ever have been thought so had it not been patronized, in a spirit of partisanship, by a particular section of religious dissenters. Wherever *that* happens the fortune of a book is made; for the sectarian impulse creates a sensible current in favor of the book;

and the general or neutral reader yields passively to the motion
of the current, without knowing or caring to know whence it is
derived. •

Our remarks must of necessity be cursory here, so that they
will not need or permit much preparation; but one distinction,
which is likely to strike on some minds, as to the two different
purposes of conversation, ought to be noticed, since otherwise
it will seem doubtful whether we have not confounded them; or,
secondly, if we have *not* confounded them, which of the two it
is that our remarks contemplate. In speaking above of conversation, we have fixed our view on those uses of conversation
which are ministerial to intellectual culture; but, in relation to
the majority of men, conversation is far less valuable as an
organ of intellectual culture than of social enjoyment. For one
man interested in conversation as a means of advancing his
studies, there are fifty men whose interest in conversation points
exclusively to convivial pleasure. This, as being a more extensive function of conversation, is so far the more dignified function; whilst, on the other hand, such a purpose as direct mental
improvement seems by its superior gravity to challenge the
higher rank. Yet, in fact, even here the more general purpose
of conversation takes precedency; for, when dedicated to the
objects of festal delight, conversation rises by its tendency to
the rank of a fine art. It is true that not one man in a million
rises to any distinction in this art; nor, whatever France may
conceit of herself, has any one nation, amongst other nations, a
real precedency in this art. The artists are rare indeed; but
still the art, as distinguished from the artist, may, by its difficulties, by the quality of its graces, and by the range of its possi-

ble brilliances, take rank as a *fine* art; or, at all events, according to its powers of execution, it tends to that rank; whereas
the best order of conversation that is simply ministerial to a
purpose of use, cannot pretend to a higher name than that of a
mechanic art. But these distinctions, though they would form
the grounds of a separate treatment in a regular treatise on
conversation, may be practically neglected on this occasion,
because the hints offered, by the generality of the terms in which
they express themselves, may be applied indifferently to either
class of conversation. The main diseases, indeed, which ob-
struct the healthy movement of conversation, recur everywhere;
and alike, whether the object be pleasure or profit in the free
interchange of thought, almost universally that free interchange
is obstructed in the very same way, by the very same defect of
any controlling principle for sustaining the general rights and
interests of the company, and by the same vices of self-indulgent
indolence, or of callous selfishness, or of insolent vanity, in the
individual talkers.

Let us fall back on the recollections of our own experience.
In the course of our life we have heard much of what was
reputed to be the select conversation of the day, and we have
heard many of those who figured at the moment as effective
talkers; yet in mere sincerity, and without a vestige of misan-
thropic retrospect, we must say, that never once has it happened
to us to come away from any display of that nature without intense disappointment; and it always appeared to us that this
failure (which soon ceased to be a *disappointment*) was inevitable
by a necessity of the case. For here lay the stress of the
difficulty: almost all depends, in most trials of skill, upon the

parity of those who are matched against each other. An ignorant person supposes that to an able disputant it must be an
advantage to have a feeble opponent; whereas, on the contrary,
it is ruin to him; for he cannot display his own powers but
through something of a corresponding power in the resistance
of his antagonist. A brilliant fencer is lost and confounded in
playing with a novice; and the same thing takes place in playing at ball, or battledore, or in dancing, where a powerless
partner does not enable you to shine the more, but reduces you
to mere helplessness, and takes the wind altogether out of your
sails. Now, if by some rare good luck the great talker — the
protagonist — of the evening has been provided with a commensurate second, it is just possible that something like a
brilliant "passage of arms" may be the result, though much,
even in that case, will depend on the chances of the moment
for furnishing a fortunate theme; and even then, amongst the
superior part of the company, a feeling of deep vulgarity and of
mountebank display is inseparable from such an ostentatious
duel of wit. On the other hand, supposing your great talker to
be received like any other visitor, and turned loose upon the
company, then he must do one of two things: either he will
talk upon *outré* subjects specially tabooed to his own private
use, in which case the great man has the air of a quack-doctor
addressing a mob from a street stage; or else he will talk like
ordinary people upon popular topics, in which case the company,
out of natural politeness, that they may not seem to be staring
at him as a lion, will hasten to meet him in the same style; the
conversation will become general; the great man will seem
reasonable and well-bred; but, at the same time, we grieve to

say it, the great man will have been extinguished by being drawn off from his exclusive ground. The dilemma, in short, is this: if the great talker attempts the plan of showing off by firing cannon-shot when everybody else is contented with musketry, then undoubtedly he produces an impression, but at the expense of insulating himself from the sympathies of the company, and standing aloof as a sort of monster hired to play tricks of funambulism for the night. Yet again, if he contents himself with a musket like other people, then for *us*, from whom he modestly hides his talent under a bushel, in what respect is he different from the man who *has* no such talent? ·

> "If she be not fair to me,
> What care I how fair she be?"

The reader, therefore, may take it upon the *a priori* logic of this dilemma, or upon the evidence of our own experience, that all reputation for brilliant talking is a visionary thing, and rests upon a sheer impossibility — namely, upon such a histrionic performance in a state of insulation from the rest of the company as could not be effected, even for a single time, without a rare and difficult collusion, and could not even for that single time, be endurable to a man of delicate and honorable sensibilities.

Yet surely Coleridge *had* such a reputation, and without needing any collusion at all; for Coleridge, unless he could have all the talk, would have none. But then this was not conversation; it was not *colloquium*, or talking *with* the company, but *alloquium*, or talking *to* the company. As Madame de Staël observed, Coleridge talked, and *could* talk, only by monologue. Such a mode of systematic trespass upon the conversational rights of a whole party, gathered together under pretence of amusement, is fatal to every purpose of social intercourse, whether that purpose be connected with direct use and the service of the intellect, or with the general graces and amenities of life. The result is the same, under whatever impulse such an outrage is practised; but the impulse is not always the same; it varies; and so far the criminal intention varies. In some people this gross excess takes its rise in pure arrogance. They are fully aware of their own intrusion upon the general privileges of the company; they are aware of the temper in which it is likely to be received; but they persist wilfully in the wrong, as a sort of homage levied compulsorily upon those who may wish to resist it but hardly *can* do so without a violent interruption, wearing the same shape of indecorum as that which they resent. In most people, however, it is not arrogance which prompts this capital offence against social rights, but a blind selfishness, yielding passively to its own instincts, without being distinctly aware of the degree in which this self-indulgence trespasses on the rights of others. We see the same temper illustrated at times in travelling; a brutal person, as we are disposed at first to pronounce him, but more frequently one who yields unconsciously to a lethargy of selfishness, plants himself at the public fireplace, so as to exclude his fellow-travellers from all but a fraction of the warmth. Yet he does not do this in a spirit of wilful aggression upon others; he has but a glimmering suspicion of the odious shape which his own act assumes to others, for the luxurious torpor of self-indulgence has extended its mists to the energy and clearness of his perceptions. Meantime, Coleridge's habit of soliloquizing through a whole evening of four or five hours had its origin neither in arrogance nor in absolute selfishness. The fact was that he *could* not talk unless he were uninterrupted, and unless he were able to count upon this concession from the company. It was a silent contract between him and his hearers, that nobody should speak but himself. If any man objected to this arrangement, why did he come? For the custom of the place, the *lex loci*, being notorious, by coming at all he was understood to profess his allegiance to the autocrat who presided. It was not, therefore, by an insolent usurpation that Coleridge persisted in monology through his whole life, but in virtue of a concession from the kindness and respect of his friends. You could not be angry with him for using his privilege, for it was a privilege confessed by others, and a privilege which he was ready to resign as soon as any man demurred to it. But though reconciled to it by these considerations, and by the ability with which he used it, you could not but feel that it worked ill for all parties. Himself it tempted oftentimes into pure garrulity of egotism, and the listeners it reduced to a state of debilitated sympathy or of absolute torpor. Prevented by the custom from putting questions, from proposing doubts, from asking for explanations, reacting by no mode of mental activity, and condemned also to the mental distress of hearing opinions or doctrines stream past them by flights which they must not arrest for a moment, so as even to take a note of them, and which yet they could not often understand, or, seeming to understand, could not always approve, the audience sank at times into a listless condition of inanimate vacuity. To be acted upon forever, but never to react, is fatal to the very powers by which sympathy must grow, or by which intelligent admiration can be evoked. For his own sake, it was Coleridge's interest to have forced his hearers into the active commerce of question and answer, of objection and demur. Not otherwise was it possible that even the attention could be kept from drooping, or the coherency and dependency of the arguments be forced into light.

The French rarely make a mistake of this nature. The graceful levity of the nation could not easily err in this direction, nor tolerate such deliration in the greatest of men. Not the gay temperament only of the French people, but the particular qualities of the French language, which (however poor for the higher purposes of passion) is rich beyond all others for purposes of social intercourse, prompt them to rapid and vivacious exchange of thought. Tediousness, therefore, above all other vices, finds no countenance or indulgence amongst the French, excepting always in two memorable cases, namely : first, the case of tragic dialogue on the stage, which is privileged to be tedious by usage and tradition ; and, secondly, the case (authorized by the best usages in living society) of narrators or *raconteurs*. This is a shocking anomaly in the code of French good taste as applied to conversation. Of all the bores whom man in his folly hesitates to hang, and heaven in its mysterious wisdom suffers to propagate their species, the most insufferable is the teller of "good stories," — a nuisance that should be put down by cudgelling, by submersion in horse-ponds, or any mode of abatement, as summarily as men would combine to suffocate a vampire or a mad dog. This case excepted, however, the French have the keenest possible sense of all that is odious and all that is ludicrous in prosing, and universally have a horror of

des longuers. It is not strange, therefore, that Madame de Staël
noticed little as extraordinary in Coleridge beyond this one capital monstrosity of unlimited soliloquy, that being a peculiarity
which she never could have witnessed in France; and, considering the burnish of her French tastes in all that concerned colloquial characteristics, it is creditable to her forbearance that she
noticed even this rather as a memorable fact than as the inhu-
man fault which it was. On the other hand, Coleridge was not
so forbearing as regarded the brilliant French lady. He spoke
of her to ourselves as a very frivolous person, and in short summary terms that disdained to linger upon a subject so inconsiderable. It is remarkable that Goethe and Schiller both
conversed with Madame de Staël, like Coleridge, and both spoke
of her afterward in the same disparaging terms as Coleridge.
But it is equally remarkable that Baron *William* Humboldt, who
was personally acquainted with all the four parties,— Madame de
Staël, Goethe, Schiller, and Coleridge, — gave it as his opinion
(in letters subsequently published) that the lady had been calum-
niated through a very ignoble cause — namely, mere ignorance
of the French language, or, at least, non-familiarity with the
fluencies of *oral* French. Neither Goethe nor Schiller, though
well acquainted with written French, had any command of it for
purposes of *rapid* conversation; and Humboldt supposes that
mere spite at the trouble which they found in limping after the
lady so as to catch one thought that she uttered, had been the
true cause of their unfavorable sentence upon her. Not malice aforethought, so much as vindictive fury for the sufferings
they had endured, accounted for their severity in the opinion of
the diplomatic baron. He did not extend the same explanation

to Coleridge's case, because, though even then in habits of intercourse with Coleridge, he had not heard of *his* interview with the lady, or of the results from that interview; else what was true of the two German wits was true *a fortiori* of Coleridge; the Germans at least *read* French and talked it slowly, and occasionally understood it when talked by others. But Coleridge did none of these things. We are all of us well aware that Madame de Staël was *not* a trifler; nay, that she gave utterance at times to truths as worthy to be held oracular as any that were uttered by the three inspired wits — all philosophers, and bound to truth — but all poets, and privileged to be wayward. This we may collect from these anecdotes, that people accustomed to colloquial despotism, and who wield a sceptre within a circle of their own, are no longer capable of impartial judgments, and do not accommodate themselves with patience, or even with justice, to the pretensions of rivals; and were it only for this result of conversational tyranny, it calls clamorously for extinction by some combined action upon the part of society.

Is such a combination on the part of society possible as a sustained effort? We imagine that it *is* in these times, and will be more so in the times which are coming. Formerly, the social meetings of men and women, except only in capital cities, were few; and even in such cities the infusion of female influence was not broad and powerful enough for the correction of those great aberrations from just ideals which disfigured social intercourse. But great changes are proceeding; were it only by the vast revolution in our *means* of intercourse, laying open every village to the contagion of social temptation, the world of Western Europe is tending more and more to a mode of living in public. Under such a law of life, conversation becomes a vital interest of every hour, that can no more suffer interruption from individual caprice or arrogance than the animal process of respiration from transient disturbances of health. Once, when travelling was rare, there was no fixed law for the usages of public rooms in inns or coffee-houses; the courtesy of individuals was the tenure by which men held their rights. If a morose person detained the newspaper for hours, there was no remedy. At present, according to the circumstances of the case, there are strict regulations, which secure to each individual his own share of the common rights.

A corresponding change will gradually take place in the usages which regulate conversation. It will come to be considered an infringement of the general rights for any man to detain the conversation, or arrest its movement, for more than a short space of time, which gradually will be more and more defined. This one curtailment of arrogant pretensions will lead to others. Egotism will no longer freeze the openings to intellectual discussions; and conversation will then become, what it never *has* been before, a powerful ally of education and generally of self-culture. The main diseases that besiege conversation at present are — 1st. The want of *timing.* Those who are not recalled, by a sense of courtesy and equity, to the continual remembrance that, in appropriating too large a share of the conversation, they are committing a fraud upon their companions, are beyond all control of monitory hints or of reproof, which does not take a direct and open shape of personal remonstrance; but this, where the purpose of the assembly is festive and convivial, bears too harsh an expression for most people's feelings. That objection, however, would not apply to any mode of admonition that was universally established. A public memento carries with it no personality. For instance, in the Roman law-courts, no advocate complained of the *clepsydra*, or water time-piece, which regulated the duration of his pleadings. Now, such a contrivance would not be impracticable at an after-dinner talk. To invert the clepsydra when all the water had run out, would be an act open to any one of the guests, and liable to no misconstruction, when this check was generally applied, and understood to be a simple expression of public defence, not of private rudeness or personality. The clepsydra ought to be filled with some brilliantly colored fluid to be placed in the centre of the table, and with the capacity, at the very most, of the little minute glasses used for regulating the boiling of eggs. It would obviously be insupportably tedious to turn the glass every two or three minutes; but to do so occasionally would avail as a sufficient memento to the company. 2d. Conversation suffers from the want of some discretional power lodged in an individual for controlling its movements. Very often it sinks into insipidity through mere accident. Some trifle has turned its current upon ground where few of the company have anything to say—the commerce of thought languishes; and the consciousness that it *is* languishing about a narrow circle, "unde pedem proferre pudor vetat," operates for the general refrigeration of the company. Now, the ancient Greeks had an officer appointed over every convivial meeting, whose functions applied to all cases of doubt or interruption that could threaten the genial harmony of the company. We also have such officers, presidents, vice-presidents, etc.; and we need only to extend their powers, so that they may exercise over the movement of the conversation the beneficial influence of the Athenian *symposiarch.* At present the evil is, that conversation has no authorized originator; it is servile to the accidents of the moment; and generally these accidents are merely verbal. Some word or some name is dropped casually in the course of an illustration; and *that* is allowed to suggest a topic, though neither interesting to the majority of the persons present, nor leading naturally into other collateral topics that are more so. Now, in such cases it will be the business of the symposiarch to restore the interest of the conversation, and to rekindle its animation, by recalling it from any tracks of dulness or sterility into which it may have rambled. The natural *excursiveness* of colloquial intercourse, its tendency to advance by subtle links of association, is one of its advantages; but mere *vagrancy* from passive acquiescence in the direction given to it by chance or by any verbal accident, is amongst its worst diseases. The business of the symposiarch will be, to watch these morbid tendencies, which are not the deviations of graceful freedom, but the distortions of imbecility and collapse. His business it will also be to derive occasions of discussion bearing a general and permanent interest from the fleeting events of the casual disputes of the day. His business again it will be to bring back a subject that has been imperfectly discussed, and has yielded but half of the interest which it promises, under the interruption of any accident which may have carried the thoughts of the party into less attractive channels. Lastly, it should be an express office of education to form a particular style, cleansed from *verbiage,* from elaborate parenthesis, and from circumlocution, as the only style fitted for a purpose which is one of pure enjoyment, and where every moment used by the speaker is deducted from a public stock.

Many other suggestions for the improvement of conversation might be brought forward within ampler limits; and especially for that class of conversation which moves by discussion a whole code of regulations might be proposed, that would equally promote the interests of the individual speakers and the public interests of the truth involved in the question discussed. Meantime nobody is more aware than we are that no style of conversation is more essentially vulgar than that which moves by disputation. This is the vice of the young and the inexperienced, but especially of those amongst them who are fresh from academic life. But discussion is not necessarily disputation; and the two orders of conversation — *that*, on the one hand, which contemplates an interest of knowledge, and of the self-developing intellect; *that*, on the other hand, which forms one. and the widest amongst the gay embellishments of life — will always advance together. Whatever there may remain of illiberal in the first (for, according to the remark of Burke, there is always something illiberal in the severer aspects of study until balanced by the influence of social amenities), will correct itself, or will tend to correct itself, by the model held up in the second; and thus the great organ of social intercourse, by means of speech, which hitherto has done little for man, except. through the channel of its ministrations to the direct *business* of daily necessities, will at length rise into a rivalship with books, and become fixed amongst the alliances of intellectual progress, not less than amongst the ornamental accomplishments of convivial life.

COMPENSATION.*

BY RALPH WALDO EMERSON.

(Born 1803, Died 1882.)

VER since I was a boy, I have wished to write a discourse on Compensation : for it seemed to me when
very young, that on this subject life was ahead of theology, and the people knew more than the preachers
taught. The documents, too, from which the doctrine is to be
drawn, charmed my fancy by their endless variety, and lay always
before me, even in sleep ; for they are the tools in our hands, the
bread in our basket, the transactions of the street, the farm, and
the dwelling-house, greetings, relations, debts, and credits, the influence of character, the nature and endowment of all men. It
seemed to me, also, that in it might be shown men a ray of
divinity, the present action of the soul of this world, clean from
all vestige of tradition, and so the heart of man might be bathed
by an inundation of eternal love, conversing with that which he
knows was always and always must be, because it really is now.
It appeared, moreover, that if this doctrine could be stated in

---

* From Emerson's Essays, first series, through the courtesy of Mess s. Houghton,.
Mifflin & Co.

terms with any resemblance to those bright intuitions in which
this truth is sometimes revealed to us, it would be a star in many
dark hours and crooked passages in our journey that would not
suffer us to lose our way.

I was lately confirmed in these desires by hearing a sermon at
church. The preacher, a man esteemed for his orthodoxy, un-
folded in the ordinary manner the doctrine of the Last Judgment. He assumed, that judgment is not executed in this
world; that the wicked are successful; that the good are miserable; and then urged from reason and from Scripture a compensation to be made to both parties in the next life. No offence
appeared to be taken by the congregation at this doctrine. As
far as I could observe, when the meeting broke up, they separated without remark on the sermon.

Yet what was the import of this teaching? What did the
preacher mean by saying that the good are miserable in the
present life? Was it that houses and lands, offices, wine, horses,
dress, luxury, are had by unprincipled men, whilst the saints
are poor and despised; and that a compensation is to be
made to these last hereafter, by giving them the like gratifica-
tions another day, — bank-stock and doubloons, venison and
champagne? This must be the compensation intended; for
what else? Is it that they are to have leave to pray and praise?
to love and serve men? Why, that they can do now. The
legitimate inference the disciple would draw was: "We are to
have *such* a good time as the sinners have now;" or, to push it
to its extreme import: "You sin now, we shall sin by and by;
we would sin now, if we could; not being successful, we expect
our revenge to-morrow."

The fallacy lay in the immense concession, that the bad are successful; that justice is not done now. The blindness of the preacher consisted in deferring to the base estimate of the market of what constitutes a manly success instead of confronting and convicting the world from the truth; announcing the presence of the soul; the omnipotence of the will : and so establishing the standard of good and ill, of success and falsehood.

I find a similar base tone in the popular religious works of the day, and the same doctrines assumed by the literary men when occasionally they treat the related topics. I think that our popular theology has gained in decorum, and not in principle, over the superstitions it has displaced. But men are better than this theology. Their daily life gives it the lie. Every ingenious and aspiring soul leaves the doctrine behind him in his own experience; and all men feel sometimes the falsehood which they cannot demonstrate. For men are wiser than they know. That which they hear in schools and pulpits without after-thought, if said in conversation, would probably be questioned in silence. If a man dogmatize in a mixed company on Providence and the divine laws, he is answered by a silence which conveys well enough to an observer the dissatisfaction of the hearer, but his incapacity to make his own statement.

I shall attempt in this and the following chapter to record some facts that indicate the path of the law of Compensation; happy beyond my expectation, if I shall truly draw the smallest arc of this circle.

POLARITY, or action and reaction, we meet in every part of nature : in darkness and light; in heat and cold; in the ebb and flow of waters; in male and female; in the inspiration and expiration of plants and animals; in the equation of quantity and quality in the fluids of the animal body; in the systole and diastole of the heart; in the undulations of fluids, and of sound; in the centrifugal and centripetal gravity; in electricity, galvanism, and chemical affinity. Superinduce magnetism at one end of a needle; the opposite magnetism takes place at the other end. If the south attracts, the north repels. To empty here, you must condense there. An inevitable dualism bisects nature, so that each thing is a half, and suggests another thing to make it whole; as, spirit, matter; man, woman; odd, even; subjective, objective; in, out; upper, under; motion, rest; yea, nay.

Whilst the world is thus dual, so is every one of its parts. The entire system of things gets represented in every particle. There is somewhat that resembles the ebb and flow of the sea, day and night, man and woman, in a single needle of the pine, in a kernel of corn, in each individual of every animal tribe. The reaction, so grand in the elements, is repeated within these small boundaries. For example, in the animal kingdom the physiologist has observed that no creatures are favorites, but a certain compensation balances every gift and every defect. A surplusage given to one part is paid out of a reduction from another part of the same creature. If the head and neck are enlarged, the trunk and extremities are cut short.

The theory of the mechanic forces is another example. What we gain in power is lost in time; and the converse. The periodic or compensating errors of the planets is another instance. The influences of climate and soil in political history are another. The cold climate invigorates. The barren soil does not breed fevers, crocodiles, tigers, or scorpions.

The same dualism underlies the nature and condition of man. Every excess causes a defect; every defect an excess. Every sweet has its sour; every evil its good. Every faculty which is a receiver of pleasure has an equal penalty put on its abuse. It is to answer for its moderation with its life. For every grain of wit there is a grain of folly. For every thing you have missed, you have gained something else; and for every thing you gain, you lose something. If riches increase, they are increased that use them. If the gatherer gathers too much, nature takes out of the man what she puts into his chest, swells the estate, but kills the owner. Nature hates monopolies and exceptions. The waves of the sea do not more speedily seek a level from their loftiest tossing, than the varieties of condition tend to equalize themselves. There is always some levelling circumstance that puts down the overbearing, the strong, the rich, the fortunate, substantially on the same ground with all others. Is a man too strong and fierce for society, and by temper and position a bad citizen, — a morose ruffian, with a dash of the pirate in him ; — nature sends him a troop of pretty sons and daughters, who are getting along in the dame's classes at the village school, and love and fear for them smooth his grim scowl to courtesy. Thus she contrives to intenerate the granite and feldspar, takes the boar out and puts the lamb in, and keeps her balance true.

The farmer imagines power and place are fine things. But the President has paid dear for his White House. It has commonly cost him all his peace, and the best of his manly attributes. To preserve for a short time so conspicuous an appearance before the world, he is content to eat dust before the real masters who stand erect behind the throne. Or, do men desire the more substantial and permanent grandeur of genius? Neither has this an immunity. He who by force of will or of thought is great, and overlooks thousands, has the charges of that eminence. With every influx of light comes new danger. Has he light? he must bear witness to the light, and always outrun that sympathy which gives him such keen satisfaction, by his fidelity to new revelations of the incessant soul. He must hate father and mother, wife and child. Has he all that the world loves and admires and covets? — he must cast behind him their admiration, and afflict them by faithfulness to his truth, and become a byword and a hissing.

This law writes the laws of cities and nations. It is in vain to build or plot or combine against it. Things refuse to be mismanaged long. *Res nolunt diu male administrari.* Though no checks to a new evil appear, the checks exist and will appear. If the government is cruel, the governor's life is not safe. If you tax too high, the revenue will yield nothing. If you make the criminal code sanguinary, juries will not convict. If the law is too mild, private vengence comes in. If the government is a terrific democracy, the pressure is resisted by an overcharge of energy in the citizen, and life glows with a fiercer flame. The true life and satisfactions of man seem to elude the utmost rigors or felicities of condition, and to establish themselves with great indifferency under all varieties of circumstances. Under all governments the influence of character remains the same, — in Turkey and in New England about alike. Under the primeval despots of Egypt, history honestly confesses that man must have been as free as culture could make him.

These appearances indicate the fact that the universe is represented in every one of its particles. Every thing in nature contains all the powers of nature. Every thing is made of one hidden stuff; as the naturalist sees one type under every metamorphosis, and regards a horse as a running man, a fish as a swimming man, a bird as a flying man, a tree as a rooted man. Each new form repeats not only the main character of the type, but part for part all the details, all the aims, furtherances, hindrances, energies, and whole system of every other. Every occupation, trade, art, transaction, is a compend of the world, and a correlative of every other. Each one is an entire emblem of human life; of its good and ill, its trials, its enemies, its course, and its end. And each one must somehow accommodate the whole man, and recite all his destiny.

The world globes itself in a drop of dew. The microscope cannot find the animalcule which is less perfect for being little. Eyes, ears, taste, smell, motion, resistance, appetite, and organs of reproduction that take hold on eternity, — all find room to consist in the small creature. So do we put our life into every act. The true doctrine of omnipresence is, that God reappears with all his parts in every moss and cobweb. The value of the universe contrives to throw itself into every point. If the good is there, so is the evil; if the affinity, so the repulsion; if the force, so the limitation.

Thus is the universe alive. All things are moral. That soul, which within us is a sentiment, outside of us is a law. We feel its inspiration; out there in history we can see its fatal strength.

" It is in the world, and the world was made by it." Justice is
not postponed. A perfect equity adjusts its balance in all parts
of life. Οι κύβοι Διὸς ἀεὶ εὐπίπτουσι, — The dice of God are
always loaded. The world looks like a multiplication-table, or
a mathematical equation, which, turn it how you will, balances
itself. Take what figure you will, its exact value, no more nor
less, still returns to you. Every secret is told, every crime is
punished, every virtue rewarded, every wrong redressed, in
silence and certainty. What we call retribution is the universal
necessity by which the whole appears wherever a part appears.
If you see smoke there must be fire. If you see a hand or a
limb, you know that the trunk to which it belongs is there behind.
╀ Every act rewards itself, or, in other words, integrates itself,
in a twofold manner: first, in the thing, or in real nature; and
secondly, in the circumstance, or in apparent nature. Men call
the circumstance the retribution. The causal retribution is in
the thing, and is seen by the soul. The retribution in the circumstance is seen by the understanding; it is inseparable from
the thing, but is often spread over a long time, and so does not
become distinct until after many years. The specific stripes
may follow late after the offence, but they follow because they
accompany it. Crime and punishment grow out of one stem.
Punishment is a fruit that unsuspected ripens within the flower
of the pleasure which concealed it. Cause and effect, means
and ends, seed and fruit, cannot be severed; for the effect already blooms in the cause, the end preëxists in the means, the
fruit in the seed.

Whilst thus the world will be whole, and refuses to be dis-
parted, we seek to act partially, to sunder, to appropriate; for

example, — to gratify the senses, we sever the pleasure of the senses from the needs of the character. The ingenuity of man has always been dedicated to the solution of one problem, — how to detach the sensual sweet, the sensual strong, the sensual bright, etc., from the moral sweet, the moral deep, the moral fair; that is, again, to contrive to cut clean off this upper surface so thin as to leave it bottomless; to get a *one end*, without an *other end*. The soul says, Eat; the body would feast. The soul says, The man and woman shall be one flesh and one soul; the body would join the flesh only. The soul says, Have dominion over all things to the ends of virtue; the body would have the power over things to its own ends.

The soul strives amain to live and work through all things. It would be the only fact. All things shall be added unto it, — power, pleasure, knowledge, beauty. The particular man aims to be somebody; to set up for himself; to truck and higgle for a private good; and, in particulars, to ride, that he may ride; to dress, that he may be dressed; to eat, that he may eat; and to govern, that he may be seen. Men seek to be great; they would have offices, wealth, power, and fame. They think that to be great is to possess one side of nature, — the sweet, — without the other side, — the bitter.

This dividing and detaching is steadily counteracted. Up to this day, it must be owned, no projector has had the smallest success. The parted water reunites behind our hand. Pleasure is taken out of pleasant things, profit out of profitable things, power out of strong things, as soon as we seek to separate them from the whole. We can no more halve things and get the sensual good, by itself, than we can get an inside that shall have no outside, or a light without a shadow. " Drive out nature with a fork, she comes running back."

Life invests itself with inevitable conditions, which the unwise seek to dodge, which one and another brags that he does not know; that they do not touch him; — but the brag is on his lips, the conditions are in his soul. If he escapes them in one part, they attack him in another more vital part. If he has escaped them in form and in the appearance, it is because he has resisted his life, and fled from himself, and the retribution is so much death. So signal is the failure of all attempts to make this separation of the good from the tax, that the experiment would not be tried, — since to try it is to be mad, — but for the circumstance, that when the disease began in the will, of rebellion and separation, the intellect is at once infected, so that the man ceases to see God whole in each object, but is able to see the sensual allurement of an object, and not see the sensual hurt; he sees the mermaid's head, but not the dragon's tail; and thinks he can cut off that which he would have, from that which he would not have. " How secret art thou who dwellest in the highest heavens in silence, O thou only great God, sprinkling with an unwearied Providence certain penal blindnesses upon such as have unbridled desires ! " [1]

'The human soul is true to these facts in the painting of fable, of history, of law, of proverbs, of conversation. It finds a tongue in literature unawares. Thus the Greeks called Jupiter, Supreme Mind; but having traditionally ascribed to him many base actions, they involuntarily made amends to reason, by tying

---

[1] St. Augustine, " Confessions," B. I.

up the hands of so bad a god. He is made as helpless as a king of England. Prometheus knows one secret which Jove must bargain for; Minerva, another. He cannot get his own thunders; Minerva keeps the key of them.

> " Of all the gods, I only know the keys
> That ope the solid doors within whose vaults
> His thunders sleep."

A plain confession of the in-working of the All, and of its moral aim. The Indian mythology ends in the same ethics; and it would seem impossible for any fable to be invented and get any currency which was not moral. Aurora forgot to ask youth for her lover, and though Tithonus is immortal, he is old. Achilles is not quite invulnerable; the sacred waters did not wash the heel by which Thetis held him. Siegfried, in the Nibelungen, is not quite immortal, for a leaf fell on his back whilst he was bathing in the dragon's blood, and that spot which it covered is mortal. And so it must be. There is a crack in everything God has made. It would seem, there is always this vindictive circumstance stealing in at unawares, even into the wild poesy in which the human fancy attempted to make bold holiday, and to shake itself free of the old laws, — this back-stroke, this kick of the gun, certifying that the law is fatal; that in nature nothing can be given, all things are sold.

This is that ancient doctrine of Nemesis, who keeps watch in the universe, and lets no offence go unchastised. The Furies, they said, are attendants on justice, and if the sun in heaven should transgress his path, they would punish him. The poets related that stone walls, and iron swords, and leathern thongs had an occult sympathy with the wrongs of their owners;

that the belt which Ajax gave Hector, dragged the Trojan
hero over the field at the wheels of the car of Achilles, and
the sword which Hector gave Ajax was that on whose point
Ajax fell. They recorded, that when the Thasians erected a
statue to Theagenes, a victor in the games, one of his rivals
went to it by night, and endeavored to throw it down by
repeated blows, until at last he moved it from its pedestal,
and was crushed to death beneath its fall.

This voice of fable has in it somewhat divine. It came from
thought above the will of the writer. That is the best part of
each writer, which has nothing private in it; that which he does
not know; that which flowed out of his constitution, and not
from his too active invention; that which in the study of a single
artist you might not easily find, but in the study of many, you
would abstract as the spirit of them all. Phidias it is not, but
the work of man in that early Hellenic world, that I would
know. The name and circumstance of Phidias, however convenient for history, embarrass when we come to the highest
criticism. We are to see that which man was tending to do in a
given period, and was hindered, or, if you will, modified
in doing, by the interfering volitions of Phidias, of Dante, of
Shakespeare, the organ whereby man at the moment wrought.

Still more striking is the expression of this fact in the proverbs of all nations, which are always the literature of reason, or
the statements of an absolute truth, without qualification.
Proverbs, like the sacred books of each nation, are the sanctuary
of the intuitions. That which the droning world, chained to
appearances, will not allow the realist to say in his own words, it
will suffer him to say in proverbs without contradiction. And

this law of laws which the pulpit, the senate, and the college deny, is hourly preached in all markets and workshops by flights of proverbs, whose teaching is as true and as omnipresent as that of birds and flies.

All things are double, one against another. — Tit for tat ; an eye for an eye; a tooth for a tooth ; blood for blood; measure for measure; love for love. — Give and it shall be given you. — He that watereth shall be watered himself. — What will you have? quoth God ; pay for it and take it. — Nothing venture, nothing have. — Thou shalt be paid exactly for what thou hast done, no more, no less. — Who doth not work shall not eat. — Harm watch, harm catch. — Curses always recoil on the head of him who imprecates them. — If you put a chain around the neck of a slave, the other end fastens itself around your own. — Bad counsel confounds the adviser. — The Devil is an ass.

It is thus written, because it is thus in life. Our action is overmastered and characterized above our will by the law of nature. We aim at a petty end quite aside from the public good, but our act arranges itself by irresistible magnetism in a line with the poles of the world.

A man cannot speak but he judges himself. With his will, or against his will, he draws his portrait to the eye of his companions by every word. Every opinion reacts on him who utters it. It is a thread-ball thrown at a mark, but the other end remains in the thrower's bag. Or, rather, it is a harpoon hurled at the whale, unwinding, as it flies, a coil of cord in the boat, and if the harpoon is not good, or not well thrown, it will go nigh to cut the steersman in twain, or to sink the boat.

You cannot do wrong without suffering wrong. "No man

had ever a point of pride that was not injurious to him," said Burke. The exclusive in fashionable life does not see that he excludes himself from enjoyment, in the attempt to appropriate it. The exclusionist in religion does not see that he shuts the door of heaven on himself, in striving to shut out others. Treat men as pawns and ninepins, and you shall suffer as well as they. If you leave out their heart, you shall lose your own. The senses would make things of all persons; of women, of children, of the poor. The vulgar proverb, "I will get it from his purse or get it from his skin," is sound philosophy.

All infractions of love and equity in our social relations are speedily punished. They are punished by fear. Whilst I stand in simple relations to my fellow-man, I have no displeasure in meeting him. We meet as water meets water, or as two currents of air mix, with perfect diffusion and interpenetration of nature. But as soon as there is any departure from simplicity, and attempt at halfness, or good for me that is not good for him, my neighbor feels the wrong; he shrinks from me as far as I have shrunk from him; his eyes no longer seek mine; there is war between us; there is hate in him and fear in me.

All the old abuses in society, universal and particular, all unjust accumulations of property and power, are avenged in the same manner. Fear is an instructor of great sagacity, and the herald of all revolutions. One thing he teaches, that there is rottenness where he appears. He is a carrion crow, and though you see not well what he hovers for, there is death somewhere. Our property is timid, our laws are timid, our cultivated classes are timid. Fear for ages has boded and mowed and gibbered over government and property. That obscene bird is not there for nothing. He indicates great wrongs which must be revised.

Of the like nature is that expectation of change which instantly follows the suspension of our voluntary activity. The terror of cloudless noon, the emerald of Polycrates, the awe of prosperity, the instinct which leads every generous soul to impose on itself tasks of a noble asceticism and vicarious virtue, are the tremblings of the balance of justice through the heart and mind of man.

Experienced men of the world know very well that it is best to pay scot and lot as they go along, and that a man often pays dear for a small frugality. The borrower runs in his own debt. Has a man gained any thing who has received a hundred favors and rendered none? Has he gained by borrowing, through indolence or cunning, his neighbor's wares, or horses or money? There arises on the deed the instant acknowledgement of benefit on the one part, and of debt on the other; that is, of superiority and inferiority. The transaction remains in the memory of himself and his neighbor; and every new transaction alters, according to its nature, their relation to each other. He may soon come to see that he had better have broken his own bones than to have ridden in his neighbor's coach, and that "the highest price he can pay for a thing is to ask for it."

A wise man will extend this lesson to all parts of life, and know that it is the part of prudence to face every claimant, and pay every just demand on your time, your talents, or your heart. Always pay; for, first or last, you must pay your entire debt. Persons and events may stand for a time between you and justice, but it is only a postponement. You must pay at last

your own debt. If you are wise, you will dread a prosperity
which only loads you with more. Benefit is the end of nature.
But for every benefit which you receive, a tax is levied. He is
great who confers the most benefits. He is base — and that is
the one base thing in the universe — to receive favors and
render none. In the order of nature we cannot render benefits
to those from whom we receive them, or only seldom. But the
benefit we receive must be rendered again, line for line, deed
for deed, cent for cent, to somebody. Beware of too much
good staying in your hand. It will fast corrupt and worm
worms. Pay it away quickly in some sort.

Labor is watched over by the same pitiless laws. Cheapest,
say the prudent, is the dearest labor. What we buy in a broom,
a mat, a wagon, a knife, is some application of good-sense to a
common want. It is best to pay in your land a skilful gardener,
or to buy good-sense applied to gardening; in your sailor, good-
sense applied to navigation; in the house, good-sense applied to
cooking, sewing, serving; in your agent, good-sense applied
to accounts and affairs. So do you multiply your presence, or
spread yourself throughout your estate. But because of the
dual constitution of things, in labor as in life there can be no
cheating. The thief steals from himself. The swindler swin-
dles himself. For the real price of labor is knowledge and
virtue, whereof wealth and credit are signs. These signs, like
paper-money, may be counterfeited or stolen, but that which
they represent, namely, knowledge and virtue, cannot be counterfeited or stolen. These ends of labor cannot be answered
but by real exertions of the mind, and in obedience to pure
motives. The cheat, the defaulter, the gambler, cannot extort

the knowledge of material and moral nature which his honest
care and pains yield to the operative. The law of nature is, Do
the thing, and you shall have the power : but they who do not
the thing have not the power.

Human labor, through all its forms, from the sharpening of a
stake to the construction of a city or an epic, is one immense
illustration of the perfect compensation of the universe. The
absolute balance of Give and Take, the doctrine that every
thing has its price, — and if that price is not paid, not that
thing but something else is obtained, and that it is impossible to
get any thing without its price, — is not less sublime in the
columns of a ledger than in the budgets of states, in the laws of
light and darkness, in all the action and reaction of nature. I
cannot doubt that the high laws which each man sees implicated
in those processes with which he is conversant, — the stern
ethics which sparkle on his chisel-edge, which are measured out
by his plumb and foot-rule, which stand as manifest in the
footing of the shop-bill as in the history of a state, — do recommend to him his trade, and though seldom named, exalt his
business to his imagination.

The league between virtue and nature engages all things
to assume a hostile front to vice. The beautiful laws and
substances of the world persecute and whip the traitor. He
finds that things are arranged for truth and benefit, but there is
no den in the wide world to hide a rogue. Commit a crime,
and the earth is made of glass. Commit a crime, and it seems
as if a coat of snow fell on the ground, such as reveals in the
woods the track of every partridge and fox and squirrel and
mole. You cannot recall the spoken word, you cannot wipe out

the foot-track, you cannot draw up the ladder, so as to leave no
inlet or clue.   Some damning circumstance always transpires.
The laws and substances of nature — water, snow, wind, gravita-
tion — become penalties to the thief.

On the other hand, the law holds with equal sureness for all
, right action.   Love, and you shall be loved.   All love is mathe-
matically just, as much as the two sides of an algebraic
equation.   The good man has absolute good, which like fire
turns every thing to its own nature, so that you cannot do him
any harm ; but as the royal armies sent against Napoleon, when·
he approached, cast down their colors and from enemies became
friends, so disasters of all kinds, as sickness, offence, poverty,
prove benefactors : —

> " Winds blow and waters roll
> Strength to the brave, and power and deity,
> Yet in themselves are nothing."

The good are befriended even by weakness and defect. As
no man had ever a point of pride that was not injurious to him,
so no man had ever a defect that was not somewhere made
useful to him.   The stag in the fable admired his horns and
blamed his feet, but when the hunter came, his feet saved him,
and afterward, caught in the thicket, his horns destroyed him.
Every man in his lifetime needs to thank his faults.   As no man
thoroughly understands a truth until he has contended against
it, so no man has a thorough acquaintance with the hindrances
or talents of men, until he has suffered from the one, and seen
the triumph of the other over his own want of the same.   Has
he a defect of temper that unfits him to live in society ?
Thereby he is driven to entertain himself alone, and acquire

habits of self-help; and thus, like the wounded oyster, he mends
his shell with pearl.

Our strength grows out of our weakness. The indignation
which arms itself with secret forces does not awaken until we
are pricked and stung and sorely assailed. A great man is
always willing to be little. Whilst he sits on the cushion of.
advantages, he goes to sleep. When he is pushed, tormented,
defeated, he has a chance to learn something; he has been put
on his wits, on his manhood;. he has gained facts; learns his
'ignorance; is cured of the insanity of conceit; has got moderation and real skill. The wise man throws himself on the side of
his assailants. It is more his interest than it is theirs to find his
weak point. The wound cicatrizes and falls off from him like a
dead skin, and when they would triumph, lo! he has passed on
invulnerable. Blame is safer than praise. I hate to be defended in a newspaper. As long as all that is said is said
against me, I feel a certain assurance of success. But as soon
as honeyed words of praise are spoken for me, I feel as one
that lies unprotected before his enemies. In general, every evil
to which we do not succumb is a benefactor. As the Sandwich
Islander believes that the strength and valor of the enemy he
kills passes into himself, so we gain the strength of the temptation we resist.

The same guards which protect us from disaster, defect, and
enmity, defend us, if we will, from selfishness and fraud. Bolts
and bars are not the best of our institutions, nor is shrewdness
in trade a mark of wisdom. Men suffer all their life long,
under the foolish superstition that they can be cheated. But it
is as impossible for a man to be cheated by any one but himself,

as for a thing to be and not to be at the same time. There is
a third silent party to all our bargains. The nature and soul of
things takes on itself the guaranty of the fulfilment of every
contract, so that honest service cannot come to loss. If you
serve an ungrateful master, serve him the more. Put God in
your debt. Every stroke shall be repaid. The longer the payment is withholden, the better for you; for compound interest
on compound interest is the rate and usage of this exchequer.

The history of persecution is a history of endeavors to cheat
nature, to make water run up hill, to twist a rope of sand. It'
makes no difference whether the actors be many or one, a
tyrant or a mob. A mob is a society of bodies voluntarily
bereaving themselves of reason, and traversing its work. The
mob is man voluntarily descending to the nature of the beast.
Its fit hour of activity is night. Its actions are insane like its
whole constitution. It persecutes a principle; it would whip a
right; it would tar and feather justice, by inflicting fire and
outrage upon the houses and persons of those who have these.
It resembles the prank of boys, who run with fire-engines to put
out the ruddy aurora streaming to the stars. The inviolate
spirit turns their spite against the wrong-doers. The martyr
cannot be dishonored. Every lash inflicted is a tongue of
fame; every prison, a more illustrious abode; every burned
book or house enlightens the world; every suppressed or
expunged word reverberates through the earth from side to side.
Hours of sanity and consideration are always arriving to communities, as to individuals, when the truth is seen, and the
martyrs are justified.

Thus do all things preach the indifferency of circumstances. The man is all. Every thing has two sides, a good and an evil. Every advantage has its tax. I learn to be content. But the doctrine of compensation is not the doctrine of indifferency. The thoughtless say on hearing these representations: " What boots it to do well? there is one event to good and evil; if I gain any good I must pay for it; if I lose any good, I gain some other; all actions are indifferent."

There is a deeper fact in the soul than compensation — to wit, its own nature. · The soul is not a compensation, but a life. The soul *is*. Under all this running sea of circumstance, whose waters ebb and flow with perfect balance, lies the aboriginal abyss of real Being. Essence, or God, is not a relation, or a part, but the whole. Being is the vast affirmative, excluding negation, self-balanced, and swallowing up all relations, parts, and times within itself. Nature, truth, virtue, are the influx from thence. Vice is the absence or departure of the same. Nothing, Falsehood, may indeed stand as the great Night or shade, on which, as a background, the living universe paints itself forth; but no fact is begotten by it; it cannot work, for it is not. It cannot work any good; it cannot work any harm. It is harm, inasmuch as it is worse not to be than to be.

We feel defrauded of the retribution due to evil acts, because the criminal adheres to his vice and contumacy, and does not come to a crisis or judgment anywhere in visible nature. There is no stunning confutation of his nonsense before men and angels. Has he therefore outwitted the law? Inasmuch as he carries the malignity and the lie with him, he so far deceases from nature. In some manner there will be a demonstration of the wrong to the understanding also; but should we not see it, this deadly deduction makes square the eternal account.

Neither can it be said, on the other hand, that the gain of rectitude must be bought by any loss. There is no penalty to virtue ; no penalty to wisdom : they are proper additions of being. In a virtuous action, I properly *am ;* in a virtuous act, I add to the world; I plant into deserts conquered from Chaos and Nothing, and see the darkness receding on the limits of the horizon. There can be no excess to love; none to knowledge ; none to beauty, when these attributes are considered in the purest sense. The soul refuses limits, and always affirms an Optimism, never a Pessimism.

Man's life is a progress, and not a station. His instinct is trust. Our instinct uses "more" and "less" in application to man, of the *presence of the soul,* and not of its absence; the brave man is greater than the coward ; the true, the benevolent, the wise, is more a man, and not less, than the fool and knave. There is no tax on the good of virtue ; for that is the incoming of God himself, or absolute existence, without any comparative. Material good has its tax, and if it came without desert or sweat, has no root in me, and the next wind will blow it away. But all the good of nature is the soul's, and may be had, if paid for in nature's lawful coin — that is, by labor which the heart and the head allow. I no longer wish to meet a good I do not earn, for example, to find a pot of buried gold, knowing that it brings with it new burdens. I do not wish more external goods, — neither possessions, nor honors, nor powers, nor persons. The gain is apparent; the tax is certain. But there is no tax on the knowledge that the compensation exists, and that it is not desirable to dig up treasure. Herein I rejoice with a serene, eternal peace. I contract the boundaries of possible mischief. I learn the wisdom of St. Bernard: "Nothing can work me damage except myself; the harm that I sustain I carry about. with me, and never am a real sufferer but by my own fault."

In the nature of the soul is the compensation for the inequalities of condition. The radical tragedy of nature seems to be the distinction of More and Less. How can Less not feel the pain; how not feel indignation or malevolence toward More? Look at those who have less faculty, and one feels sad, and knows not well what to make of it. He almost shuns their eye; he fears they will upbraid God. What should they do? It seems a great injustice. But see the facts nearly, and these mountainous inequalities vanish. Love reduces them, as the sun melts the iceberg in the sea. The heart and soul of all men being one, this bitterness of *His* and *Mine* ceases. His is mine. I am my brother, and my brother is me. If I feel overshadowed and outdone by great neighbors, I can yet love; I can still receive; and he that loveth maketh his own the grandeur he loves. Thereby I make the discovery that my brother is my guardian, acting for me with the friendliest designs, and the estate I so admired and envied is my own. It is the nature of the soul to appropriate all things. Jesus and Shakespeare are fragments of the soul, and by love I conquer and incorporate them in my own conscious domain. His virtue, — is not that mine? His wit, — if it cannot be made mine, it is not wit.

Such, also, is the natural history of calamity. The changes which break up at short intervals the prosperity of men are advertisements of a nature whose law is growth. Every soul is by this intrinsic necessity quitting its whole system of things, its friends, and home, and laws, and faith, as the shell-fish crawls out of its beautiful but stony case, because it no longer admits of its growth, and slowly forms a new house. In proportion to the vigor of the individual, these revolutions are frequent, until in some happier mind they are incessant, and all worldly relations hang very loosely about him, becoming, as it were, a transparent fluid membrane through which the living form is seen, and not, as in most men, an indurated heterogeneous fabric of many dates, and of no settled character, in which the man is imprisoned. Then there can be enlargement, and the man of to-day scarcely recognizes the man of yesterday. And such should be the outward biography of man in time, a putting off of dead circumstances day by day, as he renews his raiment day by day. But to us, in our lapsed estate, resting, not advancing, resisting, not co-operating with the divine expansion, this growth comes by shocks.

We cannot part with our friends. We cannot let our angels go. We do not see that they only go out, that archangels may come in. We are idolaters of the old. We do not believe in the riches of the soul, in its proper eternity and omnipresence. We do not believe there is any force in to-day to rival or re-create that beautiful yesterday. We linger in the ruins of the old tent, where once we had bread and shelter and organs, nor believe that the spirit can feed, cover, and nerve us again. We cannot again find aught so dear, so sweet, so graceful. But we sit and weep in vain. The voice of the Almighty saith: "Up and onward for evermore!" We cannot stay amid the ruins. Neither will we rely on the new; and so we walk ever with reverted eyes, like those monsters who look backward.

And yet the compensations of calamity are made apparent to the understanding also, after long intervals of time. A fever, a mutilation, a cruel disappointment, a loss of wealth, a loss of friends, seems at the moment unpaid loss, and unpayable. But the sure years reveal the deep remedial force that underlies all facts. The death of a dear friend, wife, brother, lover, which seemed nothing but privation, somewhat later assumes the aspect of a guide or genius; for it commonly operates revolutions in our way of life, terminates an epoch of infancy or of youth which was waiting to be closed, breaks up a wonted occupation, or a household, or style of living, and allows the formation of new ones more friendly to the growth of character. It permits or constrains the formation of new acquaintances, and the reception of new influences that prove of the first importance to the next years; and the man or woman who would have remained a sunny garden-flower, with no room for its roots and too much sunshine for its head, by the falling of the walls and the neglect of the gardener, is made the banian of the forest, yielding shade and fruit to wide neighborhoods of men.

SWEETNESS AND LIGHT.

BY MATTHEW ARNOLD.

(BORN 1822.)

HE disparagers of culture make its motive curiosity; sometimes, indeed, they make its motive mere exclusiveness and vanity. The culture which is supposed to plume itself on a smattering of Greek and Latin is a culture which is begotten by nothing so intellectual as curiosity; it is valued either out of sheer vanity and ignorance, or else as an engine of social and class distinction, separating its holder, like a badge or title, from other people who have not got it. No serious man would call this *culture*, or attach any value to it, as culture, at all. To find the real ground for the very differing estimate which serious people will set upon culture, we must find some motive for culture in the terms of which may lie a real ambiguity; and such a motive the word *curiosity* gives us.

I have before now pointed out that we English do not, like the foreigners, use this word in a good sense as well as in a bad sense. With us the word is always used in a somewhat disapproving sense. A liberal and intelligent eagerness about the

82

things of the mind may be meant by a foreigner when he speaks of curiosity, but with us the word always conveys a certain notion of frivolous and unedifying activity. In the *Quarterly Review*, some little time ago, was an estimate of the celebrated French critic, M. Sainte-Beuve, and a very inadequate estimate it in my judgment was. And its inadequacy consisted chiefly in this: that in our English way it left out of sight the double sense really involved in the word *curiosity*, thinking enough was said to stamp M. Sainte-Beuve with blame if it was said that he was impelled in his operations as a critic by curiosity, and omitting either to perceive that M. Sainte-Beuve himself, and many other people with him, would consider that this was praiseworthy and not blameworthy, or to point out why it ought really to be accounted worthy of blame and not of praise. For as there is a curiosity about intellectual matters which is futile, and merely a disease, so there is certainly a curiosity — a desire after the things of the mind simply for their own sakes and for the pleasure of seeing them as they are — which is, in an intelligent being, natural and laudable. Nay, and the very desire to see things as they are, implies a balance and regulation of mind which is not often attained without fruitful effort, and which is the very opposite of the blind and diseased impulse of mind which is what we mean to blame when we blame curiosity. Montesquieu says: "The first motive which ought to compel us to study is the desire to augment the excellence of our nature, and to render an intelligent being yet more intelligent." This is the true ground to assign for the genuine scientific passion, however manifested, and for culture, viewed simply as a fruit of this passion; and it is a worthy ground, even though we let the term *curiosity* stand to describe it.

But there is of culture another view, in which not solely the scientific passion, the sheer desire to see things as they are, natural and proper in an intelligent being, appears as the ground of it. There is a view in which all the love of our neighbor, the impulses toward action, help, and beneficence, the desire for removing human error, clearing human confusion, and diminishing human misery, the noble aspiration to leave the world better and happier than we found it, — motives eminently such as are called social, — come in as part of the grounds of culture, and the main and pre-eminent part. Culture is then properly described not as having its origin in curiosity, but as having its origin in the love of perfection; it is *a study of perfection*. It moves by the force, not merely or primarily of the scientific passion for pure knowledge, but also of the moral and social passion for doing good. As, in the first view of it, we took for its worthy motto Montesquieu's words: " To render an intelligent being yet more intelligent," so, in the second view of it, there is no better motto which it can have than these words of Bishop Wilson : " To make reason and the will of God prevail."

Only, whereas the passion for doing good is apt to be over-hasty in determining what reason and the will of God say, because its turn is for acting rather than thinking and it wants to be beginning to act; and whereas it is apt to take its own conceptions, which proceed from its own state of development and share in all the imperfections and immaturities of this, for a basis of action ; what distinguishes culture is, that it is possessed by the scientific passion, as well as by the passion of doing good; that it demands worthy notions of reason and the will of God, and does not readily suffer its own crude conceptions to substitute themselves for them. And knowing that no action or institution can be salutary and stable which are not based on reason and the will of God, it is not so bent on acting and instituting, even with the great aim of diminishing human error and misery ever before its thoughts, but that it can remember that acting and instituting are of little use, unless we know how and what we ought to act and to institute.

This culture is more interesting and more far-reaching than that other, which is founded solely on the scientific passion for knowing. But it needs times of faith and ardor, times when the intellectual horizon is opening and widening all round us, to flourish in. And is not the close and bounded intellectual horizon within which we have long lived and moved now lifting up, and are not new lights finding free passage to shine in upon us? For a long time there was no passage for them to make their way in upon us, and then it was of no use to think of adapting the world's action to them. Where was the hope of making reason and the will of God prevail among people who had a routine which they had christened reason and the will of God, in which they were inextricably bound, and beyond which they had no power of looking? But now the iron force of adhesion to the old routine — social, political, religious — has wonderfully yielded; the iron force of exclusion of all which is new has wonderfully yielded. The danger now is, not that people should obstinately refuse to allow anything but their old routine to pass for reason and the will of God, but either that they should allow some novelty or other to pass for these too easily, or else that they should underrate the importance of them altogether, and think it enough to follow action for its own sake, without troubling themselves to make reason and the will of God prevail therein. Now, then, is the moment for culture to be of service, culture which believes in making reason and the will of God prevail, believes in perfection, is the study and pursuit of perfection, and is no longer debarred, by a rigid invincible exclusion of whatever is new, from getting acceptance for its ideas, simply because they are new.

The moment this view of culture is seized, the moment it is regarded not solely as the endeavor to see things as they are, to draw toward a knowledge of the universal order which seems to be intended and aimed at in the world, and which it is a man's happiness to go along with or his misery to go counter to, — to learn, in short, the will of God, — the moment, I say, culture is considered not merely as the endeavor to *see* and *learn* this, but as the endeavor, also, to make it *prevail*, the moral, social, and beneficent character of culture becomes manifest. The mere endeavor to see and learn the truth for our own personal satisfaction is indeed a commencement for making it prevail, a preparing the way for this, which always serves this, and is wrongly, therefore, stamped with blame absolutely in itself and not only in its caricature and degeneration. But perhaps it has got stamped with blame, and disparaged with the dubious title of curiosity, because in comparison with this wider endeavor of such great and plain utility it looks selfish, petty, and unprofitable.

And religion, the greatest and most important of the efforts by which the human race has manifested its impulse to perfect itself, — religion, that voice of the deepest human experience, — does not only enjoin and sanction the aim which is the great aim of culture, the aim of setting ourselves to ascertain what perfection is and to make it prevail; but also, in determining generally in what human perfection consists, religion comes to a conclusion identical with that which culture — seeking the determination of this question through all the voices of human experience which have been heard upon it, of art, science, poetry, philosophy, history, as well as of religion, in order to give a greater fulness and certainty to its solution — likewise reaches. Religion says : *The kingdom of God is within you;* and culture, in like manner, places human perfection in an *internal* condition, in the growth and predominance of our humanity proper, as distinguished from our animality. It places it in the ever-increasing efficacy and in the general harmonious expansion of those gifts of thought and feeling, which make the peculiar dignity, wealth, and happiness of human nature. As I have said on a former occasion : " It is in making endless additions to itself, in the endless expansion of its powers, in endless growth in wisdom and beauty, that the spirit of the human race finds its ideal. To reach this ideal, culture is an indispensable aid, and that is the true value of culture." Not a having and a resting, but a growing and a becoming, is the character of perfection as culture conceives it; and here, too, it coincides with religion.

And because men are all members of one great whole, and the sympathy which is in human nature will not allow one member to be indifferent to the rest, or to have a perfect welfare independent of the rest, the expansion of our humanity, to suit the idea of perfection which culture forms, must be a *general* expansion. Perfection, as culture conceives it, is not possible while the individual remains isolated. The individual is required, under pain of being stunted and enfeebled in his own development if he disobeys, to carry others along with him in his march toward perfection, to be continually doing all he can to enlarge and increase the volume of the human stream sweeping thitherward. And here, once more, culture lays on us the same obligation as religion, which says, as Bishop Wilson has admirably put it, that "to promote the kingdom of God is to increase and hasten one's own happiness."

But, finally, perfection — as culture from a thorough disinterested study of human nature and human experience learns to conceive it — is an harmonious expansion of *all* the powers which make the beauty and worth of human nature, and is not consistent with the over-development of any one power at the expense of the rest. Here culture goes beyond religion, as religion is generally conceived by us.

If culture, then, is a study of perfection, and of harmonious perfection, general perfection, and perfection which consists in becoming something rather than in having something, in an inward condition of the mind and spirit, not in an outward set of circumstances, — it is clear that culture, instead of being the frivolous and useless thing which Mr. Bright, and Mr. Frederic Harrison and many other Liberals are apt to call it, has a very important function to fulfil for mankind. And this function is particularly important in our modern world, of which the whole civilization is, to a much greater degree than the civilization of Greece and Rome, mechanical and external, and tends constantly to become more so. But above all in our own country has culture a weighty part to perform, because here that mechanical character, which civilization tends to take everywhere, is shown in the most eminent degree. Indeed, nearly all the characters of perfection, as culture teaches us to fix them, meet in this country with some powerful tendency which thwarts them and sets them at defiance. The idea of perfection as an *inward* condition of the mind and spirit is at variance with the mechanical and material civilization in esteem with us, and nowhere, as I have said, so much in esteem as with us. The idea of perfection as a *general* expansion of the human family is at variance with our strong individualism, our hatred of all limits to the unrestrained swing of the individual's personality, our maxim of "every man for himself." Above all, the idea of perfection as an *harmonious* expansion of human nature is at variance with our want of flexibility, in our inaptitude for seeing more than one side of a thing, with our intense energetic absorption in the particular pursuit we happen to be following. So culture has a rough task to achieve in this country. Its preachers have, and are likely long to have, a hard time of it, and they will much oftener be regarded, for a great while to come, as elegant or spurious Jeremiahs, than as friends and benefactors. That, however, will not prevent their doing in the end good service if they persevere. And meanwhile, the mode of action they have to pursue, and the sort of habits they must fight against, ought to be made quite clear for every one to see, who may be willing to look at the matter attentively and dispassionately.

Faith in machinery is, I said, our besetting danger; often in machinery most absurdly disproportioned to the end which this machinery, if it is to do any good at all, is to serve; but always in machinery, as if it had a value in and for itself. What is freedom but machinery? what is population but machinery? what is coal but machinery? what are railroads but machinery? what is wealth but machinery? what are, even, religious organizations but machinery? Now almost every voice in England is accustomed to speak of these things as if they were precious ends in themselves, and therefore had some of the characters of perfection indisputably joined to them. I have before now noticed Mr. Roebuck's stock argument for proving the greatness and happiness of England as she is, and for quite stopping the mouths of all gainsayers. Mr. Roebuck is never weary of reiterating this argument of his, so I do not know why I should be weary of noticing it. "May not every man in England say what he likes?" — Mr. Roebuck perpetually asks; and that, he thinks, is quite sufficient, and when every man may say what he likes, our aspirations ought to be satisfied. But the aspirations of culture, which is the study of perfection, are not satisfied, unless what men say, when they may say what they like, is worth saying, — has good in it, and more good than bad. In the same way the *Times*, replying to some foreign strictures on the dress, looks, and behavior of the English abroad, urges that the English ideal is that every one should be free to do and to look just as he likes. But culture indefatigably tries, not to make what each raw person may like the rule by which he fashions himself; but to draw ever nearer to a sense of what is indeed beautiful, graceful, and becoming, and to get the raw person to like that.

And in the same way with respect to railroads and coal. Every one must have observed the strange language current during the late discussions as to the possible failure of our supplies of coal. Our coal, thousands of people were saying, is the real basis of our national greatness; if our coal runs short, there is an end of the greatness of England. But what *is* greatness?—culture makes us ask. Greatness is a spiritual condition worthy to excite love, interest, and admiration; and the outward proof of possessing greatness is that we excite love, interest, and admiration. If England were swallowed up by the sea to-morrow, which of the two, a hundred years hence, would most excite the love, interest, and admiration of mankind,—would most, therefore, show the evidences of having possessed greatness,—the England of the last twenty years, or the England of Elizabeth, of a time of splendid spiritual effort, but when our coal, and our industrial operations depending on coal, were very little developed? Well, then, what an unsound habit of mind it must be which makes us talk of things like coal or iron as constituting the greatness of England, and how salutary a friend is culture, bent on seeing things as they are, and thus dissipating delusions of this kind and fixing standards of perfection that are real!

Wealth, again, that end to which our prodigious works for material advantage are directed,—the commonest of commonplaces tells us how men are always apt to regard wealth as a precious end in itself; and certainly they have never been so apt thus to regard it as they are in England at the present time. Never did people believe anything more firmly, than nine Englishmen out of ten at the present day believe that our greatness and welfare are proved by our being so very rich. Now, the use of culture is that it helps us, by means of its spiritual standard of perfection, to regard wealth as but machinery, and not only to say as a matter of words that we regard wealth as but machinery, but really to perceive and feel that it is so. If it were not for this purging effect wrought upon our minds by culture, the whole world, the future as well as the present, would inevitably belong to the Philistines. The people who believe most that our greatness and welfare are proved by our being very rich, and who most give their lives and thoughts to becoming rich, are just the very people whom we call Philistines. Culture says : "Consider these people, then, their way of life, their habits, their manners, the very tones of their voice; look at them attentively; observe the literature they read, the things which give them pleasure, the words which come forth out of their mouths, the thoughts which make the furniture of their minds : would any amount of wealth be worth having with the condition that one was to become just like these people by having it?" And thus culture begets a dissatisfaction which is of the highest possible value in stemming the common tide of men's thoughts in a wealthy and industrial community, and which saves the future, as one may hope, from being vulgarized, even if it cannot save the present.

Population, again, and bodily health and vigor, are things which are nowhere treated in such an unintelligent, misleading, exaggerated way as in England. Both are really machinery; yet how many people all around us do we see rest in them and fail to look beyond them! Why, one has heard people, fresh from reading certain articles of the *Times* on the Registrar-General's returns of marriages and births in this country, who would talk of our large English families in quite a solemn strain,

as if they had something in itself beautiful, elevating, and meri-
torious in them; as if the British Philistine would have only to
present himself before the Great Judge with his twelve children,
in order to be received among the sheep as a matter of right!

But bodily health and vigor, it may be said, are not to be
classed with wealth and population as mere machinery; they
have a more real and essential value. True; but only as they
are more intimately connected with a perfect spiritual condition
than wealth or population are. The moment we disjoin them
from the idea of a perfect spiritual condition, and pursue them,
as we do pursue them, for their own sake, and as ends in
themselves, our worship of them becomes as mere worship of
machinery, as our worship of wealth or population, and as
unintelligent and vulgarizing a worship as that is. Every one
with any thing like an adequate idea of human perfection has
distinctly marked this subordination to higher and spiritual ends
of the cultivation of bodily vigor and activity. " Bodily exercise
profiteth little; but godliness is profitable unto all things," says
the author of the Epistle to Timothy. And the utilitarian
Franklin says just as explicitly: " Eat and drink such an exact
quantity as suits the constitution of thy body, *in reference to the
services of the mind.*" But the point of view of culture, keeping
the mark of human perfection simply and broadly in view, and
not assigning to this perfection, as religion or utilitarianism
assign to it, a special and limited character, — this point of view,
I say, of culture is best given by these words of Epictetus: " It
is a sign of ἀφυΐα," says he, — that is, of a nature not finely tempered, — "to give yourself up to things which relate to the body;
to make, for instance, a great fuss about exercise, a great fuss

about eating, a great fuss about drinking, a great fuss about walking, a great fuss about riding. All these things ought to be done merely by the way: the formation of the spirit and character must be our real concern." This is admirable ; and, indeed, the Greek word εὐφυΐα, a finely-tempered nature, gives exactly the notion of perfection as culture brings us to perceive it: an harmonious perfection, a perfection in which the characters of beauty and intelligence are both present, which unites "the two noblest of things," — as Swift, who of one of the two, at any rate, had himself all too little, most happily calls them in his "Battle of the Books," "the two noblest of things, *sweetness and light.*" The εὐφυής is the man who tends toward sweetness and light; the ἀφυής, on the other hand, is our Philistine. The immense spiritual significance of the Greeks is due to their having been inspired with this central and happy idea of the essential character of human perfection ; and Mr. Bright's misconception of culture, as a smattering of Greek and Latin, comes itself, after all, from this wonderful significance of the Greeks having affected the very machinery of our education, and is in itself a kind of homage to it.

In thus making sweetness and light to be characters of perfection, culture is of like spirit with poetry, follows one law with poetry. Far more than on our freedom, our population, and our industrialism, many amongst us rely upon our religious organizations to save us. I have called religion a yet more important manifestation of human nature than poetry, because it has worked on a broader scale for perfection, and with greater masses of men. But the idea of beauty and of a human nature perfect on all its sides, which is the dominant idea of poetry, is a true and invaluable idea, though it has not yet had the success that the idea of conquering the obvious faults of our animality, and of a human nature perfect on the moral side, — which is the dominant idea of religion, — has been enabled to have; and it is destined, adding to itself the religious idea of a devout energy, to transform and govern the other.

The best art and poetry of the Greeks, in which religion and poetry are one, in which the idea of beauty and of a human nature perfect on all sides adds to itself a religious and devout energy, and works in the strength of that, is on this account of such surpassing interest and instructiveness for us, though it was — as, having regard to the human race in general, and, indeed, having regard to the Greeks themselves, we must own — a premature attempt, an attempt which for success needed the moral and religious fibre in humanity to be more braced and developed than it had yet been. But Greece did not err in having the idea of beauty, harmony, and complete human perfection so present and paramount. It is impossible to have this idea too present and paramount; only, the moral fibre-must be braced too. And we, because we have braced the moral fibre, are not on that account in the right way, if at the same time the idea of beauty, harmony, and complete human perfection is wanting or misapprehended amongst us; and evidently it *is* wanting or misapprehended at present. And when we rely as we do on our religious organizations, which in themselves do not and cannot give us this idea, and think we have done enough if we make them spread and prevail, then, I say, we fall into our common fault of overvaluing machinery.

Nothing is more common than for people to confound the

inward peace and satisfaction which follow the subduing of the obvious faults of our animality with what I may call absolute inward peace and satisfaction, — the peace and satisfaction which are reached as we draw near to complete spiritual perfection, and not merely to moral perfection, or rather to relative moral perfection. No people in the world have done more and struggled more to attain this relative moral perfection than our English race has. For no people in the world has the command to *resist the devil,* to *overcome the wicked one,* in the nearest and most obvious sense of those words, had such a pressing force and reality. And we have had our reward, not only in the great worldly prosperity which our obedience to this command has brought us, but also, and far more, in great inward peace and satisfaction. But to me few things are more pathetic than to see people, on the strength of the inward peace and satisfaction which their rudimentary efforts. toward perfection have brought them, employ, concerning their incomplete perfection and the religious organizations within which they have found it, language which properly applies only to complete perfection, and is a far-off echo of the human soul's prophecy of it. Religion itself, I need hardly say, supplies them in abundance with this grand language. And very freely do they use it ; yet it is really the severest possible criticism of such an incomplete perfection as alone we have yet reached through our religious organizations.

The impulse of the English race toward moral development and self-conquest has nowhere so powerfully manifested itself as in Puritanism. Nowhere has Puritanism found so adequate an expression as in the religious organization of the Independents. The modern Independents have a newspaper, the *Nonconformist,*

written with great sincerity and ability. The motto, the standard, the profession of faith which this organ of theirs carries
aloft, is: "The Dissidence of Dissent and the Protestantism of
the Protestant Religion." There are sweetness and light, and
an ideal of complete harmonious human perfection! One need
not go to culture and poetry to find language to judge it. Religion, with its instinct for perfection, supplies language to judge
it, language, too, which is in our mouths every day. "Finally,
be of one mind, united in feeling," says St. Peter. There is an
ideal which judges the Puritan ideal: "The Dissidence of
Dissent and the Protestantism of the Protestant Religion!"
And religious organizations like this are what people believe in,
rest in, would give their lives for! Such, I say, is the wonderful
virtue of even the beginnings of perfection, of having conquered
even the plain faults of our animality, that the religious organization which has helped us to do it can seem to us something
precious, salutary, and to be propagated, even when it wears
such a brand of imperfection on its forehead as this. And men
have got such a habit of giving to the language of religion a
special application, of making it a mere jargon, that for the
condemnation which religion itself passes on the shortcomings
of their religious organizations they have no ear; they are sure
to cheat themselves and to explain this condemnation away.
They can only be reached by the criticism which culture, like
poetry, speaking a language not to be sophisticated, and resolutely testing these organizations by the ideal of a human perfection complete on all sides, applies to them.

But men of culture and poetry, it will be said, are again and
again failing, and failing conspicuously, in the necessary first

stage to an harmonious perfection, in the subduing of the great obvious faults of our animality, which it is the glory of these religious organizations to have helped us to subdue. True, they do often so fail. They have often been without the virtues as well as the faults of the Puritan; it has been one of their dangers that they so felt the Puritan's faults that they too much neglected the practice of his virtues. I will not, however, exculpate them at the Puritan's expense. They have often failed in morality, and morality is indispensible. And they have been punished for their failure, as the Puritan has been rewarded for his performance. They have been punished wherein they erred; but their ideal of beauty, of sweetness and light, and a human nature complete on all its sides, remains the true ideal of perfection still; just as the Puritan's ideal of perfection remains narrow and inadequate, although for what he did well he has been richly rewarded. Notwithstanding the mighty results of the Pilgrim Fathers' voyage, they and their standard of perfection are rightly judged when we figure to ourselves Shakespeare or Virgil, — souls in whom sweetness and light, and all that in human nature is most humane, were eminent, accompanying them on their voyage, and think what intolerable company Shakespeare and Virgil would have found them! In the same way let us judge the religious organizations which we see all around us. Do not let us deny the good and the happiness which they have accomplished; but do not let us fail to see clearly that their idea of human perfection is narrow and inadequate; and that the Dissidence of Dissent and the Protestantism of the Protestant religion will never bring humanity to its true goal. As I said with regard to wealth: Let us look at the life of those who live in and for it, — so I say with regard to the religious organizations. Look at the life imaged in such a newspaper as the *Nonconformist*, — a life of jealousy of the Establishment, disputes, tea-meetings, openings of chapels, sermons; and then think of it as an ideal of a human life completing itself on all sides, and aspiring with all its organs after sweetness, light, and perfection ! Another newspaper, representing, like the *Nonconformist*, one of the religious organizations of this country, was a short time ago giving an account of the crowd at Epsom on the Derby day, and of all the vice and hideousness which were to be seen in that crowd ; and then the writer turned suddenly round upon Professor Huxley, and asked him how he proposed to cure all this vice and hideousness without religion. I confess I felt disposed to ask the asker this question : And how do you propose to cure it with such a religion as yours ? How is the ideal of a life so unlovely, so unattractive, so incomplete, so narrow, so far removed from a true and satisfying ideal of human perfection, as is the life of your religious organization as you yourself image it, to conquer and transform all this vice and hideousness ? Indeed, the strongest plea for the study of perfection as pursued by culture, the clearest proof of the actual inadequacy of the idea of perfection held by the religious organizations, — expressing, as I have said, the most wide-spread effort which the human race has yet made after perfection, — is to be found in the state of our life and society with these in possession of it, and having been in possession of it I know not how many hundred years. We are all of us included in some religious organization or other ; we all call ourselves, in the sublime and aspiring language of religion which I have before noticed, *children of God.* Children of God; — it is an immense pretension! — and how are we to justify it? By the works which we do, and the words which we speak. And the work which we collective children of God do, our grand centre of life, our *city* which we have builded for us to dwell in, is London! London, with its unutterable external hideousness, and with its internal canker of *publicè egestas, privatim opulentia,* — to use the words which Sallust puts into Cato's mouth about Rome, — unequalled in the world! The word, again, which we children of God speak, the voice which most hits our collective thought, the newspaper with the largest circulation in England, nay, with the largest circulation in the whole world, is the *Daily Telegraph!* I say that when our religious organizations, — which I admit to express the most considerable effort after perfection that our race has yet made, — land us in no better result than this, it is high time to examine carefully their idea of perfection, to see whether it does not leave out of account sides and forces of human nature which we might turn to great use; whether it would not be more operative if it were more complete. And I say that the English reliance on our religious organizations and on their ideas of human perfection just as they stand, is like our reliance on freedom, on muscular Christianity, on population, on coal, on wealth, — mere belief in machinery, and unfruitful; and that it is wholesomely counteracted by culture, bent on seeing things as they are, and on drawing the human race onward to a more complete, an harmonious perfection.

Culture, however, shows its single-minded love of perfection, its desire simply to make reason and the will of God prevail, its freedom from fanaticism, by its attitude toward all this machinery, even while it insists that it *is* machinery. Fanatics, seeing the mischief men do themselves by their blind belief in some machinery or other, — whether it is wealth and industrialism, or whether it is the cultivation of bodily strength and activity, or whether it is a political organization, or whether it is a religious organization, — oppose with might and main the tendency to this or that political and religious organization, or to games and athletic exercises, or to wealth and industrialism, and try violently to stop it. But the flexibility which sweetness and light give, and which is one of the rewards of culture pursued in good faith, enables a man to see that a tendency may be necessary, and even, as a preparation for something in the future, salutary, and yet that the generations or individuals who obey this tendency are sacrificed to it, that they fall short of the hope of perfection by following it; and that its mischiefs are to be criticised, lest it should take too firm a hold and last after it has served its purpose.

Mr. Gladstone well pointed out, in a speech at Paris, — and others have pointed out the same thing, — how necessary is the present great movement toward wealth and industrialism, in order to lay broad foundations of material well-being for the society of the future. The worst of these justifications is, that they are generally addressed to the very people engaged, body and soul, in the movement in question; at all events, that they are always seized with the greatest avidity by these people, and taken by them as quite justifying their life; and that thus they tend to harden them in their sins. Now, culture admits the necessity of the movement toward fortune-making and exaggerated industrialism, readily allows that the future may derive benefit from it; but insists, at the same time, that the passing generations of industrialists, — forming, for the most part, the stout main body of Philistinism, — are sacrificed to it. In the same way, the result of all the games and sports which occupy the passing generation of boys and young men may be the establishment of a better and sounder physical type for the future to work with. Culture does not set itself against the games and sports; it congratulates the future, and hopes it will make a good use of its improved physical basis; but it points out that our passing generation of boys and young men is, meantime, sacrificed. Puritanism was perhaps necessary to develop the moral fibre of the English race, Nonconformity to break the yoke of ecclesiastical domination over men's minds and to prepare the way for freedom of thought in the distant future; still, culture points out that the harmonious perfection of generations of Puritans and Nonconformists have been, in consequence, sacrificed. Freedom of speech may be necessary for the society of the future, but the young lions of the *Daily Telegraph* in the meanwhile are sacrificed. A voice for every man in his country's goverment may be necessary for the society of the future, but meanwhile Mr. Beales and Mr. Bradlaugh are sacrificed.

Oxford, the Oxford of the past, has many faults : and she has heavily paid for them in defeat, in isolation, in want of hold upon the modern world. Yet we in Oxford, brought up amidst the beauty and sweetness of that beautiful place, have not failed to seize· one truth : — the truth that beauty and sweetness are essential characters of a complete human perfection. When I insist on this, I am all in the faith and tradition of Oxford. I say boldly that this our sentiment for beauty and sweetness, our sentiment against hideousness and rawness, has been at the bottom of our attachment to so many beaten causes, of our opposition to so many triumphant movements. And the sentiment is true, and has never been wholly defeated, and has shown its power even in its defeat. We have not won our political battles, we have not carried our main points, we have not stopped our adversaries' advance, we have not marched victoriously with the modern world; but we have told silently upon the mind of the country, we have prepared currents of feeling which sap our adversaries' position when it seems gained, we have kept up our own communications with the future. Look at the course of the great movement which shook Oxford to its centre some thirty years ago ! It was directed, as any one who reads Dr. Newman's "Apology" may see, against what in one word may be called "Liberalism." Liberalism prevailed ; it was the appointed force to do the work of the hour ; it was necessary, it was inevitable that it should prevail. The Oxford movement was broken, it failed; our wrecks are scattered on every shore : —

Quæ regio in terris nostri non plena laboris ?

But what was it, this liberalism, as Dr. Newman saw it, and as it really broke the Oxford movement ? It was the great middle-class liberalism, which had for the cardinal points of its belief the Reform Bill of 1832, and local self-government, in politics ; in the social sphere, free trade, unrestricted competition, and the making of large industrial fortunes ; in the religious sphere, the

Dissidence of Dissent and the Protestantism of the Protestant religion. I do not say that other and more intelligent forces than this were not opposed to the Oxford movement: but this was the force which really beat it; this was the force which Dr. Newman felt himself fighting with ; this was the force which till only the other day seemed to be the paramount force in this country, and to be in possession of the future; this was the force whose achievements fill Mr. Lowe with such inexpressible admiration, and whose rule he was so horror-struck to see threatened. And where is this great force of Philistinism now? It is thrust into the second rank, it is become a power of yesterday, it has lost the future. A new power has suddenly appeared, a power which it is impossible yet to judge fully, but which is certainly a wholly different force from middle-class liberalism; different in its cardinal points of belief, different in its tendencies in every sphere. It loves and admires neither the legislation of middle-class Parliaments, nor the local self-government of middle-class vestries, nor the unrestricted competition of middle-class industrialists, nor the Dissidence of middle-class Dissent and the Protestantism of middle-class Protestant religion. I am not now praising this new force, or saying that its own ideals are better; all I say is, that they are wholly different. And who will estimate how much the currents of feeling created by Dr Newman's movements, the keen desire for beauty and sweetness which it nourished, the deep aversion it manifested to the hardness and vulgarity of middle-class liberalism, the strong light it turned on the hideous and grotesque illusions of middle-class Protestantism, — who will estimate how much all these contributed to swell the tide of secret dissatisfaction which has mined the ground under the self-confident liberalism of the last thirty years, and has prepared the way for its sudden collapse and supersession? It is in this manner that the sentiment of Oxford for beauty and sweetness conquers, and in this manner long may it continue to conquer!

In this manner it works to the same end as culture, and there is plenty of work for it yet to do. I have said that the new and more democratic force which is now superseding our old middle-class liberalism cannot yet be rightly judged. It has its main tendencies still to form. We hear promises of its giving us administrative reform, law reform, reform of education, and I know not what; but those promises come rather from its advocates, wishing to make a good plea for it and to justify it for superseding middle-class liberalism, than from clear tendencies which it has itself yet developed. But meanwhile it has plenty of well-intentioned friends against whom culture may with advantage continue to uphold steadily its ideal of human perfection; that this is *an inward spiritual activity, having for its characters increased sweetness, increased light, increased life, increased sympathy.* Mr. Bright, who has a foot in both worlds, the world of middle-class liberalism and the world of democracy, but who brings most of his ideas from the world of middle-class liberalism in which he was bred, always inclines to inculcate that faith in machinery to which, as we have seen, Englishmen are so prone, and which has been the bane of middle-class liberalism. He complains with a sorrowful indignation of people who "appear to have no proper estimate of the value of the franchise;" he leads his disciples to believe — what the Englishman is always too ready to believe — that the having a vote, like the having a large family, or a large business, or large muscles, has in itself some edifying and perfecting effect upon human nature.   Or else he cries out to the democracy—"the men," as he calls them, "upon whose shoulders the greatness of England rests"—he cries out to them: "See what you have done!   I look over this country and see the cities you have built, the railroads you have made, the manufactures you have produced, the cargoes which freight the ships of the greatest mercantile navy the world has ever seen!   I see that you have converted by your labors what was once 'a wilderness, these islands, into a fruitful garden; I know that you have created this wealth, and are a nation whose name is a word of power throughout all the world."   Why, this is just the very style of laudation with which Mr. Roebuck and Mr. Lowe debauch the minds of the middle-classes, and make such Philistines of them. It is the same fashion of teaching a man to value himself not on what he *is*, not on his progress in sweetness and light, but on the number of railroads he has constructed, or the bigness of the tabernacle he has built.   Only the middle-classes are told they have done it all with their energy, self-reliance, and capital, and the democracy are told they have done it all with their hands and sinews.   But teaching the democracy to put its trust in achievements of this kind is merely training them to be Philistines to take the place of the Philistines whom they are superseding; and they too, like the middle-class, will be encouraged to sit down at the banquet of the future without having on a wedding garment, and nothing excellent can then come from them.   Those who know their besetting faults, those who have watched them and listened to them, or those who will read

the instructive account recently given of them by one of themselves, the "Journeyman Engineer," will agree that the idea
which culture sets before us of perfection — an increased
spiritual activity, having for its characters increased sweetness,
increased light, increased life, increased sympathy — is an idea
which the new democracy needs far more than the idea of the
blessedness of the franchise, or the wonderfulness of its own
industrial performances.

Other well-meaning friends of this new power are for leading
it, not in the old ruts of middle-class Philistinism, but in ways
which are naturally alluring to the feet of democracy, though
in this country they are novel and untried ways. I may call
them the ways of Jacobinism. Violent indignation with the
past, abstract systems of renovation applied wholesale, a new
doctrine drawn up in black and white for elaborating down to
the very smallest details a rational society for the future, —
these are the ways of Jacobinism. Mr. Frederic Harrison and
other disciples of Comte — one of them Mr. Congreve, is an old
acquaintance of mine, and I am glad to have an opportunity of
publicly expressing my respect for his talents and character —
are among the friends of democracy who are for leading it in
paths of this kind. Mr. Frederic Harrison is very hostile to
culture, and from a natural enough motive ; for culture is the
eternal opponent of the two things which are the signal marks
of Jacobinism, — its fierceness, and its addiction to an abstract
system. Culture is always assigning to system-makers and
systems a smaller share in the bent of human destiny than their
friends like. A current in people's minds sets toward new
ideas ; people are dissatisfied with their old narrow stock of Phil-

istine ideas, Anglo-Saxon ideas, or any other; and some man, some Bentham or Comte, who has the real merit of having early and strongly felt and helped the new current, but who brings plenty of narrowness and mistakes of his own into his feeling and help of it, is credited with being the author of the whole current, the fit person to be entrusted with its regulation and to guide the human race.

The excellent German historian of the mythology of Rome, Preller, relating the introduction at Rome under the Tarquins of the worship of Apollo, the god of light, healing, and reconciliation, will have us observe that it was not so much the Tarquins who brought to Rome the new worship of Apollo, as a current in the mind of the Roman people which set powerfully at that time toward a new worship of this kind, and away from the old run of Latin and Sabine religious ideas. In a similar way culture directs our attention to the natural current there is in human affairs, and to its continual working, and will not let us rivet our faith upon any one man and his doings. It makes us see, not only his good side, but also how much in him was of necessity limited and transient; nay, it even feels a pleasure, a sense of an increased freedom and of an ampler future, in so doing.

I remember when I was under the influence of a mind to which I feel the greatest obligations, the mind of a man who was the very incarnation of sanity and clear sense, a man the most considerable, it seems to me, whom America has yet produced, — Benjamin Franklin, — I remember the relief with which, after long feeling the sway of Franklin's imperturbable common-sense, I came upon a project of his for a new version of the Book of Job, to replace the old version, the style of which, says Franklin, has become obsolete, and thence less agreeable. "I give," he continues, "a few verses, which may serve as a sample of the kind of version I would recommend." We all recollect the famous verse in our translation : "Then Satan answered the Lord and said : 'Doth Job fear God for nought?'" Franklin makes this : "Does Your Majesty imagine that Job's good conduct is the effect of mere personal attachment and affection?" I well remember how when first I read that, I drew a deep breath of relief, and said to myself : "After all, there is a stretch of humanity beyond Franklin's victorious good-sense!" So, after hearing Bentham cried loudly up as the renovator of modern society, and Bentham's mind and ideas proposed as the rulers of our future, I opened the "Dentology." There I read : "While Xenophon was writing his history and Euclid teaching geometry, Socrates and Plato were talking nonsense under pretence of talking wisdom and morality. This morality of theirs consisted in words ; this wisdom of theirs was the denial of matters known to every man's experience." From the moment of reading that I am delivered from the bondage of Bentham ! the fanaticism of his adherents can touch me no longer. I feel the inadequacy of his mind and ideas for supplying the rule of human society, for perfection. ⬩

Culture tends always thus to deal with the men of a system, of disciples, of a school ; with men like Comte, or the late Mr. Buckle, or Mr. Mill. However much it may find to admire in these personages, or in some of them, it nevertheless remembers the text : "Be not ye called Rabbi!" and it soon passes on

from any Rabbi. But Jacobinism loves a Rabbi; it does not
want to pass on from its Rabbi in pursuit of a future and still
unreached perfection; it wants its Rabbi and his ideas to stand
for perfection, that they may with the more authority recast the
world; and for Jacobinism, therefore, culture — eternally passing
onward and seeking — is an impertinence and an offence. But
culture, just because it resists this tendency of Jacobinism to
impose on us a man with limitations and errors of his own
along with the true ideas of which he is the organ, really does
the world and Jacobinism itself a service.

So, too, Jacobinism, in its fierce hatred of the past and of
those whom it makes liable for the sins of the past, cannot away
with the inexhaustible indulgence proper to culture, the consideration of circumstances, the severe judgment of actions joined
to the merciful judgment of persons. "The man of culture is
in politics," cries Mr. Frederic Harrison, "one of the poorest
mortals alive!" Mr. Frederic Harrison wants to be doing
business, and he complains that the man of culture stops him
with a "turn for small fault-finding, love of selfish ease, and
indecision in action." Of what use is culture, he asks, except
for "a critic of new books or a professor of *belles-lettres* ?"
Why, it is of use because, in presence of the fierce exasperation
which breathes, or rather, I may say, hisses, through the whole
production in which Mr. Frederic Harrison asks that question,
it reminds us that the perfection of human nature is sweetness
and light. It is of use, because, like religion — that other effort
after perfection, — it testifies that, where bitter envying and strife
are, there is confusion and every evil work.

The pursuit of perfection, then, is the pursuit of sweetness and light. He who works for sweetness and light, works to make reason and the will of God prevail. He who works for machinery, he who works for hatred, works only for confusion. Culture looks beyond machinery, culture hates hatred; culture has one great passion, the passion for sweetness and light. It has one even yet greater! — the passion for making them *prevail.* It is not satisfied till we *all* come to a perfect man; it knows that the sweetness and light of the few must be imperfect until the raw and unkindled masses of humanity are touched with sweetness and light. If I have not shrunk from saying that we must work for sweetness and light, so neither have I shrunk from saying that we must have a broad basis, must have sweetness and light for as many as possible. Again and again I have insisted how those are the happy moments of humanity, how those are the marking epochs of a people's life, how those are the flowering times for literature and art and all the creative power of genius, when there is a *national* glow of life and thought, when the whole of society is in the fullest measure permeated by thought, sensible to beauty, intelligent and alive. Only it must be *real* thought and *real* beauty; *real* sweetness and *real* light. Plenty of people will try to give the masses, as they call them, an intellectual food prepared and adapted in the way they think proper for the actual condition of the masses. The ordinary popular literature is an example of this way of working on the masses. Plenty of people will try to indoctrinate the masses with the set of ideas and judgments constituting the creed of their own profession or party. Our religious and political organizations give an example of this way of working on the masses. I condemn neither way; but culture works differently. It does not try to teach down to the level of inferior classes; it does not try to win them for this or that sect of its own, with ready-made judgments and watchwords. It seeks to do away with classes; to make the best that has been taught and known in the world current everywhere; to make all men live in an atmosphere of sweetness and light, where they may use ideas, as it uses them itself, freely, — nourished, and not bound by them.

This is the *social idea;* and the men of culture are the true apostles of equality. The great men of culture are those who have had a passion for diffusing, for making prevail, for carrying from one end of society to the other, the best knowledge, the best ideas of their time; who have labored to divest knowledge of all that was harsh, uncouth, difficult, abstract, professional, exclusive; to humanize it, to make it efficient outside the clique of the cultivated and learned, yet still remaining the *best* knowledge and thought of the time, and a true source, therefore, of sweetness and light. Such a man was Abelard in the Middle Ages, in spite of all his imperfections; and thence the boundless emotion and enthusiasm which Abelard excited. Such were Lessing and Herder in Germany, at the end of the last century; and their services to Germany were in this way inestimably precious. Generations will pass, and literary monuments will accumulate, and works far more perfect than the works of Lessing and Herder will be produced in Germany; and yet the names of these two men will fill a German with a reverence and enthusiasm such as the names of the most gifted masters will hardly awaken. And why? Because they *humanized* knowledge; because they broadened the basis of life and intelligence;

because they worked powerfully to diffuse sweetness and light, to make reason and the will of God prevail. With St. Augustine they said : " Let us not leave Thee alone to make in the secret of thy knowledge, as thou didst before the creation of the firmament, the division of light from darkness; let the children of thy spirit, placed in their firmament, make their light shine upon the earth, mark the division of night and day, and announce the revolution of the times; for the old order is passed, and the new arises; the night is spent, the day is come forth; and thou shalt crown the year with thy blessing, when thou shalt send forth laborers into thy harvest sown by other hands than theirs; when thou shalt send forth new laborers to new seed-times, whereof the harvest shall be not yet."

ON POPULAR CULTURE.

An Address Delivered at the Town Hall, Birmingham (October 5, 1876), by the Writer, as President of the Midland Institute.

BY JOHN MORLEY.
(Born 1838.)

HE proceedings which have now been brought satisfactorily to an end, are of a kind which nobody who has sensibility as well as sense can take a part in without some emotion. An illustrious French philosopher, who happened to be an examiner of candidates for admission to the Polytechnic School, once confessed that, when a youth came before him eager to do his best, competently taught, and of an apt intelligence, he needed all his self-control to press back the tears from his eyes. Well, when we think how much industry, patience, and intelligent discipline; how many hard hours of self-denying toil; how many temptations to worthless pleasures resisted; how much steadfast feeling for things that are honest and true and of good report — are all represented by the young men and young women to whom I have had the honor of giving your prizes to-night, we must all feel our hearts warmed and gladdened in generous sympathy with so much excellence, so many good hopes, and so honorable a display of those qualities which make life better worth having for ourselves, and are so likely to make the world better worth living in for those who are to come after us.

If a prize-giving is always an occasion of lively satisfaction, my own satisfaction is all the greater at this moment, because your Institute, which is doing such good work in the world, and is in every respect so prosperous and so flourishing, is the creation of the people of your own district, without subsidy and without direction either from London, or from Oxford, or from Cambridge, or from any other centre whatever. Nobody in this town at any rate needs any argument of mine to persuade him that we can only be sure of advancing all kinds of knowledge, and developing our national life in all its plenitude and variety, on condition of multiplying these local centres both of secondary and higher education, and encouraging each of them to fight its own battle and do its work in its own way. For my own part I look with the utmost dismay at the concentration, not only of population, but of the treasures of instruction, in our vast city on the banks of the Thames. At Birmingham, as I am informed, one has not far to look for an example of this. One of the branches of your multifarious trades in this town is the manufacture of jewellery. Some of it is said commonly to be wanting in taste, elegance, skill; though some of it also — if I am not misinformed — is good enough to be passed off at Rome and at Paris, even to connoisseurs, as of Roman or French production. Now the nation possesses a most superb collection of all that is excellent and beautiful in jewellers' work. When I say that the nation possesses it, I mean that London possesses it. The University of Oxford, by the way, has also purchased a portion, but that is not at present accessible. If one of your craftsmen in that kind wants to profit by these admirable models, he must go to London. What happens is that he goes to the capital and stays there. Its superficial attractions are too strong for him. You lose a clever workman and a citizen, and he adds one more atom to that huge, overgrown, and unwieldy community. Now, why, in the name of common-sense, should not a portion of the Castellani collection pass six months of the year in Birmingham, the very place of all others where it is most likely to be of real service, and to make an effective mark on the national taste? [1]

---

[1] Sir Henry Cole, C. B., writes to the *Times* (Oct. 13th) on this suggestion as follows: — " In justice to the Lords President of the Council on Education, I hope you will allow me the opportunity of stating that from 1855 the Science and Art Department has done its very utmost to induce schools of art to receive deposits of works of art for study and popular examination, and to circulate its choicest objects useful to manufacturing industry. In corroboration of this assertion, please to turn to p. 435 of the Twenty-second Report of the Department, just issued. You will there find that upward of 26,907 objects of art, besides 23,911 paintings and drawings, have been circulated since 1855, and in some cases have been left for several months for exhibition in the localities. They have been seen by more than 6,000,000 of visitors, besides having been copied by students, etc., and the localities have taken the great sum of £116,182 for showing them.

" The Department besides has tried every efficient means to induce other public institutions, which are absolutely choked with superfluous specimens, to concur in a general principle of circulating the nation's works of art, but without success.

" The chief of our national storehouses of works of art, actually repudiates the idea that its objects are collected for purposes of education, and declares that they are only ' things rare and curious,' the very reverse of what common-sense says they are.

" Further, the Department, to tempt schools of art to acquire objects permanently for art museums attached to them, offered a grant in aid, of 50 per cent. of the cost price of the objects."

To pass on to the more general remarks which you are accustomed to expect from the President of the Institute on this occasion. When I consulted one of your townsmen as to the subject which he thought would be most useful and most interesting to you, he said : " Pray talk about any thing you please, if it is only not Education." There is a saying that there are two kinds of foolish people in the world, those who give advice and those who do not take it. My friend and I in this matter represent these two interesting divisions of the race, for in spite of what he said, it is upon Education after all that I propose to offer you some short observations. You will believe it no affectation on my part, when I say that I shall do so with the sincerest willingness to be corrected by those of wider practical experience in teaching. I am well aware, too, that I have very little that is new to say, but education is one of those matters on which much that has already been said, will long bear saying over and over again.

I have been looking through the report of your classes, and two things have rather struck me, which I will mention. One of them is the very large attendance in the French classes. This appears a singularly satisfactory thing, because you could scarcely do a hard-working man of whatever class a greater service than to give him easy access to French literature. Montesquieu used to say that he had never known a pain or a distress which he could not soothe by half an hour of a good book ; and perhaps it is no more of an exaggeration to say that a man who can read French with comfort need never have a dull hour. Our own literature has assuredly many a kingly name. In boundless riches and infinite imaginative variety, there is no rival to Shakespeare in the world; in energy and height and majesty Milton and Burke have no masters. But besides its great men of this loftier sort France has a long list of authors who have produced a literature whose chief mark is its agreeableness. As has been so often said, the genius of the French language is its clearness, firmness, and order; to this clearness certain circumstances in the history of French society have added the delightful qualities of liveliness in union with urbanity. Now, as one of the most important parts of popular education is to put people in the way of amusing and refreshing themselves in a rational rather than an irrational manner, it is a great gain to have given them the key to the most amusing and refreshing set of books in the world.

And here, perhaps, I may be permitted to remark, that it seems a pity that Racine is so constantly used as a school-book, instead of some of the moderns who are nearer to ourselves in ideas and manners. Racine is a great and admirable writer; but what you want for ordinary readers who have not much time, and whose faculties of attention are already largely exhausted by the more important industry of the day, is a book which brings literature more close to actual life than such a poet as Racine does. This is exactly one of the gifts and charms of modern French. To put what I mean very shortly, I would say, by way of illustration, that a man who could read the essays of Ste. Beuve with moderate comfort would have in his hands — of course I am now speaking of the active and busy part of the world, not of bookmen and students, — would, I say, have in his hands one of the very best instruments that I can think of; such work is exquisite and instructive in itself, it is a model of gracious writing, it is full of ideas, it breathes the happiest moods over us, and it is the most suggestive of guides, for those who have the capacity of extensive interests, to all the greater spheres of thought and history.

This word brings me back to the second fact that has struck me in your report, and it is this. The subject of English history has apparently so little popularity, that the class is as near being a failure as anything connected with the Midland Institute can be. On the whole, whatever may be the ability and the zeal of the teacher, this is, in my humble judgment, neither very surprising nor particularly mortifying, if we think what history in the established conception of it means. How are we to expect workmen to make their way through constitutional antiquities, through the labyrinthine shifts of party intrigue at home, and through the entanglements of intricate diplomacy abroad — "shallow village tales," as Emerson calls them? These studies are fit enough for professed students of the special subject, but such exploration is for the ordinary run of men and women impossible, and I do not know that it would lead them into very fruitful lands even if it were easy. You know what the great Duke of Marlborough said: that he had learned all the history he ever knew out of Shakespeare's historical plays. I have long thought that if we persuaded those classes who have to fight their own little Battles of Blenheim for bread every day, to make such a beginning of history as is furnished by Shakespeare's plays and Scott's novels, we should have done more to imbue them with a real interest in the past of mankind, than if he had taken them through a course of Hume and Smollett, or Hallam on the English Constitution, or even the dazzling Macaulay. What I for one should like to see in such an institution as this, would be an attempt to compress the whole history of England into a dozen or fifteen lectures — lectures of course accompanied by catechetical instruction. I am not so extravagant as to dream that a short general course of this kind would be enough to go over so many of the details as it is desirable for men to know, but details in popular instruction, though not in study of the writer or the university professor, are only important after you have imparted the largest general truths. It is the general truths that stir a life-like curiosity as to the particulars which they are the means of lighting up. Now this short course would be quite enough to present in a bold outline — and it need not be a whit the less true and real for being both bold and rapid — the great chains of events and the decisive movements, that have made of ourselves and our institutions what we and what they are — the Teutonic beginnings, the Conquest, the Great Charter, the Hundred Years' War, the Reformation, the Civil Wars and the Revolution, the Emancipation of the American Colonies from the Monarchy. If this course were framed and filled in with a true social intelligence, men would find that they had at the end of it a fair idea — an idea that might be of great value, and at any rate an idea much to be preferred to that blank ignorance which is in so many cases practically the only alternative — of the large issues of our past, of the antagonistic principles that strove with one another for mastery, of the chief material forces and moral currents of successive ages, and, above all, of those great men and our fathers that begat us — the Pyms, the Hampdens, the Cromwells, the Chathams — yes, and shall we not say the Washingtons, — to whose sagacity, bravery, and unquenchable ardor for justice and order and equal laws all our English-speaking peoples owe a debt that can never be paid.

Another point is worth thinking of, besides the reduction of history for your purposes to a comprehensive body of rightly grouped generalities. Dr. Arnold says somewhere, that he wishes the public might have a history of our present state of society *traced backward.* It is the present that really interests us ; it is the present that we seek to understand and to explain. I do not in the least want to know what happened in the past, except as it enables me to see my way more clearly through what is happening to-day. I want to know what men thought and did in the thirteenth century, not out of any dilettante or idle antiquarian's curiosity, but because the thirteenth century is at the root of what men think and do in the nineteenth. Well, then, it cannot be a bad educational rule to start from what is most interesting, and to work from that outward and backward. By beginning with the present, we see more clearly what are the two things best worth attending to in history — not party intrigues nor battles nor dynastic affairs, nor even many acts of Parliament, but the great movements of the economic forces of a society on the one hand, and on the other the forms of religious opinion and ecclesiastical organization. All the rest are important, but their importance is subsidiary.

Allow me to make one more remark on this subject. If a dozen or a score of wise lectures would suffice for a general picture of the various phrases through which our own society has passed, there ought to be added to the course of popular instruction as many lectures more, which would trace the

history, not of England, but of the world. And the history of
the world ought to go before the history of England. This is no
paradox, but the deliberate opinion of many of those who
have thought most deeply about the far-reaching chain of human
progress. When I was on a visit to the United States some
years ago — things may have improved since then — I could not
help noticing that the history classes in their common-schools
all began their work with the year 1776, when the American
colonies formed themselves into an independent confederacy.
The teaching assumed that the creation of the universe occurred
about that date. What could be more absurd, more narrow and
narrowing, more mischievously misleading as to the whole purport and significance of history? As if the laws, the representative institutions, the religious uses, the scientific methods, the
moral ideas, which give to an American citizen his character and
mental habits and social surroundings, had not all their roots in
the deeds and thoughts of wise and brave men, who lived in
centuries which are of course just as much the inheritance of the
vast continent of the West, as they are of the little island
whence its first colonizers sailed forth.

Well, there is something nearly as absurd, if not quite, in our
common plan of taking for granted that people should begin
their reading of history, not in 1776, but in 1066. As if this
could bring into our minds what is after all the greatest lesson
of history, namely, the fact of its oneness; of the independence
of all the elements that have in the course of long ages made
the European of to-day what we see him to be. It is no doubt
necessary for clear and definite comprehension to isolate your
phenomenon, and to follow the stream of our own history

separately. But that cannot be enough. We must also see that this stream is the effluent of a far broader and mightier flood — whose springs and sources and great tributaries lay higher up in the history of mankind. ✓

"We are learning," says Mr. Freeman, whose little book on the "Unity of History" I cannot be wrong in warmly recommending even to the busiest among you, "that European history, from its first glimmerings to our own day, is one unbroken drama, no part of which can be rightly understood without reference to the other parts which come before and after it. We are learning that of this great drama Rome is the centre, the point to which all roads lead and from which all roads lead no less. The world of independent Greece stands on one side of it; the world of modern Europe stands on another. But the history alike of the great centre itself, and of its satellites on either side, can never be fully grasped except from a point of view wide enough to take in the whole group, and to mark the relations of each of its members to the centre and to one another."

Now the counsel which our learned historian thus urges upon the scholar and the leisured student, equally represents the point of view which is proper for the more numerous classes of whom we are thinking to-night. The scale will have to be reduced; all save the very broadest aspects of things will have to be left out; none save the highest ranges and the streams of most copious volume will find a place in that map. Small as is the scale and many as are its omissions, yet if a man has intelligently followed the very shortest course of universal history, it will be the fault of his teacher if he has not acquired an

impressive conception, which will never be effaced, of the destinies of man upon the earth; of the mighty confluence of forces
working on from age to age, which have their meeting in every
one of us here to-night; of the order in which each state of
society has followed its foregoer, according to great and change-
less laws "embracing all things and all times;" of the thousand
faithful hands that have, one after another, each in their several
degrees, orders, and capacities, trimmed the silver lamp of
knowledge and kept its sacred flame bright from generation to
generation and age to age, now in one land and now in another,
from its early spark among far-off dim Chaldeans down to
Goethe and Faraday and Darwin and all the other good workers
of our own day.

The shortest course of universal history will let him see
how he owes to the Greek civilization, on the shores of the
Mediterranean two thousand years back, a debt extending from
the architectural forms of this very Town Hall to some of the
most systematic operations of his own mind; will let him see
the forum of Rome, its roads and its gates —

> "What conflux issuing forth or entering in,
> Prætors, Proconsuls to their provinces
> Hasting or on return, in robs of state, — "

all busily welding an empire together in a marvellous framework
of citizenship, manners, and laws, that laid assured foundations
for a still higher civilization that was to come after. He
will learn how when the Roman Empire declined, then at
Damascus and Bagdad and Seville the Mahometan conquerors
took up the torch of science and learning, and handed it on to
Western Europe when the new generations were ready. He will

learn how in the meantime, during ages which we both wrongly and ungratefully call dark, from Rome again, that other great organization, the mediæval Church, had arisen, which amid many imperfections and some crimes did a work that no glory of physical science can equal, and no instrument of physical science can compass, in purifying men's appetites, in setting discipline and direction on their lives, and in offering to humanity new types of moral obligation and fairer ideals of saintly perfection, whose light still shines like a star to guide our own poor voyages. It is only by this contemplation of the life of our race as a whole that men see the beginnings and the ends of things; learn not to be near-sighted in history, but to look before and after; see their own part and lot in the rising up and going down of empires and faiths since first recorded time began; and what I am contending for is that even if you can take your young men and women no further than the mere vestibule of this ancient and ever venerable temple of many marvels, you will have opened to them the way to a kind of knowledge that not only enlightens the understanding, but enriches the character—which is a higher thing than mere intellect — and makes it constantly alive with the spirit of beneficence.

I know it is said that such a view of collective history is true, but that you will never get plain people to respond to it; it is a thing for intellectual *dilettanti* and moralizing *virtuosi*. Well, we do not know, because we have never yet honestly tried, what the commonest people will or will not respond to. When Sir Richard Wallace's pictures were being exhibited at Bethnal Green, after people had said that the workers had no souls for art and would not appreciate its treasures, a story is told of a female in very poor clothes gazing intently at a picture of the Infant Jesus in the arms of his Mother, and then exclaiming, " *Who would not try to be a good woman, who had such a child as that?* " We have never yet, I say, tried the height and pitch to which our people are capable of rising.

I have thought it well to take this opportunity of saying a word for history, because I cannot help thinking that one of the most narrow, and what will eventually be one of the most impoverishing, characteristics of our day is the excessive supremacy claimed for physical science. This is partly due, no doubt, to a most wholesome reaction against the excessive supremacy that has hitherto been claimed for literature, and held by literature, in our schools and universities. At the same time, it is well to remember that the historic sciences are making strides not unworthy of being compared with those of the physical sciences, and not only is there room for both, but any system is radically wrong which excludes or depresses either to the advantage of the other.[1]

And now there is another idea which I should like to throw out, if you will not think it too tedious and too special. It is an old saying that, after all, the great end and aim of the British

---

[1] A very eminent physicist writes to me on this passage: "I cannot help smiling when I think of the place of physical science in the endowed schools," etc. My reference was to the great prevalence of such assertions as that human progress depends upon increase of our knowledge of the conditions of material phenomena (Dr. Draper, for instance, lays this down as a fundamental axiom of history): as if moral advance, the progressive elevation of types of character and ethical ideals, were not at least an equally important cause of improvement in civilization. The type of Saint Vincent de Paul is plainly as indispensible to progress as the type of Newton.

Constitution is to get twelve honest men into a box. That is really a very sensible way of putting the theory, that the first end of government is to give security to life and property, and to make people keep their contracts. But with this view it is not only important that you should get twelve honest men into a box: the twelve honest men must have in their heads some notions as to what constitutes evidence. Now it is surely a striking thing that while we are so careful to teach physical science and literature; while men want to be endowed in order to have leisure to explore our spinal cords, and to observe the locomotor system of Medusæ, — and I have no objection against those who urge on all these studies, — yet there is no systematic teaching, very often no teaching at all, in the principles of evidence and reasoning, even for the bulk of those who would be very much offended if we were to say that they are not educated. Of course I use the term evidence in a wider sense than the testimony in crimes and contracts, and the other business of courts of law. Questions of evidence are rising at every hour of the day. As Bentham says, it is a question of evidence with the cook whether the joint of meat is roasted enough. It has been excellently said that the principal and most characteristic difference between one human intellect and another consists in their ability to judge correctly of evidence. Most of us, Mr. Mill says, are very unsafe hands at estimating evidence, if appeal cannot be made to actual eyesight. Indeed, if we think of some of the tales that have been lately diverting the British Association, we might perhaps go further, and describe many of us as very bad hands at estimating evidence, even where appeal can be made to actual eyesight. Eyesight, in fact, is the least part of the matter. The senses are as often the tools as the guides of reason. One of the longest chapters in the history of vulgar error would contain the cases in which the eyes have only seen what old prepossessions inspired them to see, and were blind to all that would have been fatal to the prepossessions. "It is beyond all question or dispute," says Voltaire, "that magic words and ceremonies are quite capable of most effectually destroying a whole flock of sheep, if the words be accompanied by a sufficient quantity of arsenic." Sorcery has no doubt been exploded — at least we assume that it has — but the temper that made men attribute all the efficacy to the magic words, and entirely overlook the arsenic, still prevails in a great host of moral and political affairs, into which it is not convenient to enter here. The stability of a government for instance is constantly set down to some ornamental part of it, when in fact the ornamental part has no more to do with stability than the incantations of the soothsayer.

You have heard, again, that for many generations the people of the Isle of St. Kilda believed that the arrival of a ship in the harbor inflicted on the islanders epidemic colds in the head, and many ingenious reasons were from time to time devised by clever men why the ship should cause colds among the population. At last it occurred to somebody that the ship might not be the cause of the colds, but that both might be the common effects of some other cause, and it was then remembered that a ship could only enter the harbor when there was a strong northeast wind blowing.

However faithful the observation, as soon as ever a man uses words he may begin at that moment to go wrong. "A village

apothecary," it has been said, " and if possible in a still greater
degree, an experienced nurse, is seldom able to describe the
plainest case without employing a phraseology of which every
word is a theory; the simplest narrative of the most illiterate
observer involves more or less of hypothesis ;" — yet both by
the observer himself and by most of those who listen to him,
each of these conjectural assumptions is treated as respectfully
as if it were an established axiom. We are supposed to deny
the possibility of a circumstance, when in truth we only deny
the evidence alleged for it. We allow the excellence of reasoning from certain data to captivate our belief in the truth of the
data themselves, even when they are unproved and unprovable.
There is no end, in short, of the ways in which men habitually
go wrong in their reasoning, tacit or expressed. The greatest
boon that any benefactor could confer on the human race would
be to teach men — and especially women — to quantify their
propositions. It sometimes seems as if Swift were right when
he said that mankind were just as fit for flying as for thinking.

Now it is quite true that mother-wit and the common
experiences of life do often furnish people with a sort of shrewd
and sound judgment that carries them very creditably through
the world. They come to good conclusions, though perhaps
they would give bad reasons for them if they were forced to find
their reasons. But you cannot count upon mother-wit in everybody; perhaps not even in a majority. And then as for the
experience of life, — there are a great many questions, and those
of the deepest ultimate importance to mankind, in which the
ordinary experience of life sheds no light, until it has been
interrogated and interpreted by men with trained minds. " It

is far easier," as has been said, "to acquire facts than to judge what they prove." What is done in our systems of training to teach people how to judge what facts prove? There is mathematics, no doubt; anybody who has done even no more than the first book of Euclid's geometry, ought to have got into his head the notion of a demonstration, of the rigorously close connection between a conclusion and its premises, of the necessity of being able to show how each link in the chain comes to be where it is, and that it has a right to be there. This, however, is a long way from the facts of real life, and a man might well be a great geometer, and still be a thoroughly bad reasoner in practical questions.

Again, in other of your classes, in chemistry, in astronomy, in natural history, besides acquiring groups of facts, the student has a glimpse of the method by which they were discovered, of the type of inference to which the discovery conforms, so that the discovery of a new comet, the detection of a new species, the invention of a new chemical compound, — each becomes a lesson of the most beautiful and impressive kind in the art of reasoning. And it would be superfluous and impertinent for me here to point out how valuable such lessons are in the way of mental discipline, apart from the fruit they bear in other ways. But here again the relation to the judgments we have to form in the moral, political, practical sphere is too remote and too indirect. The judgments, in this region, of the most brilliant and successful explorers in physical science, seem to be exactly as liable to every kind of fallacy as those of other people. The application of scientific method and conception to society is yet in its infancy, and the "Novum Organum" or the "Principia" of moral and social phenomena will perhaps not be wholly disclosed to any of us now alive. In any case it is clear that for the purposes of such an institution as this, if the rules of evidence and proof and all the other safeguards for making your propositions true and relevant, are to be taught at all, they must be taught not only in an elementary form, but with illustrations that shall convey their own direct reference and application to practical life. If everybody could find time to master Mill's "Logic" or so instructive and interesting a book as Professor Jevons' "Principles of Science," a certain number at any rate of the bad mental habits of people would be cured; and for those of you here who have leisure enough, and want to find a worthy keystone of your culture, it would be hard to find a better thing to do for the next six months than to work through one or both of the books I have just named—pen in hand. The ordinary text-books of formal logic do not seem to meet the special aim which I am now trying to impress as desirable — namely, the habit of valuing, not merely speculative or scientific truth, but the truth of practical life; a practising of the intellect in forming and expressing the opinions and judgments that form the staple of our daily discourse.

It is now accepted that the most effective way of learning a foreign language is to begin by reading books written in it, or by conversing in it—and then after a certain empirical familiarity with vocabulary and construction has been acquired, one may proceed to master the grammar. Just in the same way it would seem to be the best plan to approach the art of practical reasoning in concrete examples, in cases of actual occurrence and living interest; and then after the processes of disentangling a complex group of propositions, of dividing and sifting, of scenting a fallacy, have all become familiar, it may be worth while to find names for them all, and to set out rules for reasoning rightly, just as in the former illustration the rules of writing correctly follow a certain practice, rather than precede it.

Now it has long seemed to me that the best way of teaching carefulness and precision in dealing with propositions might be found through the medium of the argumentation in the courts of justice. This is reasoning in real matter. There is a famous book well known to legal students — Smith's " Leading Cases "— which contains a selection of important decisions, and sets forth the grounds on which the courts arrived at them. I have often thought that a dozen or a score of cases might be collected from this book into a small volume, that would make such a manual as no other matter could, for opening plain men's eyes to the logical pitfalls among which they go stumbling and crashing, when they think they are disputing like Socrates or reasoning like Newton. They would see how a proposition or an expression that looks straightforward and unmistakable, is yet on examination found to be capable of bearing several distinct interpretations and meaning several distinct things; how the same evidence may warrant different conclusions, and what kinds of evidence carry with them what degrees of validity; how certain sorts of facts can only be proved in one way, and certain other sorts of facts in some other way; how necessary it is, before you set out, to know exactly what it is you intend to show, or what it is you intend to dispute; how there may be many argumentative objections to a proposition, yet the balance be in favor of its adoption. It is from the generality of people having neglected to practise the attention on these and the like matters, that interest and prejudice find so ready an instrument of sophistry in that very art of speech which ought to be the organ of reason and truth. To bring the matter to a point, then, I submit that it might be worth while in this and all such institutions to have a class for the study of logic, reasoning, evidence, and that such a class might well find its best material in selections from " Leading Cases," and from Bentham's " Rationale of Judicial Evidence," elucidated by those special sections in Mill's " Logic," or smaller manuals such as those of Mr. Fowler, the Oxford Professor of Logic, which treat of the department of fallacies. Perhaps Bentham's " Book of Fallacies" is too political for me to commend it to you here. But if there happens to be any one in Birmingham who is fond of meeting proposed changes by saying that they are Utopian; that they are good in theory, but bad in practice; that they are too good to be realized, and so forth, then I can promise him that he will in that book hear of something very much to his advantage.[1]

An incidental advantage — which is worth mentioning — of making legal instances the medium of instruction in practical logic, would be that people would — not learn law, of course, in

---

[1] This suggestion has fortunately found favor in a quarter where shrewd and critical common-sense is never wanting. The *Economist* (Oct. 14th) writes : — " Such a text-book commented on to a class by a man trained to estimate the value of evidence, would form a most valuable study, and not, we should imagine, at all less fascinating than valuable. Of course the class suggested would not be a class in English law, but in the principles on which evidence should be estimated, and the special errors to which, in common life, average minds are most liable. We regard this suggestion as a most useful one, and as one which would not only greatly contribute to the educational worth of an institute for adults, but also to its popularity."

the present state of our system, but they would have their attention called in a direct and business-like way to the lawyer's point of view, and those features of procedure in which every man and woman in the land has so immediate an interest. Perhaps if people interested themselves more seriously than is implied by reading famous cases in the newspapers, we should get rid, for one thing, of the rule which makes the accused person in a criminal case incompetent to testify; and, for another, of that infamous license of cross-examination to credit, which is not only barbarous to those who have to submit to it, but leads to constant miscarriage of justice in the case of those who, rather than submit to it, will suffer wrong.

It will be said, I dare say, that overmuch scruple about our propositions and the evidence for them will reduce men, especially the young, to the intellectual condition of the great philosopher, Marphurius, in Molière's comedy. Marphurius rebukes Saganarelle for saying he had come into the room : " What you should say is, that it *seems* I am come into the room." Instead of the downright affirmation and burly negations so becoming to Britons, he would bring down all our propositions to the attenuation of a possibility or a perhaps. We need not fear such an end. The exigencies of practical affairs will not allow this endless balancing. They are always driving men to the other extreme, making us like the new judge, who first heard the counsel on one side and made up his mind on the merits of the case, until the turn of the opposing counsel came, and then the new counsel filled the judge with so many doubts and perplexities, that he suddenly vowed that nothing would induce him to pay any heed to evidence again as long as he lived.

I do not doubt that I shall be blamed in what I have said about French, and about history, for encouraging a spirit of superficiality, and of contentment with worthless smatterings of things. To this I should answer that, as Archbishop Whately pointed out long ago, it is a fallacy to mistake general truths for superficial truths, or a knowledge of the leading propositions of a subject for a superficial knowledge. " To have a general knowledge of a subject is to know only its leading truths, but to know these thoroughly, so as to have a true conception of the subject in its great features." (*Mill.*) And I need not point out that instruction may be of the most general kind, and still possess that most important quality of all instruction — namely, being *methodical.*

I think popular instruction has been made much more repulsive than it need have been, and more repulsive than it ought to have been, because those who have had the control of the movement for the last fifty years, have been too anxious to make the type of popular instruction conform to the type of academic instruction proper to learned men. The principles of instruction have been too rigorously ascetic and puritanical, and instead of making the access to knowledge as easy as possible, we have delighted in forcing every pilgrim to make his journey to the shrine of the Muses with a hair shirt on his back and peas in his shoes. Nobody would say that Macaulay had a superficial knowledge of the things best worth knowing in ancient litera-ture, yet we have his own confession that when he became a busy man — as you are all busy — then he read his classics, not like a collegian, but like a man of the world ; if he did not know a word he passed it over, and if a passage refused to give up its meaning at the second reading, then he let it alone. Now the aims of academic education and those of popular education are — it is obvious if you come to think of it — quite different. The end of the one is rather to increase knowledge; of the other to diffuse it, and to increase men's interest in what is already known. If, therefore, I am for making certain kinds of instruction as general as they can possibly be made in these local centres, I should give to the old seats of learning a very special function indeed.

It would be absurd to attempt to discuss academic organization here at this hour. I only want to ask you as politicians whose representatives in Parliament will ultimately settle the matter — to reflect whether the money now consumed in idle fellowships might not be more profitably employed in endowing enquirers. The favorite argument of those who support prize fellowships is that they are the only means by which a child of the working-class can raise himself to the highest position in the land. My answer to this would be that, in the first place, it is of questionable expediency to invite the cleverest members of any class to leave it — instead of making their abilities available in it, and so raising the whole class along with, and by means of, their own rise. Second, these prize fellowships will continue, and must continue, to be carried off by those who can afford time and money to educate their sons for the competition. Third, I doubt the expediency — and the history of Oxford within the last twenty-five years strikingly confirms this doubt — of giving to a young man of any class what is practically a premium on indolence, and the removal of a motive to self-reliant and energetic spirit of enterprise. The best thing that I can

think of as happening to a young man is this : that he should
have been educated at a day-school in his own town ; that he
should have opportunities of following also the higher education in his own town ; and that at the earliest convenient time
he should be taught to earn his own living.

The universities might then be left to their proper business of
study. Knowledge for its own sake is clearly an object which
only a very small portion of society can be spared to pursue ;
only a very few men in a generation have that devouring passion
for knowing, which is the true inspirer of fruitful study and
exploration. Even if the passion were more common than it
is, the world could not afford on any very large scale that men
should indulge in it : the great business of the world has to be
carried on. One of the greatest of all hindrances to making
things better, is the habit of taking for granted that plans or
ideas, simply because they are different and approach the matter
from different sides, are therefore the rivals and enemies, instead
of being the friends and complements of one another. But a
great and wealthy society like ours ought very well to be able
to nourish one or two great seats for the augmentation of true
learning, and at the same time make sure that young men — and
again I say, especially young women — should have a good education of the higher kind within reach of their own hearths.

It is not necessary for me here, I believe, to dwell upon any
of the great commonplaces which the follower of knowledge
does well to keep always before his eyes, and which represent
the wisdom of many generations of studious experience. You
may have often heard from others, or may have found out, how
good it is to have on your shelves, however scantily furnished

they may be, three or four of those books, to which it is well to give ten minutes every morning, before going down into the battle and choking dust of the day. Men will name these books for themselves. One will choose the Bible, another Goethe, one the "Imitation of Christ," another Wordsworth. Perhaps it matters little what it be, so long as your writer has cheerful seriousness, elevation, calm, and, above all, a sense of size and strength, which shall open out the day before you and bestow gifts of fortitude and mastery.

Then, to turn to the intellectual side. You know as well as I or any one can tell you, that knowledge is worth little until you have made it so perfectly your own, as to be capable of reproducing it in precise and definite form. Goethe said that in the end we only retain of our studies, after all, what we practically employ of them. And it is at least well that in our serious studies we should have the possibility of practically turning them to a definite destination, clearly before our eyes. Nobody can be sure that he has got clear ideas on a subject, unless he has tried to put them down on a piece of paper in independent words of his own. It is an excellent plan, too, when you have read a good book, to sit down and write a short abstract of what you can remember of it. It is a still better plan, if you can make up your minds to a slight extra labor, to do what Lord Strafford, and Gibbon, and Daniel Webster did. After glancing over the title, subject, or design of a book, these eminent men would take a pen and write roughly what questions they expected to find answered in it, what difficulties solved, what kind of information imparted. Such practices keep us from reading with the eye only, gliding vaguely over the page·

and they help us to *place* our new acquisitions in relation with what we knew before. It is almost always worth while to read a thing twice over, to make sure that nothing has been missed or dropped on the way, or wrongly conceived or interpreted. And if the subject be serious, it is often well to let an interval elapse. Ideas, relations, statements of fact, are not to be taken by storm. We have to steep them in the mind, in the hope of thus extracting their inmost essence and significance. If one lets an interval pass, and then returns, it is surprising how clear and ripe that has become, which, when we left it, seemed crude, obscure, full of perplexity.

All this takes trouble, no doubt, but then it will not do to deal with ideas that we find in books or elsewhere as a certain bird does with its eggs — leave them in the sand for the sun to hatch and chance to rear. People who follow this plan possess nothing better than ideas half-hatched, and convictions reared by acci- dent. They are like a man who should pace up and down the world in the delusion that he is clad in sumptuous robes of purple and velvet, when in truth he is only half-covered by the rags and tatters of other people's cast-off clothes.

Apart from such mechanical devices as these I have mentioned, there are habits and customary attitudes of mind which a con- scientious reader will practice, if he desires to get out of a book still greater benefits than the writer of it may have designed or thought of. For example, he should never be content with mere aggressive and negatory criticism of the page before him. The page may be open to such criticism, and in that case it is natural to indulge in it; but the reader will often find an unexpected profit by asking himself — What does this error teach me? How comes that fallacy to be here? How came the writer to fall into this defect of taste? To ask such questions gives a reader a far healthier tone of mind in the long run, more seriousness, more depth, more moderation of judgment, more insight into other men's ways of thinking as well as into his own, than any amount of impatient condemnation and hasty denial, even when both condemnation and denial may be in their place.

Again, let us not be too ready to detect an inconsistency in our author, but rather let us teach ourselves to distinguish between inconsistency and having two sides to an opinion. " Before I admit that two and two are four," some one said, " I must first know to what use you are going to put the proposition." That is to say, even the plainest proposition needs to be stated with a view to the drift of the discussion in hand, or with a view to some special part of the discussion. When the turn of some other part of the matter comes, it will be convenient and often necessary to bring out into full light another side of your opinion, not contradictory, but complementary, and the great distinction of a candid disputant or of a reader of good faith, is his willing-ness to take pains to see the points of reconciliation among different aspects and different expressions of what is substan-tially the same judgment.

Then, again, nobody here needs to be reminded that the great successes of the world have been affairs of a second, a third, nay, a fiftieth trial. The history of literature, of science, of art, of industrial achievements, — all testify to the truth that success is only the last term of what looked like a series of failures. What is true of the great achievements of history, is true also of the little achievements of the observant cultivator of his own understanding. If a man is despondent about his work, the best remedy that I can prescribe to him is to turn to a good biography; there he will find that other men before him have known the dreary reaction that follows long-sustained effort, and he will find that one of the differences between the first-rate man and the fifth-rate lies in the vigor with which the first-rate man recovers from this reaction, and crushes it down, and again flings himself once more upon the breach. I remember the wisest and most virtuous man I have ever known, or am ever likely to know, — Mr. Mill, — once saying to me that whenever he had written any thing, he always felt profoundly dissatisfied with it, and it was only by reflecting that he had felt the same about other pieces of which the world had thought well, that he could bring himself to send the new production to the printer. The heroism of the scholar and the truth-seeker is not less admirable than the heroism of the man-at-arms.

Finally, you none of you need to be reminded of the most central and important of all the commonplaces of the student — that the stuff of which life is made is Time; that it is better, as Goethe said, to do the most trifling thing in the world, than to think half an hour a trifling thing. Nobody means by this that we are to have no pleasures. Where time is lost and wasted is where many people lose and waste their money — in things that are neither pleasure nor business — in those random and officious sociabilities, which neither refresh nor instruct nor invigorate, but only fret and benumb and wear all edge off the mind. All these things, however, you have all of you often thought about; yet, alas, we are so ready to forget, both in these matters and in other and weightier, how irrevocable are our mistakes.

> " The moving Finger writes, and having writ,
> Moves on ; nor all your piety nor wit
> Can lure it back to cancel half a line,
> Nor all your tears wipe out a word of it."

And now I think I cannot ask you to listen any longer. I will only add that these ceremonial anniversaries, when they are over, sometimes slightly tend to depress us, unless we are on our guard. When the prizes of the year are all distributed, and the address is at an end, we perhaps ask ourselves, Well, and what then? It is not to be denied that the expectations of the first fervent promoters of popular instruction by such institutes as this — of men like Lord Brougham and others, a generation ago — were not fulfilled. The principal reason was that the elementary instruction of the country was not then sufficiently advanced to supply a population ready to take advantage of education in the higher subjects. Well, we are in a fair way for removing that obstacle. It is true that the old world moves tardily on its arduous way, but even if the results of all our efforts in the cause of education were smaller than they are, there are still two considerations that ought to weigh with us and encourage us.

For one thing, you never know what child in rags and pitiful squalor that meets you in the street may have in him the germ of gifts that might add new treasures to the store-house of beautiful things or noble acts. In that great storm of terror that swept over France in 1793, a certain man who was every hour expecting to be led off to the guillotine, uttered this memorable sentiment: "Even at this incomprehensible moment," he said "when mortality, enlightenment, love of country, — all of them only make death at the prison-door or on the scaffold more certain — yes, on the fatal tumbril itself, with nothing free but my voice, I could still cry *Take care*, to a child that should come too near the wheel ; perhaps I may save his life, perhaps he may one day save his country." This is a generous and inspiring thought — one to which the roughest-handed man or woman in Birmingham may respond as honestly and heartily as the philosopher who wrote it. It ought to shame the listlessness with which so many of us see the great phantasmagoria of life pass before us.

There is another thought to encourage us, still more direct, and still more positive. The boisterous old notion of hero-worship, which has been preached by so eloquent a voice in our age, is, after all, now seen to be a half-truth, and to contain the less edifying and the less profitable half of the truth. The world will never be able to spare its hero, and the man with the rare and inexplicable gift of genius will always be as command-ing a figure as he has ever been. What we see every day with increasing clearness is that not only the well-being of the many, but the chances of exceptional genius, moral or intellectual, in the gifted few, are highest in a society where the *average* interest, curiosity, capacity, are all highest. The moral of this for you. and for me is plain. We cannot, like Beethoven or Handel, lift the soul by the magic of divine melody into the seventh heaven of ineffable vision and hope incommensurable ; we cannot, like Newton, weigh the far-off stars in a balance, and measure the heavings of the eternal flood ; we cannot, like Voltaire, scorch up what is cruel and false by a word as a flame ; nor, like Milton or Burke, awaken men's hearts with the note of an organ-trumpet; we cannot, like the great saints of the churches and the great sages of the schools, add to those acquisitions of spiritual beauty and intellectual mastery which have, one by one, and little by little, raised man from being no higher than the brute to be only a little lower than the angels. But what we can do — the humblest of us in this great hall — is by diligently using our own minds and diligently seeking to extend our own opportunities to others, to help to swell that common tide, on the force and the set of whose currents depends the prosperous voyaging of humanity. When our names are blotted out, and our place knows us no more, the energy of each social service will remain, and so too, let us not forget, will each social disservice remain, like the unending stream of one of nature's forces. The thought that this is so, may well lighten the poor perplexities of our daily life, and even soothe the pang of its calamities; it lifts us from our feet as on wings, opening a larger meaning to our private toil and a higher purpose to our public endeavor; it makes the morning as we awake to its welcome, and the evening like a soft garment as it wraps us about; it nerves our arm with boldness against oppression and injustice, and strengthens our voice with deeper accents against falsehood, while we are yet in the full noon of our days — yes, and perhaps it will shed some ray of consolation, when our eyes are growing dim to it all, and we go down into the Valley of Darkness.

ON A CERTAIN CONDESCENSION IN FOREIGNERS.*

BY JAMES RUSSELL LOWELL.

(BORN 1819.)

ALKING one day toward the Village, as we used to call it in the good old days when almost every dweller in the town had been born in it, I was enjoying that delicious sense of disenthralment from the actual which the deepening twilight brings with it, giving as it does a sort of obscure novelty to things familiar. The coolness, the hush, broken only by the distant bleat of some belated goat, querulous to be disburthened of her milky load, the few faint stars, more guessed as yet than seen, the sense that the coming dark would so soon fold me in the secure privacy of its disguise, — all things combined in a result as near absolute peace as can be hoped for by a man who knows that there is a writ out against him in the hands of the printer's devil. For the moment, I was enjoying the blessed privilege of thinking without being called on to stand and deliver what I thought

---

* From "My Study Windows," through the courtesy of Messrs. Houghton, Mifflin, & Co.

to the small public who are good enough to take any interest therein. I love old ways, and the path I was walking felt kindly to the feet it had known for almost fifty years. How many fleeting impressions it had shared with me ! How many times I had lingered to study the shadows of the leaves mezzo-tinted upon the turf that edged it by the moon, of the bare boughs etched with a touch beyond Rembrandt by the same unconscious artist on the smooth page of snow! If I turned round, through dusky tree-gaps came the first twinkle of evening lamps in the dear old homestead. On Corey's hill I could see these tiny pharoses of love and home and sweet domestic thoughts flash out one by one across the blackening salt-meadow between. How much has not kerosene added to the cheerfulness of our evening landscape ! A pair of night-herons flapped heavily over me toward the hidden river. The war was ended. I might walk townward without that aching dread of bulletins that had darkened the July sunshine and twice made the scarlet leaves of October seem stained with blood. I remembered with a pang, half proud, half painful, how, so many years ago, I had walked over the same path and felt round my finger the soft pressure of a little hand that was one day to harden with faithful grip of sabre. On how many paths, leading to how many homes where proud Memory does all she can to fill up the fireside gaps with shining shapes, must not men be walking in just such pensive mood as I? Ah, young heroes, safe in immortal youth as those of Homer, you at least carried your ideal hence untarnished ! It is locked for you beyond moth or rust in the treasure-chamber of Death.

Is not a country, I thought, that has had such as they in it, that could give such as they a brave joy in dying for it, worth something then? And as I felt more and more the soothing magic of evening's cool palm upon my temples, as my fancy came home from its revery, and my senses, with reawakened curiosity, ran to the front windows again from the viewless closet of abstraction, and felt a strange charm in finding the old tree and shabby fence still there under the travesty of falling night, nay, were conscious of an unsuspected newness in familiar stars and the fading outlines of hills my earliest horizon, I was conscious of an immortal soul, and could not but rejoice in the unwaning goodliness of the world into which I had been born without any merit of my own. ˙I thought of dear Henry Vaughan's rainbow, "Still young and fine!" I remembered people who had to go over to the Alps to learn what the divine silence of snow was, who must run to Italy before they were conscious of the miracle wrought every day under their very noses by the sunset, who must call upon the Berkshire hills to teach them what a painter autumn was, while close at hand the Fresh Pond meadows made all oriels cheap with hues that showed as if a sunset-cloud had been wrecked among their maples. One might be worse off than even in America, I thought. There are some things so elastic that even the heavy roller of democracy cannot flatten them altogether down. The mind can weave itself warmly in the cocoon of its own thoughts and dwell a hermit anywhere. A country without traditions, without ennobling associations, a scramble of *parvenus*, with a horrible consciousness of shoddy running through politics, manners, art, literature, nay, religion itself? I confess, it did not seem to me there in that illimitable quiet, that serene self-possession of nature, where Collins might have brooded his "Ode to Evening," or where those verses on Solitude in Dodsley's Collection, that Hawthorne liked so much, might have been composed. Traditions? Granting that we had none, all that is worth having in them is the common property of the soul, — an estate in gavelkind for all the sons of Adam, — and, moreover, if a man cannot stand on his two feet (the prime quality of whoever has left any tradition behind him), were it not better for him to be honest about it at once, and go down on all fours? And for associations, if one have not the wit to make them for himself out of his native earth, no ready-made ones of other men will avail him much. Lexington is none the worse to me for not being in Greece, nor Gettysburg that its name is not Marathon. "Blessed old fields," I was just exclaiming to myself, like one of Mrs. Radcliffe's heroes, "dear acres, innocently secure from history, which these eyes first beheld, may you be also those to which they shall at last slowly darken!" when I was interrupted by a voice which asked me in German whether I was the Herr Professor, Doctor So-and-so? The "Doctor" was my brevet of vaticination, to make the grade easier to my pocket.

One feels so intimately assured that he is made up, in part, of shreds and leavings of the past, in part of the interpolations of other people, that an honest man would be slow in saying *yes* to such a question. But "my name is So-and-so" is a safe answer, and I gave it. While I had been romancing with myself, the street-lamps had been lighted, and it was under one of these detectives that have robbed the Old Road of its privilege of sanctuary after nightfall that I was ambushed by my foe. The inexorable villain had taken my description, it appears, that

I might have the less chance to escape him. Dr. Holmes tells us that we change our substance, not every seven years, as was once believed, but with every breath we draw. Why had I not the wit to avail myself of the subterfuge, and, like Peter, to renounce my identity, especially, as in certain moods of mind, I have often more than doubted of it myself? When a man is, as it were, his own front door, and is thus knocked at, why may he not assume the right of that sacred wood to make every house a castle, by denying himself to all visitations? I was truly not at home when the question was put to me, but had to recall myself from all out-of-doors, and to piece my self-consciousness hastily together as well as I could before I answered it.

I knew perfectly well what was coming. It is seldom that debtors or good Samaritans waylay people under gas-lamps in order to force money upon them, so far as I have seen or heard. I was also aware, from considerable experience, that every foreigner is persuaded, that by doing this country the favor of coming to it, he has laid every native thereof under an obligation, pecuniary or other, as the case may be, whose discharge he is entitled to on demand duly made in person or by letter. Too much learning (of this kind) has made me mad in the provincial sense of the word. I had begun life with the theory of giving something to every beggar that came along, though sure of never finding a native-born countryman among them. In a small way I was resolved to emulate Hatem Tai's tent, with its three hundred and sixty-five entrances, one for every day in the year, — I know not whether he was astronomer enough to add another for leap-years. The beggars were a kind of German-silver aristocracy; not real plate, to be sure, but better than nothing. Where everybody was over-worked, they supplied the comfortable equipoise of absolute leisure, so æsthetically need-ful. Besides, I was but too conscious of a vagrant fibre in myself, which too often thrilled me in my solitary walks with the temptation to wander on into infinite space, and by a single spasm of resolution to emancipate myself from the drudgery of prosaic serfdom to respectability and the regular course of things. This prompting has been at times my familiar demon, and I could not but feel a kind of respectful sympathy for men who had dared what I had only sketched out to myself as a splendid possibility. For seven years I helped maintain one heroic man on an imaginary journey to Portland, — as fine an example as I have ever known of hopeless loyalty to an ideal. I assisted another so long in a fruitless attempt to reach Meck-lenburg-Schwerin, that at last we grinned in each other's faces when we met, like a couple of augurs. He was possessed by this harmless mania as some are by the North Pole, and I shall never forget his look of regretful compassion (as for one who was sacrificing his higher life to the fleshpots of Egypt) when I at last advised him somewhat strenuously to go to the D——, whither the road was so much travelled that he could not miss it. General Banks, in his noble zeal for the honor of his coun-try, would confer on the Secretary of State the power of impris-oning, in case of war, all these seekers of the unattainable, thus by a stroke of the pen annihilating the single poetic element in our humdrum life. Alas! not everybody has the genius to be a Bobbin-Boy, or, doubtless, all these also would have chosen that more prosperous line of life! But moralists, sociologists, polit-ical economists, and taxes have slowly convinced me that my

beggarly sympathies were a sin against society. Especially was
the Buckle doctrine of averages (so flattering to our free-will)
persuasive with me; for as there must be in every year a certain
number who would bestow an alms on these abridged editions
of the Wandering Jew, the withdrawal of my quota could make
no possible difference, since some destined proxy must always
step forward to fill my gap. Just so many misdirected letters
every year and no more! Would it were as easy to reckon up
the number of men on whose backs fate has written the wrong
address, so that they arrive by mistake in Congress and other
places where they do not belong! May not these wanderers of
whom I speak have been sent into the world without any proper
address at all? Where is our Dead-Letter Office for such?
And if wiser social arrangements should furnish us with something of the sort, fancy (horrible thought!) how many a working
man's friend (a kind of industry in which the labor is light and
the wages heavy) would be sent thither because not called for in
the office where he at present lies.

But. I am leaving my new acquaintance too long under the
lamp-post. The same Gano which had betrayed me to him
revealed to me a well-set young man of about half my own age,
as well dressed, so far as I could see, as I was, and with every
natural qualification for getting his own livelihood as good, if not
better, than my own. He had been reduced to the painful
necessity of calling upon me by a series of crosses beginning
with the Baden Revolution (for which, I own, he seemed rather
young, — but perhaps he referred to a kind of revolution practised every season at Baden-Baden), continued by repeated
failures in business, for amounts which must convince me of his

entire respectability, and ending with our Civil War. During
the latter, he had served with distinction as a soldier, taking a
main part in every important battle, with a rapid list of which he
favored me, and no doubt would have admitted that, impartial
as Jonathan Wild's great ancestor, he had been on both sides,
had I baited him with a few hints of conservative opinions on a
subject so distressing to a gentleman wishing to profit by one's
sympathy and unhappily doubtful as to which way it might lean.
For all these reasons, and, as he seemed to imply, for his merit
in consenting to be born in Germany, he considered himself my
natural creditor to the extent of five dollars, which he would
handsomely consent to accept in greenbacks, though he preferred specie. The offer was certainly a generous one, and the
claim presented with an assurance that carried conviction. But,
unhappily, I had been led to remark a curious natural phenomenon. If I was ever weak enough to give any thing to a
petitioner of whatever nationality, it always rained decayed
compatriots of his for a month after. *Post hoc ergo propter hoc*
may not be always safe logic, but here I seemed to perceive a
natural connection of cause and effect. Now, a few days before I had been so tickled with a paper (professedly written by
a benevolent American clergyman) certifying that the bearer, a
hard-working German, had long "sofered with rheumatic paints
in his limps," that, after copying the passage into my note-book,
I thought it but fair to pay a trifling *honorarium* to the author.
I had pulled the string of the shower-bath! It had been running shipwrecked sailors for some time, but forthwith it began
to pour Teutons, redolent of *lager-bier.* I could not help associating the apparition of my new friend with this series of other-

wise unaccountable phenomena. I accordingly made up my
mind to deny the debt, and modestly did so, pleading a native
bias toward impecuniosity to the full as strong as his own. He
took a high tone with me at once, such as an honest man would
naturally take with a confessed repudiator. He even brought
down his proud stomach so far as to join himself to me for the
rest of my townward walk, that he might give me his views of
the American people, and thus inclusively of myself.

· I know not whether it is because I am pigeon-livered and lack
gall, or whether it is from an overmastering sense of drollery,
but I am apt to submit to such bastings with a patience which
afterward surprises me, being not without my share of warmth
in the blood. Perhaps it is because I so often meet with young
persons who know vastly more than I do, and especially with so
many foreigners whose knowledge of this country is superior to
my own. However it may be, I listened for some time with
tolerable composure as my self-appointed lecturer gave me in
detail his opinions of my country and its people. America, he
informed me, was without arts, science, literature, culture, or any
native hope of supplying them. We were a people wholly given
to money-getting, and who, having got it, knew no other use for
it than to hold it fast. I am fain to confess that I felt a sensible
itching of the biceps, and that my fingers closed with such a
grip as he had just informed me was one of the effects of our
unhappy climate. But happening just then to be where I could
avoid temptation by dodging down a by-street, I hastily left him
to finish his diatribe to the lamp-post, which could stand it better
than I. That young man will never know how near he came to
being assaulted by a respectable gentleman of middle age, at

the corner of Church Street. I have never felt quite satisfied
that I did all my duty by him in not knocking him down. But
perhaps he might have knocked *me* down, and then?

The capacity of indignation makes an essential part of the
outfit of every honest man, but I am inclined to doubt whether
he is a wise one who allows himself to act upon its first hints.
It should be rather, I suspect, a *latent* heat in the blood, which
makes itself felt in character, a steady reserve for the brain,
warming the ovum of thought to life, rather than cooking it by
a too hasty enthusiasm in reaching the boiling-point. As my
pulse gradually fell back to its normal beat, I reflected that I
had been uncomfortably near making a fool of myself, — a
handy salve of euphuism for our vanity, though it does not
always make a just allowance to Nature for her share in the
business. What possible claim had my Teutonic friend to rob
me of my composure? I am not, I think, especially thin-skinned
as to other people's opinions of myself, having, as I conceive,
later and fuller intelligence on that point than anybody else can
give. Life is continually weighing us in very sensitive scales,
and telling every one of us precisely what his real weight is to
the last grain of dust. Whoever at fifty does not rate himself
quite as low as most of his acquaintance would be likely to put
him, must be either a fool or a great man, and I humbly disclaim
being either. But if I was not smarting in person from any
scattering shot of my late companion's commination, why should
I grow hot at any implication of my country therein? Surely
her shoulders are broad enough if yours or mine are not, to bear
up under a considerable avalanche of this kind. It is the bit of
truth in every slander, the hint of likeness in every caricature,

that makes us smart. "Art thou *there*, old Truepenny?" How
did your blade know its way so well to that one loose rivet in our
armor? I wondered whether Americans were over-sensitive in
this respect, whether they were more touchy than other folks.
On the whole, I thought we were not. Plutarch, who at least
had studied philosophy, if he had not mastered it, could not
stomach something Herodotus had said of Bœotia, and devoted
an essay to showing up the delightful old traveller's malice and
ill-breeding. French editors leave out of Montaigne's "Travels"
some remarks of his about France, for reasons best known to
themselves. Pachydermatous Deutschland, covered with trophies from every field of letters, still winces under that question
which Père Bouhours put two centuries ago, *Si un Allemand
peut être bel-esprit?* John Bull grew apoplectic with angry
amazement at the audacious persiflage of Pückler-Muskau. To
be sure he was a prince, — but that was not all of it, for a
chance phrase of gentle Hawthorne sent a spasm through all
the journals of England. Then this tenderness is not peculiar
to *us?* Console yourself, dear man and brother, whatever you
may be sure of, be sure at least of this, that you are dreadfully
like other people. Human nature has a much greater genius
for sameness than for originality, or the world would be at a sad
pass shortly. The surprising thing is, that men have such a
taste for this somewhat musty flavor, that an Englishman, for
example, should feel himself defrauded, nay, even outraged,
when he comes over here and finds a people speaking what he
admits to be something like English, and yet so very different
from (or, as he would say, to) those he left at home. Nothing,
I am sure, equals *my* thankfulness when I meet an Englishman

who is *not* like every other or, I may add, an American of the
same odd turn.

Certainly it is no shame to a man that he should be as nice
about his country as about his sweetheart ; and who ever heard
even the friendliest appreciation of that unexpressive she that
did not seem to fall infinitely short ? Yet it would hardly be
wise to hold every one an enemy who could not see her with our
own enchanted eyes. It seems to be the common opinion of
foreigners that Americans are *too* tender upon this point. Perhaps we are ; and if so, there must be a reason for it. Have we
had fair-play ? Could the eyes of what is called Good Society
(though it is so seldom true either to the adjective or noun) look
upon a nation of democrats with any chance of receiving an
undistorted image ? Were not those, moreover, who found in
the old order of things an earthly paradise, paying them quarterly dividends for the wisdom of their ancestors, with the
punctuality of the seasons, unconsciously bribed to misunder-
stand if not to misrepresent us ? Whether at war or at peace,
there we were, a standing menace to all earthly paradises of
that kind, fatal underminers of the very credit on which the
dividends were based, all the more hateful and terrible that our
destructive agency was so insidious, working invisible in the
elements, as it seemed, active while they slept, and coming upon
them in the darkness like an armed man. *Could* Laius have
the proper feelings of a father toward Œdipus, announced as
his destined destroyer by infallible oracles, and felt to be such
by every conscious fibre of his soul ? For more than a century
the Dutch were the laughing-stock of polite Europe. They
were butter-firkins, swillers of beer and schnaps, and their

vrouws from whom Holbein painted the all-but loveliest of Madonnas, Rembrandt the graceful girl who sits immortal on his knee in Dresden, and Rubens his abounding goddesses, were the synonymes of clumsy vulgarity. Even so late as Irving, the ships of the greatest navigators in the world were represented as sailing equally well stern-foremost. That the aristocratic Venetians should have

> "Riveted with gigantic piles
> Thorough the centre their new-catchèd miles,"

was heroic. But the far more marvellous achievement of the Dutch in the same kind was ludicrous even to republican Marvell. Meanwhile, during that very century of scorn, they were the best artists, sailors, merchants, bankers, printers, scholars, jurisconsults, and statesmen in Europe, and the genius of Motley has revealed them to us, earning a right to themselves by the most heroic struggle in human annals. But, alas! they were not merely simple burghers who had fairly made themselves High Mightinesses, and could treat on equal terms with anointed kings, but their commonwealth carried in its bosom the germs of democracy. They even unmuzzled, at least after dark, that dreadful mastiff, the Press, whose scent is, or ought to be, so keen for wolves in sheep's clothing and for certain other animals in lions' skins. They made fun of Sacred Majesty, and, what was worse, managed uncommonly well without it. In an age when periwigs made so large a part of the natural dignity of man, people with such a turn of mind were dangerous. How could they seem other than vulgar and hateful?

In the natural course of things we succeeded to this unenviable position of general butt. The Dutch had thriven under it pretty well, and there was hope that we could at least contrive to worry along. And we certainly did in a very redoubtable fashion. Perhaps we deserved some of the sarcasm more than our Dutch predecessors in office. We had nothing to boast of in arts or letters, and were given to bragging overmuch of our merely material prosperity, due quite as much to the virtue of our continent as to our own. There was some truth in Carlyle's sneer, after all. Till we had succeeded in some higher way than this, we had only the success of physical growth. Our greatness, like that of enormous Russia, was greatness on the map, — barbarian mass only; but had we gone down, like that other Atlantis, in some vast cataclysm, we should have covered but a pin's point on the chart of memory, compared with those ideal spaces occupied by tiny Attica and cramped England. At the same time, our critics somewhat too easily forgot that material must make ready the foundation for ideal triumphs, that the arts have no chance in poor countries. But it must be allowed that democracy stood for a great deal in our shortcoming. The *Edinburgh Review* never would have thought of asking, "Who reads a Russian book?" and England was satisfied with iron from Sweden without being impertinently inquisitive after her painters and statuaries. Was it that they expected too much from the mere miracle of Freedom? Is it not the highest art of a Republic to make men of flesh and blood, and not the marble ideals of such. It may be fairly doubted whether we have produced this higher type of man yet. Perhaps it is the collective, not the individual, humanity that is to have a chance of nobler development among us. We shall see. We have a vast amount of imported ignorance, and, still worse, of

native ready-made knowledge, to digest before even the prelimi-
naries of such a consummation can be arranged. We have got
to learn that statesmanship is the most complicated of all arts,
and to come back to the apprenticeship system too hastily
abandoned. At present, we trust a man with making constitutions
on less proof of competence than we should demand before we
gave him our shoe to patch. We have nearly reached the limit of
the reaction from the old notion which paid too much regard to
birth and station as qualifications for office, and have touched
the extreme point in the opposite direction, putting the highest
of human functions up at auction to be bid for by any creature
capable of going upright on two legs. In some places, we have
arrived at a point at which civil society is no longer possible,
and already another reaction has begun, not backward to the old
system, but toward fitness either from natural aptitude or special
training. But will it always be safe to let evils work their own
cure by becoming unendurable ? Every one of them leaves its
taint in the constitution of the body-politic, each in itself,
perhaps, trifling, yet altogether powerful for evil.

But whatever we might do or leave undone, we were not gen-
teel, and it was uncomfortable to be continually reminded that,
though we should boast that we were the Great West till we
were black in the face, it did not bring us an inch nearer to the
world's West End. That sacred enclosure of respectability was
tabooed to us. The Holy Alliance did not inscribe us on its
visiting-list. The Old World of wigs and orders and liveries
would shop with us, but we must ring at the area-bell, and not
venture to awaken the more august clamors of the knocker.
Our manners, it must be granted, had none of those graces that

stamp the caste of Verē de Vere, in whatever museum of British antiquities they may be hidden.   In short, we were vulgar.

This was one of those horribly vague accusations, the victim of which has no defence.   An umbrella is of no avail against a Scotch mist.   It envelops you, it penetrates at every pore, it wets you through without seeming to wet you at all.   Vulgarity is an eighth deadly sin, added to the list in these latter days, and worse than all the others put together, since it perils your salvation in *this* world, — far the more important of the two in the minds of most men.   It profits nothing to draw nice distinctions between essential and conventional, for the convention in this case *is* the essence, and you may break every command of the decalogue with perfect good-breeding, nay, if you are adroit, without losing caste.   We, indeed, had it not to lose, for we had never gained it.   "*How* am I vulgar?" asks the culprit, shudderingly.   "Because thou art not like unto Us," answers Lucifer, Son of the Morning, and there is no more to be said.   The god of this world may be a fallen angel, but he has us *there!*   We were as clean — so far as my observation goes, I think we were cleaner — morally and physically, than the English, and therefore, of course, than everybody else.   But we did not pronounce the diphthong *ou* as they did, and we said *eether* and not *eyther*, following therein the fashion of our ancestors, who unhappily could bring over no English better than Shakespeare's; and we did not stammer as they had learned to do from the courtiers, who in this way flattered the Hanoverian king, a foreigner among the people he had come to reign over.   Worse than all, we might have the noblest ideas and the finest sentiments in the world, but we vented them through that organ by which men are led rather than leaders, though some physiologists would persuade us that Nature furnishes her captains with a fine handle to their faces that Opportunity may get a good purchase on them for dragging them to the front.

This state of things was so painful that excellent people were not wanting who gave their whole genius to reproducing here the original Bull, whether by gaiters, the cut of their whiskers, by a factitious brutality in their tone, or by an accent that was forever tripping and falling flat over the tangled roots of our common tongue. Martyrs to a false ideal, it never occurred to them that nothing is more hateful to gods and men than a second-rate Englishman, and for the very reason that this planet never produced a more splendid creature than the first-rate one, witness Shakespeare and the Indian Mutiny. Witness that truly sublime self-abnegation of those prisoners lately among the bandits of Greece, where average men gave an example of quiet fortitude for which all the stoicism of antiquity can show no match. If we could contrive to be not too unobtrusively our simple selves, we should be the most delightful of human beings, and the most original; whereas, when the plating of Anglicism rubs off, as it always will in points that come to much wear, we are liable to very unpleasing conjectures about the quality of the metal underneath. Perhaps one reason why the average Briton spreads himself here with such an easy air of superiority, may be owing to the fact that he meets with so many bad imitations as to conclude himself the only real thing in a wilderness of shams. He fancies himself moving through an endless Bloomsbury, where his mere apparition confers honor as an avatar of the court-end of the universe. Not a Bull of them all but is persuaded he bears Europa upon his back. This is the sort of fellow whose patronage is so divertingly insufferable. Thank Heaven he is not the only specimen of cater-cousinship from the dear old Mother Island that is shown to us! Among genuine things, I know nothing more genuine than the better men whose limbs were made in England. So manly-tender, so brave, so true, so warranted to wear, they make us proud to feel that blood is thicker than water.

But it is not merely the Englishman ; every European candidly admits in himself some right of primogeniture in respect to us, and pats this shaggy continent on the back with a lively sense of generous unbending. The German who plays the bass-viol has a well-founded contempt, which he is not always nice in concealing, for a country so few of whose children ever take that noble instrument between their knees. His cousin, the Ph. D. from Göttingen, cannot help despising a people who do not grow loud and red over Aryans and Turanians, and are indifferent about their descent from either. The Frenchman feels an easy mastery in speaking his mother-tongue, and attributes it to some native superiority of parts that lifts him high above us barbarians of the West. The Italian *prima donna* sweeps a courtesy of careless pity to the over-facile pit which unsexes her with the *bravo !* innocently meant to show a familiarity with foreign usage. But all without exception make no secret of regarding us as the goose bound to deliver them a golden egg in return for *their* cackle. Such men as Agassiz, Guyot, and Goldwin Smith come with gifts in their hands; but since it is commonly European failures who bring hither their remarkable gifts and acquirements, this view of the case is sometimes just the least bit in the world provoking. To think what a delicious seclusion of contempt we enjoyed till California and our own ostentatious *parvenus*, flinging gold away in Europe that might have endowed libraries at home, gave us the ill-repute of riches! What a shabby downfall from the Arcadia which the French officers of our Revolutionary War fancied they saw here through Rousseau-tinted spectacles! Something of Arcadia there really was, something of the Old Age; and that divine provincialism were cheaply repurchased could we have it back again in exchange for the tawdry upholstery that has taken its place.

For some reason or other, the European has rarely been able to see America except in caricature. Would the first review of the world have printed the *niaiseries* of Mr. Maurice Sand as a picture of society in any civilized country? Mr. Sand, to be sure, has inherited nothing of his famous mother's literary outfit, except the pseudonym. But since the conductors of the *Revue* could not have published his story because it was clever, they must have thought it valuable for its truth. As true as the last-century Englishman's picture of Jean Crapaud? We do not ask to be sprinkled with rose-water, but may perhaps fairly protest against being drenched with the rinsings of an unclean imagination. The next time the *Revue* allows such ill-bred persons to throw their slops out of its first-floor windows, let it honestly preface the discharge with a *gare de l'eau!* that we may run from under in season. And Mr. Duvergier d'Hauranne, who knows how to be entertaining! I know *le Français est plutôt indiscret que confiant*, and the pen slides too easily when indiscretions will fetch so much a page; but should

we not have been *tant-soit-peu* more cautious had we been
writing about people on the other side of the Channel? But
then it is a fact in the natural history of the American long
familiar to Europeans, that he abhors privacy, knows not the
meaning of reserve, lives in hotels because of their greater publicity, and is never so pleased as when his domestic affairs (if he
may be said to have any), are paraded in the newspapers.
Barnum, it is well known, represents perfectly the average
national sentiment in this respect. However it be, we are not
treated like other people, or perhaps I should say like people
who are ever likely to be met with in society.

Is it in the climate? Either I have a false notion of European manners, or else the atmosphere affects them strangely
when exported hither. Perhaps they suffer from the sea-voyage
like some of the more delicate wines. During our Civil War an
Englishman of the highest description was kind enough to call
upon me, mainly, as it seemed, to inform me how entirely he
sympathized with the Confederates, and how sure he felt that
we could never subdue them, — " they were the *gentlemen* of the
country, you know." Another, the first greetings hardly over,
asked me how I accounted for the universal meagreness of my
countrymen. To a thinner man than I, or from a stouter man
than he, the question *might* have been offensive. The Marquis
of Hartington [1] wore a secession badge at a public ball in New

---

[1] One of Mr. Lincoln's neatest strokes of humor was his treatment of this gentleman when a laudable curiosity induced him to be presented to the President of the
Broken Bubble. Mr. Lincoln persisted in calling him Mr. Partington. Surely the
refinement of good-breeding could go no farther. Giving the young man his real name
(already notorious in the newspapers) would have made his visit an insult. Had
Henri IV done this, it would have been famous.

York. In a civilized country he might have been roughly handled; but here, where the *bienséances* are not so well understood, of course nobody minded it. A French traveller told me he had been a good deal in the British colonies, and had been astonished to see how soon the people became Americanized. He added, with delightful *bonhomie*, and as if he were sure it would charm me, that "they even began to talk through their noses, just like you!" I was naturally ravished with this testimony to the assimilating power of democracy, and could only reply that I hoped they would never adopt our democratic patent-method of seeming to settle one's honest debts, for they would find it paying through the nose in the long-run. I am a man of the New World, and do not know precisely the present fashion of Mayfair, but I have a kind of feeling that if an American (*mutato nomine, de te* is always frightfully possible) were to do this kind of thing under a European roof, it would induce some disagreeable reflections as to the ethical results of democracy. I read the other day in print the remark of a British tourist who had eaten large quantities of our salt, such as it is (I grant it has not the European savor), that the Americans were hospitable, no doubt, but that it was partly because they longed for foreign visitors to relieve the tedium of their dead-level existence, and partly from ostentation. What shall we do? Shall we close our doors? Not I, for one, if I should so have forfeited the friendship of L. S., most lovable of men. He somehow seems to find us human, at least, and so did Clough, whose poetry will one of these days, perhaps, be found to have been the best utterance in verse of this generation. And T. H., the mere grasp of whose manly hand carries

with it the pledge of frankness and friendship, of an abiding
simplicity of nature as affecting as it is rare!

The fine old Tory aversion of former times was not hard to
bear. There was something even refreshing in it, as in a north-
easter to a hardy temperament. When a British parson, travelling in Newfoundland while the slash of our separation was still
raw, after prophesying a glorious future for an island that continued to dry its fish under the ægis of Saint George, glances
disdainfully over his spectacles in parting at the U. S. A., and
forebodes for them a "speedy relapse into barbarism," now that
they have madly cut themselves off from the humanizing influences of Britain, I smile with barbarian self-conceit. But this
kind of thing became by degrees an unpleasant anachronism.
For meanwhile the young giant was growing, was beginning
indeed to feel tight in his clothes, was obliged to let in a gore
here and there in Texas, in California, in New Mexico, in
Alaska, and had the scissors and needle and thread ready for
Canada when the time came. His shadow loomed like a
Brocken-spectre over against Europe, — the shadow of what
they were coming to, that was the unpleasant part of it. Even
in such misty image as they had of him, it was painfully evident
that his clothes were not of any cut hitherto fashionable, nor
conceivable by a Bond Street tailor, — and this in an age, too,
when every thing depends upon clothes, when, if we do not
keep up appearances, the seeming-solid frame of this universe,
nay, your very God, would slump into himself, like a mockery
king of snow, being nothing, after all, but a prevailing mode.
From this moment the young giant assumed the respectable
aspect of a phenomenon, to be got rid of if possible, but at any

rate as legitimate a subject of human study as the glacial period, or the silurian what-d'ye-call-ems. If the man of the primeval drift-heaps is so absorbingly interesting, why not the man of the drift that is just beginning, of the drift into whose irresistible current we are just being sucked whether we will or no? If I were in their place, I confess I should not be frightened. Man has survived so much, and contrived to be comfortable on this planet after surviving so much! I am something of a protestant in matters of government also, and am willing to get rid of vestments and ceremonies and to come down to bare benches, if only faith in God take the place of a general agreement to profess confidence in ritual and sham. Every mortal man of us holds stock in the only public debt that is absolutely sure of payment, and that is the debt of the Maker of this Universe to the Universe he has made. I have no notion of selling out my stock, in a panic.

It was something to have advanced even to the dignity of a phenomenon, and yet I do not know that the relation of the individual American to the individual European was bettered by it ; and that, after all, must adjust itself comfortably before there can be a right understanding between the two. We had been a desert, we became a museum. People came hither for scientific, and not social ends. The very cockney could not complete his education without taking a vacant stare at us in passing. But the sociologists (I think they call themselves so) were the hardest to bear. There was no escape. I have even known a professor of this fearful science to come disguised in petticoats. We were cross-examined as a chemist cross-examines a new substance. Human? Yes, all the elements are present,

though abnormally combined. Civilized? Hm! that needs a
stricter assay. No entomologist could take a more friendly
interest in a strange bug. After a few such experiences, I, for
one, have felt as if I were merely one of those horrid things
preserved in spirits (and very bad spirits, too) in a cabinet. I
was not the fellow-being of these explorers: I was a curiosity;
I was a *specimen*. Hath not an American organs, dimensions,
senses, affections, passions even as a European hath? If you
prick us, do we not bleed? If you tickle us, do we not laugh?
I will not keep on with Shylock to his next question but one.

Till after our Civil War it never seemed to enter the head of
any foreigner, especially of any Englishman, that an American
had what could be called a country, except as a place to eat,
sleep, and trade in. Then it seemed to strike them suddenly.
"By Jove, you know, fellahs don't fight like that for a shop-
till!" No, I rather think not. To Americans America is something more than a promise and an expectation. It has a past and
traditions of its own. A descent from men who sacrificed every
thing and came hither, not to better their fortunes, but to plant
their idea in virgin soil, should be a good pedigree. There was
never colony save this that went forth, not to seek gold, but God.
Is it not as well to have sprung from such as these as from some
burly beggar who came over with Wilhelmus Conquestor, unless,
indeed, a line grow better as it runs farther away from stalwart
ancestors? And for history, it is dry enough, no doubt, in the
books, but, for all that, is of a kind that tells in the blood. I
have admitted that Carlyle's sneer had a show of truth in it.
But what does he himself, like a true Scot, admire in the
Hohenzollerns? First of all, that they were *canny*, a thrifty,

forehanded race. Next, that they made a good fight from generation to generation with the chaos around them. That is
precisely the battle which the English race on this continent has
been carrying doughtily on for two centuries and a half.
Doughtily and silently, for you cannot hear in Europe "that
crash, the death-song of the perfect tree," that has been going
on here from sturdy father to sturdy son, and making this continent habitable for the weaker Old World breed that has swarmed
to it during the last half-century. If ever men did a good stroke,
of work on this planet, it was the forefathers of those whom
you are wondering whether it would not be prudent to acknowledge as far-off cousins. Alas, man of genius, to whom we owe
so much, could you see nothing more than the burning of a foul
chimney in that clash of Michael and Satan which flamed up
under your very eyes?

Before our war we were to Europe but a huge mob of adventurers and shop-keepers. Leigh Hunt expressed it well enough
when he said that he could never think of America without seeing a gigantic counter stretched all along the seaboard. Feu-
dalism had by degrees made commerce, the great civilizer,
contemptible. But a tradesman with sword on thigh, and very
prompt of stroke was not only redoubtable, he had become
respectable also. Few people, I suspect, alluded twice to a
needle in Sir John Hawkwood's presence, after that doughty
fighter had exchanged it for a more dangerous tool of the same
metal. Democracy had been hitherto only a ludicrous effort to
reverse the laws of nature by thrusting Cleon into the place of
Pericles. But a democracy that could fight for an abstraction,
whose members held life and goods cheap compared with that

larger life which we call country, was not merely unheard-of,
but portentous. It was the nightmare of the Old World taking
upon itself flesh and blood, turning out to be substance and not
dream. Since the Norman crusader clanged down upon the
throne of the *porphyro-geniti*, carefully draped appearances had
never received such a shock, had never been so rudely called
on to produce their titles to the empire of the world. Authority
has had its periods not unlike those of geology, and at last
comes Man claiming kingship in right of his mere manhood.
The world of the Saurians might be in some respects more picturesque, but the march of events is inexorable, and it is by-
gone.

The young giant had certainly got out of long-clothes. He
had become the *enfant terrible* of the human household. It was
not and will not be easy for the world (especially for our British
cousins) to look upon us as grown up. The youngest of nations,
its people must also be young and to be treated accordingly,
was the syllogism, — as if libraries did not make all nations
equally old in all those respects, at least, where age is an advantage and not a defect. Youth, no doubt has its good qualities,
as people feel who are losing it, but boyishness is another thing.
We had been somewhat boyish as a nation, a little loud, a little
pushing, a little braggart. But might it not partly have been
because we felt that we had certain claims to respect that were
not admitted? The war which established our position as a
vigorous nationality has also sobered us. A nation, like a man,
cannot look death in the eye for four years, without some
strange reflections, without arriving at some clearer consciousness of the stuff it is made of, without some great moral change.

Such a change, or the beginning of it, no observant person can fail to see here. Our thought and our politics, our bearing as a people, are assuming a manlier tone. We have been compelled to see what was weak in democracy as well as what was strong. We have begun obscurely to recognize that things do not go of themselves, and that popular government is not in itself a panacea, is no better than any other form except as the virtue and wisdom of the people make it so, and that when men undertake to do their own kingship, they enter upon the dangers and responsibilities as well as the privileges of the function. Above all, it looks as if we were on the way to be persuaded that no government can be carried on by declamation. It is noticeable also that facility of communication has made the best English and French thought far more directly operative here than ever before. Without being Europeanized, our discussion of important questions in statesmanship, in political economy, in æsthetics, is taking a broader scope and a higher tone. It had certainly been provincial, one might almost say local, to a very unpleasant extent. Perhaps our experience in soldiership has taught us to value training more than we have been popularly wont. We may possibly come to the conclusion, one of these days, that self-made men may not be always equally skilful in the manufacture of wisdom, may not be divinely commissioned to fabricate the higher qualities of opinion on all possible topics of human interest.

So long as we continue to be the most common-schooled and the least cultivated people in the world, I suppose we must consent to endure this condescending manner of foreigners toward us. The more friendly they mean to be, the more ludicrously prominent it becomes. They can never appreciate the immense amount of silent work that has been done here, making this continent slowly fit for the abode of man, and which will demonstrate itself, let us hope, in the character of the people. Outsiders can only be expected to judge a nation by the amount it has contributed to the civilization of the world; the amount, that is, that can be seen and handled. A great place in history can only be achieved by competitive examinations, nay, by a long course of them. How much new thought have we contributed to the common stock? Till that question can be triumphantly answered, or needs no answer, we must continue to be simply interesting as an experiment, to be studied as a problem, and not respected as an attained result or an accomplished solution. Perhaps, as I have hinted, their patronizing manner toward us is the fair result of their failing to see here anything more than a poor imitation, a plaster-cast, of Europe. And are they not partly right? If the tone of the uncultivated American has too often the arrogance of the barbarian, is not that of the cultivated as often vulgarly apologetic? In the America they meet with is there the simplicity, the manliness, the absence of sham, the sincere human nature, the sensitiveness to duty and implied obligation, that in any way distinguishes us from what our orators call the "effete civilization of the Old World?" Is there a politician among us daring enough (except a Dana here and there) to risk his future on the chance of our keeping our word with the exactness of superstitious communities like England? Is it certain that we shall be ashamed of a bankruptcy of honor, if we can only keep the letter of our bond? I hope we shall be able to answer all these

questions with a frank *yes.* At any rate, we would advise our
visitors that we are not merely curious creatures, but belong to
the family of man, and that, as individuals, we are not to be
always subjected to the competitive examination above mentioned, even if we acknowledged their competence as an
examining board. Above all, we beg them to remember that
America is not to us, as to them, a mere object of external
interest to be discussed and analyzed, but *in* us, part of our very
marrow. Let them not suppose that we conceive of ourselves
as exiles from the graces and amenities of an older date than
we, though very much at home in a state of things not yet all it
might be or should be, but which we mean to make so, and
which we find both wholesome and pleasant for men (though
perhaps not for *dilettanti*) to live in. " The full tide of human
existence " may be felt here as keenly as Johnson felt it at
Charing Cross, and in a larger sense. I know one person who
is singular enough to think Cambridge the very best spot on the
habitable globe. "Doubtless God *could* have made a better,
but doubtless he never did."

It will take England a great while to get over her airs of
patronage toward us, or even passably to conceal them. She
cannot help confounding the people with the country, and
regarding us as lusty juveniles. She has a conviction that whatever good there is in us is wholly English, when the truth is that
we are worth nothing except so far as we have disinfected ourselves of Anglicism. She is especially condescending just now,
and lavishes sugar-plums on us as if we had not outgrown them.
I am no believer in sudden conversions, especially in sudden
conversions to a favorable opinion of people who have just

proved you to be mistaken in judgment and therefore unwise in policy. I never blamed her for not wishing well to democracy, — how could she ? — but Alabamas are not wishes. Let her not be too hasty in believing Mr. Reverdy Johnson's pleasant words. Though there is no thoughtful man in America who would not consider a war with England the greatest of calamities, yet the feeling toward her here is very far from cordial, whatever our Minister may say in the effusion that comes after ample dining. Mr. Adams, with his famous "My Lord, this means war," perfectly represented his country. Justly or not, we have a feeling that we have been wronged, not merely insulted. The only sure way of bringing about a healthy relation between the two countries is for Englishmen to clear their minds of the notion that we are always to be treated as a kind of inferior and deported Englishman whose nature they perfectly understand, and whose back they accordingly stroke the wrong way of the fur with amazing perseverance. Let them learn to treat us naturally on our merits as human beings, as they would a German or a Frenchman, and not as if we were a kind of counterfeit Briton whose crime appeared in every shade of difference, and before long there would come that right feeling which we naturally call a good understanding. The common blood, and still more the common language, are fatal instruments of misapprehension. Let them give up *trying* to understand us, still more thinking that they do, and acting in various absurd ways as the necessary consequence, for they will never arrive at that devoutly-to-be-wished consummation, till they learn to look at us as we are, and not as they suppose us to be. Dear old long-estranged mother-in-law, it is a great many years since we parted.

Since 1660, when you married again, you have been a step-mother to us. Put on your spectacles, dear madam. Yes, we *have* grown, and changed likewise. You would not let us darken your doors, if you could help it. We know that perfectly well. But pray, when we look to be treated as men, don't shake that rattle in our faces, nor talk baby to us any longer.

> " Do, child, go to it grandam, child;
> Give grandam kingdom, and it grandam will
> Give it a plum, a cherry, and a fig!"

ON HISTORY.
[1830.]

BY THOMAS CARLYLE.

(Born 1795, Died 1882.)

LIO was figured by the ancients as the eldest daughter of Memory, and chief of the Muses; which dignity, whether we regard the essential qualities of her art, or its practice and acceptance among men, we shall still find to have been fitly bestowed. History, as it lies at the root of all science, is also the first distinct product of man's spiritual nature; his earliest expression of what can be called Thought. It is a looking both before and after; as, indeed, the coming Time already waits, unseen, yet definitely shaped, predetermined, and inevitable, in the Time come; and only by the combination of both is the meaning of either completed. The Sibylline Books, though old, are not the oldest. Some nations have prophecy, some have not; but of all mankind, there is no tribe so rude that it has not attempted History, though several have not arithmetic enough to count Five. History has been written with quipo-threads, with feather-pictures, with wampum-belts; still oftener with earth-mounds and monumental stone-heaps, whether as pyramid or cairn; for the Celt and the Copt, the Red man as well as the White, lives between two eternities, and warring against Oblivion, he would fain unite himself in clear conscious relation, as in dim unconscious relation he is already united, with the whole Future and the whole Past.

A talent for History may be said to be born with us, as our chief inheritance. In a certain sense all men are historians. Is not every memory written quite full with Annals, wherein joy and mourning, conquest and loss manifoldly alternate; and, with or without philosophy, the whole fortunes of one little inward Kingdom, and all its politics, foreign and domestic, stand ineffaceably recorded? Our very speech is curiously historical. Most men, you may observe, speak only to narrate; not in imparting what they have thought, which indeed were often a very small matter, but in exhibiting what they have undergone or seen, which is a quite unlimited one, do talkers dilate. Cut us off from Narrative, how would the stream of conversation, even among the wisest, languish into detached handfuls, and among the foolish utterly evaporate! Thus, as we do nothing but enact History, we say little but recite it: nay, rather, in that widest · sense, our whole spiritual life is built thereon. For, strictly considered, what is all Knowledge too but recorded Experience, and a product of History; of which, therefore, Reasoning and Belief, no less than Action· and Passion, are essential materials?

Under a limited, and the only practicable shape, History proper, that part of History which treats of remarkable action, has, in all modern as well as ancient times, ranked among the highest arts, and perhaps never stood higher than in these times

of ours. For whereas, of old, the charm of History lay chiefly
in gratifying our common appetite for the wonderful, for the unknown ; and her office was but as that of a Minstrel and Story-
teller, she has now further become a Schoolmistress, and professes to instruct in gratifying. Whether with the stateliness of
that venerable character, she may not have taken up something
of its austerity and frigidity ; whether in the logical terseness of
a Hume or Robertson, the graceful ease and gay pictorial hearti-
ness of a Herodotus or Froissart may not be wanting, is not
the question for us here. Enough that all learners, all inquiring
minds of every order, are gathered round her footstool, and
reverently pondering her lessons, as the true basis of Wisdom.
Poetry, Divinity, Politics, Physics, have each their adherents
and adversaries ; each little guild supporting a defensive and
offensive war for its own special domain ; while the domain of
History is as a Free Emporium, where all these belligerents
peaceably meet and furnish themselves ; and Sentimentalist and
Utilitarian, Sceptic and Theologian, with one voice advise us :
Examine History, for it is " Philosophy teaching by Experience."

Far be it from us to disparage such teaching, the very attempt
at which must be precious. Neither shall we too rigidly inquire :
How much it has hitherto profited ? Whether most of what
little practical wisdom men have, has come from study of
professed History, or from other less boasted sources, whereby,
as matters now stand, a Marlborough may become great in the
world's business with no History save what he derives from
Shakspeare's plays ? Nay, whether in that same teaching by
Experience, historical Philosophy has yet properly deciphered

the first element of all science in this kind: What the aim and
significance of that wondrous changeful Life it investigates and
paints may be? Whence the course of man's destinies in this
Earth originated, and whither they are tending? Or, indeed,
if they have any course and tendency, are really guided forward
by an unseen mysterious Wisdom, or only circle in blind mazes
without recognizable guidance? Which questions, altogether
fundamental, one might think, in any Philosophy of History,
have, since the era when Monkish Annalists were wont to
answer them by the long-ago extinguished light of their Missal
and Breviary, been by most philosophical Historians only
glanced at dubiously and from afar; by many, not so much as
glanced at.

The truth is, two difficulties, never wholly surmountable lie in
the way. Before Philosophy can teach by Experience, the Phi-
osophy has to be in readiness, the Experience must be gathered
and intelligibly recorded. Now, overlooking the former consideration, and with regard only to the latter, let any one who has
examined the current of human affairs, and how intricate, perplexed, unfathomable, even when seen into with our own eyes,
are their thousand-fold blending movements, say whether the
true representing of it is easy or impossible. Social Life is the
aggregate of all the individual men's Lives who constitute society; History is the essence of innumerable Biographies. But
if one Biography, nay, our own Biography, study and recapit-
ulate it as we may, remains in so many points unintelligible to us,
how much more must these million, the very facts of which, to
say nothing of the purport of them, we know not, and cannot
know!

Neither will it adequately avail us to assert that the general inward condition of Life is the same in all ages; and that only the remarkable deviations from the common endowment and common lot, and the more important variations which the outward figure of Life has from time to time undergone, deserve memory and record. The inward condition of Life, it may rather be affirmed, the conscious or half-conscious aim of mankind, so far as men are not mere digesting-machines, is the same in no two ages; neither are the more important outward variations easy to fix on, or always well capable of representation. Which was the greater innovator, which was the more important personage in man's history, he who first led armies over the Alps, and gained the victories of Cannæ and Thrasymene; or the nameless boor who first hammered out for himself an iron-spade? When the oak-tree is felled, the whole forest echoes with it; but a hundred acorns are planted silently by some unnoticed breeze. Battles and war-tumults, which for the time din every ear, and with joy or terror intoxicate every heart, pass away like tavern-brawls; and, except some few Marathons and Morgartens, are remembered by accident, not by desert. Laws themselves, political Constitutions, are not our Life, but only the house wherein our Life is led: nay, they are but the bare walls of the house; all whose essential furniture, the inventions and traditions, and daily habits that regulate and support our existence, are the work not of Dracos and Hampdens, but of Phœnician mariners, of Italian masons and Saxon metallurgists, of philosophers, alchymists, prophets, and all the long-forgotten train of artists and artisans, who from the first have been jointly teaching us how to think and how to act, how to rule over spirit-

ual and over physical Nature. Well may we say that of our
History the more important part is lost without recovery; and,
—as thanksgivings were once wont to be offered "for unrecognized mercies," — look with reverence into the dark untenanted
places of the Past, where, in formless oblivion, our chief benefactors, with all their sedulous endeavors, but not with the fruit
of these, lie entombed.

⁊ So imperfect is that same Experience, by which Philosophy is
to teach. Nay, even with regard to those occurrences which do
stand recorded, which, at their origin have seemed worthy of
record, and the summary of which constitutes what we now call
History, is not our understanding, of them altogether incomplete; is it even possible to represent them as they were? The
old story of Sir Walter Raleigh's looking from his prison window
on some street tumult, which afterward three witnesses reported
in three different ways, himself differing from them all, is still a
true lesson to us. Consider how it is that historical documents
and records originate; even honest records, where the reporters
were unbiased by personal regard; a case which, were nothing
more wanted, must ever be among the rarest. The real leading
features of an historical Transaction, whose movements that
essentially characterize it, and alone deserve to be recorded, are
nowise the foremost to be noted. At first, among the various
witnesses, who are also parties interested, there is only vague
wonder, and fear of hope, and the noise of Rumor's thousand
tongues; till, after a season, the conflict of testimonies has subsided into some general issue; and then it is settled, by majority
of votes, that such and such a "Crossing of the Rubicon," an
"Impeachment of Strafford," a "Convocation of the Notables,"

are epochs in the world's history, cardinal points on which grand world-revolutions have hinged. Suppose, however, that the majority of votes was all wrong ; that the real cardinal points lay far deeper ; and had been passed over unnoticed, because no Seer, but only mere Onlookers, chanced to be there ! (Our clock strikes when there is a change from hour to hour ; but no hammer in the horologe of Time peals through the universe when there is a change from Era to Era. Men understand not what is among their hands ; as calmness is the characteristic of strength, so the weightiest causes may be most silent. It is, in no case, the real historical Transaction, but only some more or less plausible scheme and theory of the Transaction, or the harmonized result of many such schemes, each varying from the other and all varying from truth, that we can ever hope to behold.

Nay, were our faculty of insight into passing things never so complete, there is still a fatal discrepancy between our manner of observing these, and their manner of occurring. The most gifted man can observe, still more can record, only the *series* of his own impressions : his observation, therefore, to say nothing of its other imperfections, must be *successive*, while the things done were often *simultaneous;* the things done were not a series, but a group. It is not in acted, as it is in written History ; actual events are nowise so simply related to each other as parent and offspring are ; every single event is the offspring not of one, but of all other events prior or contemporaneous, and will in its turn combine with all others to give birth to new : it is an ever-living, ever-working Chaos of Being, wherein shape after shape bodies itself forth from innumerable elements. And

this Chaos, boundless as the habitation and duration of man,
unfathomable as the soul and destiny of man, is what the historian will depict, and scientifically gauge, we may say, by
threading it with single lines of a few ells in length! For as
all action is, by its nature, to be figured as extended in breadth
and in depth, as well as in length; that is to say, is based on
Passion and Mystery, if we investigate its origin; and spreads
abroad on all hands, modifying and modified; as well as advances toward completion, — so all Narrative is, by its nature,
of only one dimension; only travels forward toward one, or
toward successive points : Narrative is *linear*, Action is *solid*.
Alas for our "chains," or chainlets, of "causes and effects,"
which we so assiduously track through certain handbreadths of
years and square miles, when the whole is a broad, deep Immen-
sity, and each atom is "chained" and complected with all'!
Truly, if History is Philosophy teaching by Experience, the
writer fitted to compose History is hitherto an unknown man.
The experience itself would require All-knowledge to record it,
— were the All-wisdom needful for such Philosophy as would
interpret it, to be had for asking. Better were it that mere
earthly Historians should lower such pretensions, more suitable
for Omniscience than for human science; and aiming only at
some picture of the things acted, which picture itself will at best
be a poor approximation, leave the inscrutable purport of them
an acknowledged secret ; or at most, in reverent Faith, far different from that teaching of Philosophy, pause over the mysterious
vestiges of Him, whose path is in the great deep of Time, whom
History indeed reveals, but only all History, and in Eternity,
will clearly reveal.

Such considerations truly were of small profit, did they, instead of teaching us vigilance and reverent humility in our inquiries into History, abate our esteem for them, or discourage us from unweariedly prosecuting them.   Let us search more and more into the Past; let all men explore it, as the true fountain of knowledge; by whose light alone, consciously or unconsciously employed, can the Present and the Future be interpreted or guessed at.   For though the whole meaning lies far beyond our ken; yet in that complex Manuscript, covered over with formless inextricably entangled unknown characters — nay, which is a *Palimpsest*, and had once prophetic writing, still dimly legible there, — some letters, some words, may be deciphered; and if no complete Philosophy, here and there an intelligible precept, available in practice, be gathered : well understanding, in the meanwhile, that it is only a little portion we have deciphered; that much still remains to be interpreted; that History is a real Prophetic Manuscript, and can be fully interpreted by no man.

But the Artist in History may be distinguished from the Artisan in History ; for here, as in all other provinces, there are Artists and Artisans; men who labor mechanically in a department, without eye for the Whole, not feeling that there is a Whole; and men who inform and ennoble the humblest department with an Idea of the Whole, and habitually know that only in the Whole is the Partial to be truly discerned.   The proceedings and the duties of these two, in regard to History, must be altogether different.   Not, indeed, that each has not a real worth, in his several degree.   The simple husbandman can till his field, and by knowledge he has gained of its soil, sow it with the fit grain, though the deep rocks and central fires are unknown to him : his little crop hangs under and over the firmament of stars, and sails through whole untracked celestial spaces, between Aries and Libra; nevertheless, it ripens for him in due season, and he gathers it safe into his barn. As a husbandman he is blameless in disregarding those higher wonders ; but as a thinker, and faithful inquirer into Nature, he were wrong. So likewise is it with the Historian, who examines some special aspect of History; and from this or that combination of circumstances, political, moral, economical, and the issues it has led to, infers that such and such properties belong to human society, and that the like circumstances will produce the like issue; which inference, if other trials confirm it, must be held true and practically valuable. He is wrong only, and an artisan, when he fancies that these properties, discovered or discoverable, exhaust the matter; and sees not, at every step, that it is inexhaustible. *a* However, that class of cause-and-effect speculators, with whom no wonder would remain wonderful, but all things in Heaven and Earth must be computed and "accounted for;" and even the Unknown, the Infinite in man's Life, had, under the words *enthusiasm, superstition, spirit of the age*, and so forth, obtained, as it were, an algebraical symbol and given value, — have now wellnigh played their part in European culture ; and may be considered, as in most countries, even in England itself, where they linger the latest, verging toward extinction. He who reads the inscrutable Book of Nature as if it were a Merchant's Ledger, is justly suspected of having never seen that Book, but only some school Synopsis thereof; from which, if taken for the real Book, more error than insight is to be derived.

⟨⟩ Doubtless, also, it is with a growing feeling of the infinite nature of History, that in these times, the old principle, division of labor, has been so widely applied to it. The Political Historian, once almost the sole cultivator of History, has now found various associates, who strive to elucidate other phases of human Life; of which, as hinted above, the political conditions it is passed under are but one, and though the primary, perhaps not the most important, of the many outward arrangements. Of this Historian himself, moreover, in his own special department, new and higher things are beginning to be expected. From of old, it was too often to be reproachfully observed of him, that he dwelt with disproportionate fondness in Senate-houses, in Battle-fields, nay even in King's Antechambers; forgetting, that far away from such scenes, the mighty tide of Thought and Action was still rolling on its wondrous course, in gloom and brightness; and in its thousand remote valleys, a whole world of Existence, with or without an earthly sun of Happiness to warm it, with or without a heavenly sun of Holiness to purify and sanctify it, was blossoming and fading, whether the "famous victory" were won or lost. The time seems coming when much of this must be amended; and he who sees no world but that of courts and camps; and writes only how soldiers were drilled and shot, and how this ministerial conjuror out-conjured that other, and then guided, or at least held, something which he called the rudder of Government, but which was rather the spigot of Taxation, wherewith, in place of steering, he could tap, and the more cunningly the nearer the lees, — will pass for a more or less instructive Gazetteer, but will no longer be called an Historian.

However, the political Historian, were his work performed with all conceivable perfection, can accomplish but a part, and still leaves room for numerous fellow-laborers. Foremost among these comes the Ecclesiastical Historian; endeavoring with catholic or sectarian view, to trace the progress of the Church; of that portion of the social establishments, which respects our religious condition ; as the other portion does our civil, or rather, in the long-run, our economical condition. Rightly conducted, this department were undoubtedly the more important of the two ; inasmuch as it concerns us more to understand how man's moral well-being had been and might be promoted, than to understand in the like sort his physical well-being; which latter is ultimately the aim of all Political arrangements. For the physically happiest is simply the safest, the strongest; and, in all conditions of Government, Power (whether of wealth as in these days, or of arms and adherents as in old days) is the only outward emblem and purchase-money of Good. True Good, however, unless we reckon pleasure synonymous with it, is said to be rarely, or rather never, offered for sale in the market where that coin passes current. So that, for man's true advantage, not the outward condition of his life, but the inward and spiritual, is of prime influence; not the form of Government he lives under, and the power he can accumulate there, but the Church he is a member of, and the degree of moral elevation he can acquire by means of its instruction. Church history, then, did it speak wisely, would have momentous secrets to teach us: nay, in its highest degree, it were a sort of continued Holy writ; our Sacred Books being, indeed, only a History of the primeval Church, as it first arose in man's soul, and symbolically embodied itself in his external life. How far our actual Church Historians fall below such unattainable standards, nay, below quite attainable approximations thereto, we need not point out. Of the Ecclesiastical Historian we have to complain, as we did of his Political fellow-craftsman, that his inquiries turn rather on. the outward mechanism, the mere hulls and superficial accidents of the object, than on the object itself: as if the Church lay in Bishops' Chapter-houses, and Ecumenic Council-halls, and Cardinals' Conclaves, and not far more in the hearts of Believing Men; in whose walk and conversation, as influenced thereby, its chief manifestations were to be looked for, and its progress or decline ascertained. The History of the Church is a History of the Invisible as well as of the Visible Church; which latter, if disjoined from the former, is but a vacant edifice; gilded, it may be, and overhung with old votive gifts, yet useless, nay, pestilentially unclean; to write whose history is less important than to forward its downfall.

Of a less ambitious character are the Histories that relate to special separate provinces of human Action; to Sciences, Practical Arts, Institutions, and the like; matters which do not imply an epitome of man's whole interest and form of life; but wherein, though each is still connected with all, the spirit of each, at least its material results, may be in some degree evolved without so strict a reference to that of the others. Highest in dignity and difficulty, under this head, would be our histories of Philosophy, of man's opinions and theories respecting the nature of his Being, and relations to the Universe Visible and Invisible: which History, indeed, were it fitly treated, or fit for right treatment, would be a province of Church History; the logical or dogmatical province thereof; for Philosophy, in its true sense, is or should be the soul, of which Religion, Worship is the body; in the healthy state of things the Philosopher and Priest were one and the same. But Philosophy itself is far enough from wearing this character; neither have its Historians been men, generally speaking, that could in the smallest degree approximate it thereto. Scarcely since the rude era of the Magi and Druids has that same healthy identification of Priest and Philosopher had place in any country: but rather the worship of divine things, and the scientific investigation of divine things, have been in quite different hands, their relations not friendly but hostile. Neither have the Brückers and Bühles, to say nothing of the many unhappy Enfields who have treated of that latter department, been more than barren reporters, often unintelligent and unintelligible reporters, of the doctrine uttered; without force to discover how the doctrine originated, or what reference it bore to its time and country, to the spiritual position of mankind there and then. Nay, such a task did not perhaps lie before them, as a thing to be attempted.

Art also and Literature are intimately blended with Religion; as it were, outworks and abutments, by which that highest pinnacle in our inward world gradually connects itself with the general level, and becomes accessible therefrom. He who should write a proper History of Poetry, would depict for us the successive Revelations which man had obtained of the Spirit of Nature; under what aspects he had caught and endeavored to body forth some glimpse of that unspeakable Beauty, which in its highest clearness is Religion, is the inspiration of a Prophet, yet in one or the other degree must inspire every true Singer,

were his theme never so humble. We should see by what steps
men had ascended to the Temple; how near they had approached; by what ill-hap they had, for long periods, turned
away from it, and grovelled on the plain with no music in the
air, or blindly struggled toward other heights. That among all
our Eichhorns and Wartons there is no such Historian, must be
too clear to every one. Nevertheless, let us not despair of far
nearer approaches to that excellence. Above all, let us keep
the Ideal of it ever in our eye; for thereby alone have we even a
chance to reach it.

Our histories of Laws and Constitutions, wherein many a
Montesquieu and Hallam have labored with acceptance, are of
a much simpler nature; yet deep enough if thoroughly investiga-
ted; and useful, when authentic, even with little depth. Then
we have Histories of Medicine, of Mathematics, of Astronomy,
Commerce, Chivalry, Monkery; and Goguets and Beckmanns
have come forward with what might be the most bountiful
contribution of all, a History of Inventions. Of all which sorts,
and many more not here enumerated, not yet devised and put in
practice, the merit and the proper scheme may, in our present
limits, require no exposition.

In this manner, though, as above remarked, all Action is
extended three ways, and the general sum of human Action is a
whole Universe, with all limits of it unknown, does History
strive by running path after path, through the Impassable, in
manifold directions and intersections, to secure for us some
oversight of the Whole; in which endeavor, if each Historian
look well around him from his path, tracking it out with the *eye*,
not, as is more common, with the *nose*, she may at last prove

not altogether unsuccessful. Praying only that increased division of labor do not here, as elsewhere, aggravate our already strong Mechanical tendencies, so that in the manual dexterity for parts we lose all command over the whole, and the hope of any Philosophy of History be farther off than ever—let us all wish her great and greater success.

HISTORY.

BY THOMAS BABINGTON MACAULAY.

(BORN 1800, DIED 1859.)

O write history respectably — that is, to abbreviate despatches, and make extracts from speeches, to intersperse in due proportion epithets of praise and abhorrence, to draw up antithetical characters of great men, setting forth how many contradictory virtues and vices they united, and abounding in *withs* and *withouts ;* all this is very easy. But to be a really great historian is perhaps the rarest of intellectual distinctions. Many scientific works are, in their kind, absolutely perfect. There are poems which we should be inclined to designate as faultless, or as disfigured only by blemishes which pass unnoticed in the general blaze of excellence. There are speeches, some speeches of Demosthenes particularly, in which it would be impossible to alter a word without altering it for the worse. But we are acquainted with no history which approaches to our notion of what a history ought to be — with no history which does not widely depart, either on the right hand or on the left, from the exact line.

The cause may easily be assigned. This province of literature

is a debatable land. It lies on the confines of two distinct territories. It is under the jurisdiction of two hostile powers; and,
like other districts similarly situated, it is ill-defined, ill-culti-
vated, and ill-regulated. Instead of being equally shared
between its two rulers, the Reason and the Imagination, it falls
alternately under the sole and absolute dominion of each. It is
sometimes fiction. It is sometimes theory.

History, it has been said, is philosophy teaching by examples.
Unhappily, what the philosophy gains in soundness and depth,
the examples generally lose in vividness. A perfect historian
must possess an imagination sufficiently powerful to make his
narrative affecting and picturesque. Yet he must control it so
absolutely as to content himself with the materials which he
finds, and to refrain from supplying deficiencies by additions of his
own. He must be a profound and ingenious reasoner. Yet he
must possess sufficient self-command to abstain from casting his
facts in the mould of his hypothesis. Those who can justly
estimate these almost insuperable difficulties will not think it
strange that every writer should have failed, either in the narrative or in the speculative department of history.

It may be laid down as a general rule, though subject to
considerable qualifications and exceptions, that history begins in
Novel, and ends in Essay. Of the romantic historians Herodotus is the earliest and the best. His animation, his simple-
hearted tenderness, his wonderful talent for description and
dialogue, and the pure, sweet flow of his language, place him at
the head of narrators. He reminds us of a delightful child.
There is a grace beyond the reach of affectation in his awkward-
ness, a malice in his innocence, an intelligence in his nonsense,

an insinuating eloquence in his lisp. We know of no writer who makes such interest for himself and his book in the heart of the reader. At the distance of three-and-twenty centuries, we feel for him the same sort of pitying fondness which Fontaine and Gay are said to have inspired in society. He has written an incomparable book. He has written something better perhaps than the best history; but he has not written a good history; he is, from the first to the last chapter, an inventor. We do not here refer merely to those gross fictions, with which he has been reproached by the critics of later times. We speak of that coloring which is equally diffused over his whole narrative, and which perpetually leaves the most sagacious reader in doubt what to reject and what to receive. The most authentic parts of his work bear the same relation to his wildest legends which Henry the Fifth bears to the Tempest. There was an expedition undertaken by Xerxes against Greece; and there was an invasion of France. There was a battle at Platea; and there was a battle at Agincourt. Cambridge and Exeter, the Constable and the Dauphin, were persons as real as Demaratus and Pausanias. The harangue of the Archbishop on the Salic Law and the Book of Numbers differs much less from the orations which have in all ages proceeded from the Right Reverend bench, than the speeches of Mardonius and Artabanus from those which were delivered at the Council-board of Susa. Shakespeare gives us enumerations of armies, and returns of killed and wounded, which are not, we suspect, much less accurate than those of Herodotus. There are passages in Herodotus nearly as long as acts of Shakespeare, in which everything is told dramatically, and in which the narrative serves only the purpose of stage directions. It is possible, no doubt, that the substance of some real conversations may have been reported to the historian. But events which, if they ever happened, happened in ages and nations so remote that the particulars could never have been known to him, are related with the greatest minuteness of detail. We have. all that Candaules said to Gyges, and all that passed between Astyagus and Harpagus. We are, therefore, unable to judge whether, in the account which he gives of transactions respecting which he might possibly have been well informed, we can trust to anything beyond the naked outline; whether, for example, the answer of Gelon to the ambassadors of the Grecian confederacy, or the expressions which passed between Aristides and Themistocles at their famous interview, have been correctly transmitted to us. The great events are no doubt faithfully related. So, probably, are many of the slighter circumstances; but which of them it is impossible to ascertain. The fictions are so much like the facts, and the facts so much like the fictions, that, with respect to many most interesting particulars, our belief is neither given nor withheld, but remains in an uneasy and interminable state of abeyance. We know that there is truth, but we cannot exactly decide where it lies.

The faults of Herodotus are the faults of a simple and imaginative mind. Children and servants are remarkably Herodotean in their style of narration. They tell everything dramatically. Their *says hes* and *says shes* are proverbial. Every person who has had to settle their disputes knows that, even when they have no intention to deceive, their reports of conversation always require to be carefully sifted. If an educated man were giving

an account of the late change of administration, he would say:
"Lord Goderich resigned ; and the King, in consequence, sent
for the Duke of Wellington." A porter tells the story as if he
had been hid behind the curtains of the royal bed at Windsor :
" So Lord Goderich says: ' I cannot manage this business; I
must go out.' So the King says, — says he: 'Well, then, I
must send for the Duke of Wellington — that's all.' " This is
in the very manner of the father of history.

Herodotus wrote as it was natural that he should write. He
wrote for a nation susceptible, curious, lively, insatiably desirous
of novelty and excitement; for a nation in which the fine arts
had attained their highest excellence, but in which philosophy
was still in its infancy. His countrymen had but recently begun
to cultivate prose composition. Public transactions had generally been recorded in verse. The first historians might, therefore, indulge, without fear of censure, in the license allowed to
their predecessors the bards. Books were few. The events of
former times were learned from tradition and from popular
ballads ; the manners of foreign countries from the reports of
travellers. It is well known that the mystery which overhangs
what is distant, either in space or time, frequently prevents us
from censuring as unnatural what we perceive to be impossible.
We stare at a dragoon who has killed three French cuirassiers,
as a prodigy ; yet we read, without the least disgust, how Godfrey slew his thousands, and Rinaldo his ten thousands. Within
the last hundred years, stories about China and Bantam, which
ought not to have imposed on an old nurse, were gravely laid
down as foundations of political theories by eminent philosophers. What the time of the crusades is to us, the generation

of Crœsus and Solon was to the Greeks of the time of Herodotus. Babylon was to them what Pekin was to the French Academicians of the last century.

For such a people was the book of Herodotus composed; and, if we may trust to a report, not sanctioned indeed by writers of high authority, but in itself not improbable, it was composed not to be read, but to be heard. It was not to the slow circulation of a few copies, which the rich only could possess, that the aspiring author looked for his reward. The great Olympian festival — the solemnity which collected multitudes, proud of the Grecian name, from the wildest mountains of Doris, and the remotest colonies of Italy and Libya, — was to witness his triumph. The interest of the narrative, and the beauty of the style, were aided by the imposing effect of recitation, — by the splendor of the spectacle, — by the powerful influence of sympathy. A critic who could have asked for authorities in the midst of such a scene, must have been of a cold and sceptical nature; and few such critics were there. As was the historian, such were the auditors, — inquisitive, credulous, easily moved by religious awe or patriotic enthusiasm. They were the very men to hear with delight of strange beasts, and birds, and trees, — of dwarfs, and giants, and cannibals, — of gods, whose very names it was impiety to utter, — of ancient dynasties, which had left behind them monuments surpassing all the works of later times, — of towns like provinces, — of rivers like seas, — of stupendous walls, and temples, and pyramids, — of the rites which the Magi performed at daybreak on the tops of the mountains, — of the secrets inscribed on the eternal obelisks of Memphis. With equal delight they would have listened to the

graceful romances of their own country. They now heard of
the exact accomplishment of obscure predictions, of the punishment of crimes over which the justice of heaven had seemed to
slumber, — of dreams, omens, warnings from the dead, — of
princesses, for whom noble suitors contended in every generous
exercise of strength and skill, — of infants, strangely preserved
from the dagger of the assassin, to fulfil high destinies.

As the narrative approached their own times, the interest
became still more absorbing. The chronicler had now to tell
the story of that great conflict, from which Europe dates its
intellectual and political supremacy, — a story which, even at
this distance of time, is the most marvellous and the most touching in the annals of the human race, — a story, abounding with
all that is wild and wonderful, with all that is pathetic and
animating; with the gigantic caprices of infinite wealth and despotic power, — with the mightier miracles of wisdom, of virtue,
and of courage. He told them of rivers dried up in a day, —
of provinces famished for a meal, — of a passage for ships hewn
through the mountains, — of a road for armies spread upon the
waves, — of monarchies and commonwealths swept away, — of
anxiety, of terror, of confusion, of despair! — and then of proud
and stubborn hearts tried in that extremity of evil, and not
found wanting, — of resistance long maintained against desperate odds, — of lives dearly sold, when resistance could be
maintained no more, — of signal deliverance, and of unsparing
revenge. Whatever gave a stronger air of reality to a narrative
so well calculated to inflame the passions, and to flatter national
pride, was certain to be favorably received.

Between the time at which Herodotus is said to have composed his history, and the close of the Peloponnesian War, about forty years elapsed — forty years, crowded with great military and political events. The circumstances of that period produced a great effect on the Grecian character; and nowhere was this effect so remarkable as in the illustrious democracy of Athens. An Athenian, indeed, even in the time of Herodotus, would scarcely have written a book so romantic and garrulous as that of Herodotus. As civilization advanced, the citizens of that famous republic became still less visionary, and still less simple-hearted. They aspired to know, where their ancestors had been content to doubt; they began to doubt, where their ancestors had thought it their duty to believe. Aristophanes is fond of alluding to this change in the temper of his countrymen. The father and son, in "The Clouds," are evidently representatives of the generations to which they respectively belonged. Nothing more clearly illustrates the nature of this moral revolution, than the change which passed upon tragedy. The wild sublimity of Æschylus became the scoff of every young Phidippides. Lectures on abstruse points of philosophy, the fine distinctions of casuistry, and the dazzling fence of rhetoric, were substituted for poetry. The language lost something of that infantine sweetness which had characterized it. It became less like the ancient Tuscan, and more like the modern French.

The fashionable logic of the Greeks was, indeed, far from strict. Logic never can be strict where books are scarce, and where information is conveyed orally. We are all aware how frequently fallacies which, when set down on paper, are at once detected, pass for unanswerable arguments when dexterously and volubly urged in Parliament, at the bar, or in private conversation. The reason is evident. We cannot inspect them closely enough to perceive their inaccuracy. We cannot readily compare them with each other. We lose sight of one part of the subject, before another, which ought to be received in connection with it, comes before us ; and as there is no immutable record of what has been admitted, and of what has been denied, direct contradictions pass muster with little difficulty. Almost all the education of a Greek consisted in talking and listening. His opinions on government were picked up in the debates of the assembly. If he wished to study metaphysics, instead of shutting himself up with a book, he walked down to the market-place to look for a sophist. So completely were men formed to these habits, that even writing acquired a conversational air. The philosophers adopted the form of dialogue, as the most natural mode of communicating knowledge. Their reasonings have the merits and the defects which belong to that species of composition; and are characterized rather by quickness and subtlety, than by depth and precision. Truth is exhibited in parts, and by glimpses. Innumerable clever hints are given ; but no sound and durable system is erected. The *argumentum ad hominem*, a kind of argument most efficacious in debate, but utterly useless for the investigation of general principles, is among their favorite resources. Hence, though nothing can be more admirable than the skill which Socrates displays in the conversations which Plato has reported or invented, his victories, for the most part, seem to us unprofitable. A trophy is set up; but no new province is added to the dominions of the human mind.

Still, where thousands of keen and ready intellects were constantly employed in speculating on the qualities of actions, and on the principles of government, it was impossible that history should retain its old character. It became less gossiping and less picturesque; but much more accurate, and somewhat more scientific.

The history of Thucydides differs from that of Herodotus as a portrait differs from the representation of an imaginary scene; as the Burke or Fox of Reynolds differs from his Ugolino or his Beaufort. In the former case, the archetype is given; in the latter, it is created. The faculties which are required for the latter purpose are of a higher and rarer order than those which suffice for the former, and indeed necessarily comprise them. He who is able to paint what he sees with the eye of the mind, will surely be able to paint what he sees with the eye of the body. He who can invent a story, and tell it well, will also be able to tell, in an interesting manner, a story which he has not invented. If, in practice, some of the best writers of fiction have been among the worst writers of history, it has been because one of their talents had merged in another so completely, that it could not be severed; because, having long been habituated to invent and narrate at the same time, they found it impossible to narrate without inventing.

Some capricious and discontented artists have affected to consider portrait-painting as unworthy of a man of genius. Some critics have spoken in the same contemptuous manner of history. Johnson puts the case thus: The historian tells either what is false or what is true. In the former case he is no historian. In the latter, he has no opportunity for displaying his abilities. For truth is one: and all who tell the truth must tell it alike.

It is not difficult to elude both the horns of this dilemma.
We will recur to the analogous art of portrait-painting. Any
man with eyes and hands may be taught to take a likeness.
The process, up to a certain point, is merely mechanical. If
this were all, a man of talents might justly despise the occupation. But we could mention portraits which are resemblances,
—but not mere resemblances; faithful,—but much more than
faithful; portraits which condense into one point of time, and
exhibit, at a single glance, the whole history of turbid and
eventful lives — in which the eye seems to scrutinize us, and the
mouth to command us — in which the brow menaces, and the
lip almost quivers with scorn — in which every wrinkle is a
comment on some important transaction. The account which
Thucydides has given of the retreat from Syracuse, is, among
narratives, what Vandyke's Lord Strafford is among paintings.

Diversity, it is said, implies error : truth is one, and admits of
no degrees. We answer, that this principle holds good only in
abstract reasonings. When we talk of the truth of imitation in
the fine arts, we mean an imperfect and a graduated truth. No
picture is exactly like the original : nor is a picture good in
proportion as it is like the original. When Sir Thomas Lawrence
paints a handsome peeress, he does not contemplate her through
a powerful microscope, and transfer to the canvas the pores of
the skin, the blood-vessels of the eye, and all the other beauties
which Gulliver discovered in the Brobdignaggian maids of
honor. If he were to do this, the effect would not merely be
unpleasant, but unless the scale of the picture were proportion-
ately enlarged, would be absolutely *false.* And, after all, a
microscope of greater power than that which he had employed,

would convict him of innumerable omissions. The same may be said of history. Perfectly and absolutely true it cannot be : for to be perfectly and absolutely true it ought to record *all* the slightest particulars of the slightest transactions — all the things done and all the words uttered during the time of which it treats. The omission of any circumstance, however insignificant, would be a defect. ᴠ If history were written thus, the Bodleian Library would not contain the occurrences of a week. What is told in the fullest and most accurate annals bears an infinitely small proportion to what is suppressed. The difference between the copious work of Clarendon, and the account of the civil wars in the abridgment of Goldsmith, vanishes, when compared with the immense mass of facts, respecting which both are equally silent.

, No picture, then, and no history, can present us with the whole truths : but those are the best pictures and the best histories which exhibit such parts of the truth as most nearly produce the effect of the whole. He who is deficient in the art of selection may, by showing nothing but the truth produce all the effect of the grossest falsehood. It perpetually happens that one writer tells less truth than another, merely because he tells more truths. · In the imitative arts we constantly see this. There are lines in the human face, and objects in landscape, which stand in such relations to each other, that they ought either to be all introduced into a painting together, or all omitted together. A sketch into which none of them enters, may be excellent; but if some are given and others left out, though there are more points of likeness, there is less likeness. An outline scrawled with a pen, which seizes the marked features of a countenance, will give a much stronger idea of it than a bad painting in oils. Yet the worst painting in oils that ever hung at Somerset House resembles the original in many more particulars. A bust of white marble may give an excellent idea of a blooming face. Color the lips and cheeks of the bust, leaving the hair and eyes unaltered, and the similarity, instead of being more striking, will be less so.

History has its foreground and its background; and it is principally in the management of its perspective that one artist differs from another. Some events must be represented on a large scale, others diminished; the great majority will be lost in the dimness of the horizon; and a general idea of their joint effect will be given by a few slight touches.

In this respect, no writer has ever equalled Thucydides. He was a perfect master of the art of gradual diminution. His history is sometimes as concise as a chronological chart; yet it is always perspicuous. It is sometimes as minute as one of Lovelace's letters; yet it is never prolix. He never fails to contract and to expand it in the right place.

Thucydides borrowed from Herodotus the practice of putting speeches of his own into the mouths of his characters. In Herodotus this usage is scarcely censurable. It is of a piece with his whole manner. But it is altogether incongruous in the work of his successor, and violates, not only the accuracy of history, but the decencies of fiction. When once we enter into the spirit of Herodotus, we find no inconsistency. The conventional probability of his drama is preserved from the beginning to the end. The deliberate orations, and the familiar dialogues are in strict keeping with each other. But the speeches of

Thucydides are neither preceded nor followed by anything with which they harmonize. They give to the whole book something of the grotesque character of those Chinese pleasure-grounds, in which perpendicular rocks of granite start up in the midst of a soft green plain. Invention is shocking, where truth is in such close juxtaposition with it.

Thucydides honestly tells us that some of these discourses are purely fictitious. He may have reported the substance of others correctly. But it is clear from the internal evidence that he has preserved no more than the substance. His own peculiar habits of thought and expression are everywhere discern-ible. Individual and national peculiarities are seldom to be traced in the sentiments, and never in the diction. The oratory of the Corinthians and Thebans is not less Attic, either in matter or in manner, than that of the Athenians. The style of Cleon is as pure, as austere, as terse, and as significant as that of Pericles.

In spite of this great fault it must be allowed that Thucydides has surpassed all his rivals in the art of historical narration, in the art of producing an effect on the imagination, by skilful selection and disposition, without indulging in the license of invention. But narration, though an important part of the business of an historian, is not the whole. To append a moral to a work of fiction, is either useless or superfluous. A fiction may give a more impressive effect to what is already known, but it can teach nothing new. If it presents to us characters and trains of events to which our experience furnishes us with nothing similar, instead of deriving instruction from it we pronounce it unnatural. We do not form our opinions from it, but we try it by our preconceived opinions. Fiction, therefore, is essentially imitative. Its merit consists in its resemblance to a model with which we are already familiar, or to which at least we can instantly refer. Hence it is that the anecdotes which interest us most strongly in authentic narrative, are offensive when introduced into novels ; that which is called the romantic part of the history is in fact the least romantic. It is delightful as history, because it contradicts our previous notions of human nature, and of the connection of causes and effects. It is, on that very account, shocking and incongruous in fiction. In fiction, the principles are given to find the facts : in history, the facts are given to find the principles ; and the writer who does not explain the phenomena as well as state them, performs only one half of his office. Facts are the mere dross of history. It is from the abstract truth which interpenetrates them, and lies latent among them, like gold in the ore, that the mass derives its whole value. And the precious particles are generally combined with the baser in such a manner that the separation is a task of the utmost difficulty.

Here Thucydides is deficient : the deficiency, indeed, is not discreditable to him. It was the inevitable effect of circumstances. It was in the nature of things necessary that, in some part of its progress through political science, the human mind should reach that point which it attained in his time. Knowledge advances by steps, and not by leaps. The axioms of an English debating club would have been startling and mysterious paradoxes to the most enlightened statesmen of Athens. But it would be as absurd to speak contemptuously of the Athenian on this account, as to ridicule Strabo for not having given us an

account of Chili, or to talk of Ptolemy as we talk of Sir Richard
Phillips. Still, when we wish for solid geographical information, we must prefer the solemn coxcombry of Pinkerton, to the
noble work of Strabo. If we wanted instruction respecting
the solar system, we should consult the silliest girl from a
boarding-school, rather than Ptolemy.

.' Thucydides was undoubtedly a sagacious and reflecting man.
This clearly appears from the ability with which he discusses
practical questions. But the talent of deciding on the circum-
tances of a particular case is often possessed in the highest
perfection by persons destitute of the power of generalization.
Men skilled in the military tactics of civilized nations have been
amazed at the far-sightedness and penetration which a Mohawk
displays in concerting his stratagems, or in discerning those of
his enemies. In England, no class possesses so much of that
peculiar ability which is required for constructing ingenious
schemes and for obviating remote difficulties, as the thieves and
the thief-takers. Women have more of this dexterity than men.
Lawyers have more of it than statesmen : statesmen have more
of it than philosophers. Monk had more of it than Harrington
and all his club. Walpole had more of it than Adam Smith or
Beccaria. Indeed, the species of discipline by which this dexterity is acquired, tends to contract the mind and to render it
incapable of abstract reasoning.

The Grecian statesmen of the age of Thucydides were distinguished by their practical sagacity, their insight into motives,
their skill in devising means for the attainment of their ends.
A state of society in which the rich were constantly planning
the oppression of the poor, and the poor the spoliation of the

rich, in which the ties of party had superseded those of country, in which revolutions and counter-revolutions were events of daily occurrence, was naturally prolific in desperate and crafty political adventurers. This was the very school in which men were likely to acquire the dissimulation of Mazarin, the judicious temerity of Richelieu, the penetration, the exquisite tact, the almost instinctive presentiment of approaching events which gave so much authority to the counsel of Shaftesbury, that "it was as if a man had inquired of the oracle of God." In this school Thucydides studied; and his wisdom is that which such a school would naturally afford. He judges better of circumstances than of principles. The more a question is narrowed, the better he reasons upon it. His work suggests many most important considerations respecting the first principles of government and morals, the growth of factions, the organization of armies, and the mutual relations of communities. Yet all his general observations on these subjects are very superficial. His most judicious remarks differ from the remarks of a really philosophical historian, as a sum correctly cast up by a bookkeeper, from a general expression discovered by an algebraist. The former is useful only in a single transaction; the latter may be applied to an infinite number of cases.

This opinion will, we fear, be considered as heterodox. For, not to speak of the illusion which the sight of a Greek type, or the sound of a Greek diphthong, often produces, there are some peculiarities in the manner of Thucydides, which in no small degree have tended to secure to him the reputation of profundity. His book is evidently the book of a man and a statesman; and in this respect presents a remarkable contrast to the delightful childishness of Herodotus. Throughout it there is an air of matured power, of grave and melancholy reflection, of impartiality and habitual self-command. His feelings are rarely indulged, and speedily repressed. Vulgar prejudices of every kind, and particularly vulgar superstitions, he treats with a cold and sober disdain peculiar to himself. His style is weighty, condensed, antithetical, and not unfrequently obscure. But when we look at his political philosophy, without regard to these circumstances, we find him to have been, what indeed it would have been a miracle if he had not been, simply an Athenian of the fifth century before Christ.

Xenophon is commonly placed, but we think without much reason, in the same rank with Herodotus and Thucydides. He resembles them, indeed, in the purity and sweetness of his style; but in spirit, he rather resembles that later school of historians, whose works seem to be fables, composed for a moral, and who, in their eagerness to give us warnings and example, forgot to give us men and women. The life of Cyrus, whether we look upon it as a history or a romance, seems to us a very wretched performance. The Expedition of the Ten Thousand, and the History of Grecian Affairs, are certainly pleasant reading; but they indicate no great power of mind. In truth Xenophon, though his taste was elegant, his disposition amiable, and his intercourse with the world extensive, had, we suspect, rather a weak head. Such was evidently the opinion of that extraordinary man to whom he early attached himself, and for whose memory he entertained an idolatrous veneration. He came in only for the milk with which Socrates nourished his babes in philosophy. A few saws of morality, and a few of the simplest

doctrines of natural religion, were enough for the good young
man.   The strong meat, the bold speculations on physical and
metaphysical science, were reserved for auditors of a different
description.   Even the lawless habits of a captain of mercenary
troops could not change the tendency which the character
of Xenophon early acquired.   To the last, he seems to have
retained a sort of heathen Puritanism.   The sentiments of piety
and virtue which abound in his works, are those of a well-meaning man, somewhat timid and narrow-minded, devout from
constitution rather than from rational conviction.   He was as
superstitious as Herodotus, but in a way far more offensive.
The very peculiarities which charm us in an infant, the toothless
mumbling, the stammering, the tottering, the helplessness, the
causeless tears and laughter, are disgusting in old age.   In the
same manner, the absurdity which precedes a period of general
intelligence is often pleasing ; that which follows it is contemptible.   The nonsense of Herodotus is that of a baby.   The
nonsense of Xenophon is that of a dotard.   His stories about
dreams, omens, and prophecies, present a strange contrast to
the passages in which the shrewd and incredulous Thucydides
mentions the popular superstitions.   It is not quite clear that
Xenophon was honest in his credulity ; his fanaticism was in
some degree politic.   He would have made an excellent member
of the Apostolic Camarilla.   An Alarmist by nature, and Aris-
tocrat by party, he carried to an unreasonable excess his horror
of popular turbulence.   The quiet atrocity of Sparta did not
shock him in the same manner ; for he hated tumult more than
crimes.   He was desirous to find restraints which might curb the
passions of the multitude ; and he absurdly fancied that he had

found them in a religion without evidences or sanction, precepts or example, in a frigid system of Theophilanthropy, supported by nursery tales.

Polybius and Arrian have given us authentic accounts of facts, and here their merit ends. They were not men of comprehensive minds; they had not the art of telling a story in an interesting manner. They have in consequence been thrown into the shade by writers who, though less studious of truth than themselves, understood far better the art of producing effect, — by Livy and Quintus Curtius.

Yet Polybius and Arrian deserve high praise, when compared with the writers of that school of which Plutarch may be considered as the head. For the historians of this class we must confess that we entertain a peculiar aversion. They seem to have been pedants, who, though destitute of those valuable qualities which are frequently found in conjunction with pedantry, thought themselves great philosophers and great politicians. They not only mislead their readers in every page, as to particular facts, but they appear to have altogether misconceived the whole character of the times of which they write. They were inhabitants of an empire bounded by the Atlantic Ocean and the Euphrates, by the ice of Scythia and the sands of Mauritania; composed of nations whose manners, whose languages, whose religion, whose countenance and complexions, were widely different, governed by one mighty despotism, which had risen on the ruins of a thousand commonwealths and kingdoms. Of liberty, such as it is in small democracies; of patriotism, such as it is in small independent communities of any kind, they had, and they could have, no experimental knowledge. But

they had read of men who exerted themselves in the cause of
their country, with an energy unknown in latter times, who had
violated the dearest of domestic charities, or voluntarily devoted
themselves to death for the public good; and they wondered at
the degeneracy of their contemporaries. It never occurred to
them, that the feelings which they so greatly admired, sprung
from local and occasional causes; that they will always grow up
spontaneously in small societies; and that, in large empires,
though they may be forced into existence for a short time by
peculiar circumstances, they cannot be general or permanent.
It is impossible that any man should feel for a fortress on a
remote frontier, as he feels for his own house; that he should
grieve for a defeat in which ten thousand people whom he never
saw have fallen, as he grieves for a defeat which has half un-
peopled the street in which he lives; that he should leave his
home for a military expedition, in order to preserve the balance
of power, as cheerfully as he would leave it to repel invaders
who had begun to burn all the cornfields in his neighborhood.

The writers of whom we speak should have considered this.
They should have considered, that in patriotism, such as it existed
amongst the Greeks, there was nothing essentially and eternally
good; that an exclusive attachment to a particular society, though
a natural, and, under certain restrictions, a most useful sentiment,
implies no extraordinary attainments in wisdom or virtue; that
where it has existed in an intense degree, it has turned states
into gangs of robbers, whom their mutual fidelity has rendered
more dangerous, has given a character of peculiar atrocity to
war, and has generated that worst of all political evils, the
tyranny of nations over nations.

Enthusiastically attached to the name of liberty, these historians troubled themselves little about its definition. The Spar-
tans, tormented by ten thousand absurd restraints, unable to
please themselves in the choice of their wives, their suppers, or
their company, compelled to assume a peculiar manner, and to
talk in a peculiar style, gloried in their liberty. The aristocracy
of Rome repeatedly made liberty a plea for cutting off the
favorites of the people. In almost all the little commonwealths
of antiquity, liberty was used as a pretext for measures directed
against every thing which makes liberty valuable, for measures
which stifled discussion, corrupted the administration of justice,
and discouraged the accumulation of property. The writers,
whose works we are considering, confounded the sound with the
substance, and the means with the end. Their imaginations
were inflamed by mystery. They conceived of liberty as monks
conceive of love, as Cockneys conceive of the happiness and
innocence of rural life, as novel-reading seamstresses conceive
of Almack's and Grosvenor Square, accomplished Marquesses
and handsome Colonels of the Guards. In the relation of
events, and the delineation of characters, they have paid little
attention to facts, to the costume of the times of which they
pretend to treat, or to the general principles of human nature.
They have been faithful only to their own puerile and extravagant doctrines. Generals and statesmen are metamorphosed
into magnanimous coxcombs, from whose fulsome virtues we
turn away with disgust. The fine sayings and exploits of their
heroes remind us of the insufferable perfections of Sir Charles
Grandison, and effect us with a nausea, similar to that which we
feel when an actor, in one of Morton's or Kotzebue's plays, lays

his hand on his heart, advances to the ground-lights, and mouths a moral sentence for the edification of the gods.

These writers, men who knew not what it was to have a country, men who have never enjoyed political rights, brought into fashion an offensive cant about patriotism and zeal for freedom. What the English Puritans did for the language of Christianity, what Scuderi did for the language of love, they did for the language of public spirit. By habitual exaggeration they made it mean. By monotonous emphasis they made it feeble. They abused it till it became scarcely possible to use it with effect.

Their ordinary rules of morality are deduced from extreme cases. The common regimen which they prescribe for society, is made up of those desperate remedies which only its most desperate distempers require. They look with peculiar complacency on actions, which even those who approve them consider as exceptions to laws of almost universal application — which bear so close an affinity to the most atrocious crimes, that even where it may be unjust to censure them, it is unsafe to praise them. It is not strange, therefore, that some flagitious instances of perfidy and cruelty should have been passed unchallenged in such company, that grave moralists, with no personal interest at stake, should have extolled, in the highest terms, deeds of which the atrocity appalled even the infuriated factions in whose cause they were perpetrated. The part which Timoleon took in the assassination of his brother, shocked many of his own partisans. The recollection of it preyed long on his own mind. But it was reserved for historians who lived some centuries later to discover that his conduct was a glorious display of virtue, and to lament

that, from the frailty of human nature, a man who could perform
so great an exploit could repent of it.

The writings of these men, and of their modern imitators, ·
have produced effects which deserve some notice. The English
have been so long accustomed to political speculation, and have
enjoyed so large a measure of practical liberty, that such works
have produced little effect on their minds. We have classical
associations and great names of our own, which we can confidently oppose to the most splendid of ancient times. Senate
has not to our ears a sound so venerable as Parliament. We
respect the Great Charter more than the laws of Solon. The
Capitol and the Forum impress us with less awe than our own
Westminster Hall and Westminster Abbey, the place where the · ·
great men of twenty generations have contended, the place
where they sleep together! The list of warriors and statesmen
by whom our constitution was founded or preserved, from De
Monfort down to Fox, may well stand a comparison with the
Fasti of Rome. The dying thanksgiving of Sydney is as noble
as the libation which Thrasea poured to Liberating Jove; and
we think with far less pleasure of Cato tearing out his entrails,
than of Russell saying, as he turned away from his wife, that
the bitterness of death was past. Even those parts of our
history, over which, on some accounts, we would gladly throw a
veil, may be proudly opposed to those on which the moralists of
antiquity loved most to dwell. The enemy of English liberty
was not murdered by men whom he pardoned and loaded with
benefits. He was not stabbed in the back by those who smiled
and cringed before his face. He was vanquished on fields of
stricken battle; he was arraigned, sentenced, and executed in the

face of heaven and earth. Our liberty is neither Greek nor
Roman, but essentially English. It has a character of its own,
—a character which has taken a tinge from the sentiments of
the chivalrous ages, and which accords with the peculiarities of
our manners and of our insular situation. It has a language,
too, of its own, and a language singularly idiomatic, full of
meaning to ourselves, scarcely intelligible to strangers.

Here, therefore, the effect of books such as those which we
have been considering, has been harmless. They have, indeed,
given currency to many very erroneous opinions with respect to
ancient history. They have heated the imaginations of boys.
They have misled the judgment, and corrupted the taste, of
some men of letters, such as Akenside and Sir William Jones.
But on persons engaged in public affairs they have had very
little influence. The foundations of our constitution were laid
by men who knew nothing of the Greeks, but that they denied
the orthodox procession, and cheated the Crusaders; and nothing of Rome, but that the Pope lived there. Those who
followed, contented themselves with improving on the original
plan. They found models at home, and therefore they did not
look for them abroad. But when enlightened men on the
Continent began to think about political reformation, having no
patterns before their eyes in their domestic history, they naturally
had recourse to those remains of antiquity, the study of which
is considered throughout Europe as an important part of education. The historians of whom we have been speaking had been
members of large communities, and subjects of absolute sovereigns. Hence it is, as we have already said, that they commit
such gross errors in speaking of the little publics of antiquity.

Their works were now read in the spirit in which they had been written. They were read by men placed in circumstances closely resembling their own, unacquainted with the real nature of liberty, but inclined to believe every thing good which could be told respecting it. How powerfully these books impressed these speculative reformers, is well known to all who have paid any attention to the French literature of the last century. But, perhaps, the writer on whom they produced the greatest effect, was Vittoria Alfieri. In some of his plays, particularly in "Virginia," "Timoleon," and "Brutus the Younger," he has even caricatured the extravagance of his masters.

It was not strange that the blind, thus led by the blind, should stumble. The transactions of the French Revolution, in some measure, took their character from these works. Without the assistance of these works, indeed, a revolution would have taken place, — a revolution productive of much good and much evil: tremendous, but short-lived evil; dearly purchased, but durable good. But it would not have been exactly such a revolution. The style, the accessories, would have been in many respects different. There would have been less of bombast in language, less of affectation in manner, less of solemn trifling and ostentatious simplicity. The acts of legislative assemblies, and the correspondence of diplomatists, would not have been disgraced by rants worthy only of a college declamation. The government of a great and polished nation would not have rendered itself ridiculous, by attempting to revive the usages of a world which had long passed away, or rather of a world which had never existed except in the description of a fantastic school of writers. These second-hand imitations resembled the originals about as much as the classical feast with which the Doctor in Peregrine Pickle turned the stomachs of all his guests, resembled one of the suppers of Lucullus in the Hall of Apollo.

These were mere follies. But the spirit excited by these writers produced more serious effects. The greater part of the crimes which disgraced the revolution sprung indeed from the relaxation of law, from popular ignorance, from the remembrance of past oppression, from the fear of foreign conquest, from rapacity, from ambition, from party-spirit. But many atrocious proceedings must, doubtless, be ascribed to heated imagination, to perverted principle, to a distaste for what was vulgar in morals, and a passion for what was startling and dubious. Mr. Burke has touched on this subject with great felicity of expression. "The gradation of their republic," says he, "is laid in moral paradoxes. All those instances to be found in history, whether real or fabulous, of a doubtful public spirit, at which morality is perplexed, reason is staggered, and from which affrighted nature recoils, are their chosen and almost sole examples, for the instruction of their youth." The evil, we believe, is to be directly ascribed to the influence of the historians whom we have mentioned, and their modern imitators.

Livy had some faults in common with these writers. But on the whole he must be considered as forming a class by himself. No historian with whom we are acquainted has shown so complete an indifference to truth. He seems to have cared only about the picturesque effect of his book, and the honor of his country. On the other hand, we do not know, in the whole range of literature, an instance of a bad thing so well done.

The painting of the narrative is beyond description vivid and graceful. The abundance of interesting sentiments and splendid imagery in the speeches is almost miraculous. His mind is a soil which is never overteemed, a fountain which never seems to trickle. It pours forth profusely ; yet it gives no sign of exhaustion. It was probably to this exuberance of thought and language always fresh, always sweet, always pure, no sooner yielded than repaired, that the critics applied that expression which has been so much discussed, *lactea ubertas*.

. , All the merits and all the defects of Livy take a coloring from the character of his nation. He was a writer peculiarly Roman; the proud citizen of a commonwealth which had indeed lost the reality of liberty, but which still sacredly preserved its forms — in fact, the subject of an arbitrary prince, but in his own estimation one of the masters of the world, with a hundred kings below him, and only the gods above him. He, therefore, looked back on former times with feelings far different from those which were naturally entertained by his Greek contemporaries, and which at a later period became general among men of letters throughout the Roman Empire. He contemplated the past with interest and delight, not because it furnished a contrast to the present, but because it had led to the present. He recurred to it, not to lose in proud recollections the sense of national degradation, but to trace the progress of national glory. It is true that his veneration for antiquity produced on him some of the effects which it produced on those who arrived at it by a very different road. He has something of their exaggeration, something of their cant, something of their fondness for anomalies and *lusus naturæ* in morality. Yet even here we perceive a difference. They talk rapturously of patriotism and liberty in the abstract. He does not seem to think any country but Rome deserving of love: nor is it for liberty as liberty, but for liberty as a part of the 'Roman institutions, that he is zealous.

Of the concise and elegant accounts of the campaigns of Cæsar little can be said. They are incomparable models for military despatches. But histories they are not, and do not pretend to be.

The ancient critics placed Sallust in the same rank with Livy; and unquestionably the small portion of his works which has come down to us is calculated to give a high opinion of his talents. But his style is not very pleasant, and his most powerful work, the account of the Conspiracy of Catiline, has rather the air of a clever party pamphlet than that of a history. It abounds with strange inconsistencies, which, unexplained as they are, necessarily excite doubts as to the fairness of the narrative. It is true, that many circumstances now forgotten may have been familiar to his contemporaries, and may have rendered passages clear to them which to us appear dubious and perplexing. But a great historian should remember that he writes for distant generations, for men who will preserve the apparent contradictions, and will possess no means of reconciling them. We can only vindicate the fidelity of Sallust at the expense of his skill. But, in fact, all the information which we have from contemporaries, respecting this famous plot is liable to the same objection, and is read by discerning men with the same incredulity. It is all on one side. No answer has reached our times. Yet, on the showing of the accusers, the accused seem entitled to acquittal. Catiline, we are told, intrigued with a Vestal virgin, and murdered his own son. His house was a den of gamblers and debauchees. No young man could cross his threshold without danger to his fortune and reputation. Yet this is the man with whom Cicero was willing to coalesce in a contest for the first magistracy of the republic; and whom he described long after the fatal termination of the conspiracy, as an accomplished hypocrite, by whom he had himself been deceived; and who had acted with consummate skill the character of a good citizen and a good friend. We are told that the plot was the most wicked and desperate ever known, and, almost in the same breath, that the great body of the people, and many of the nobles, favored it; that the richest citizens of Rome were eager for the spoliation of all property, and its highest functionaries for the destruction of all order; that Crassus, Cæsar, the Prætor Lentulus, one of the consuls of the year, one of the consuls elect, were proved or suspected to be engaged in a scheme for subverting institutions to which they owed the highest honors, and introducing universal anarchy. We are told, that a government which knew all this suffered the conspirator, whose rank, talents, and courage rendered him most dangerous, to quit Rome without molestation. We are told, that bondmen and gladiators were to be armed against the citizens. Yet we find that Catiline rejected the slaves who crowded to enlist in his army, lest, as Sallust himself expresses it, "he should seem to identify their cause with that of the citizens." Finally, we are told that the magistrate, who was universally allowed to have saved all classes of his countrymen from conflagration and massacre, rendered himself so unpopular by his conduct, that a marked insult was offered to him at the expiration of his office, and a severe punishment inflicted on him shortly after.

Sallust tells us what, indeed, the letters and speeches of Cicero sufficiently prove,. that some persons considered the shocking and atrocious parts of the plot as mere inventions of the government, designed to excuse its unconstitutional measures. We must confess ourselves to be of that opinion. There was, undoubtedly, a strong party desirous to change the administration. While Pompey held the command of an army, they could not effect their purpose without preparing means for repelling force, if necessary, by force. In all this there is nothing different from the ordinary practice of Roman factions. The other charges brought against the conspirators are so inconsistent and improbable, that we give no credit whatever to them. If our readers think this scepticism unreasonable, let them turn to the contemporary accounts of the Popish Plot. Let them look over the votes of Parliament, and the speeches of the King; the charges of Scroggs, and the harangues of the managers employed against Strafford. A person who should form his judgment from these pieces alone, would believe that London was set on fire by the Papists, and that Sir Edmondbury Godfrey was murdered for his religion. Yet these stories are now altogether exploded. They have been abandoned by statesmen to aldermen, by aldermen to clergymen, by clergymen to old women, and by old women to Sir Harcourt Lees.

Of the great Latin historians, Tacitus was certainly the greatest. His style, indeed, is not only faulty in itself, but is, in some respects, peculiarly unfit for historical composition. He carries his love of effect far beyond the limits of moderation. He tells

a fine story finely; but he cannot tell a plain story plainly. He
stimulates till stimulants lose their power. Thucydides, as we
have already observed, relates ordinary transactions with the
unpretending clearness and succinctness of a gazette. His
great powers of painting he reserves for events, of which the
slightest details are interesting. The simplicity of the setting
gives additional lustre to the brilliants. There are passages in
the narrative of Tacitus superior to the best which can be quoted
from Thucydides. But they are not enchased and relieved with
the same skill. , They are far more striking when extracted from
the body of the work to which they belong, than when they
occur in their place, and are read in connection with what precedes and follows.

. In the delineation of character, Tacitus is unrivalled among
historians, and has very few superiors among dramatists and
novelists. By the delineation of character, we do not mean the
practice of drawing up epigrammatic catalogues of good and
bad qualities, and appending them to the names of eminent
men. No writer, indeed, has done this more skilfully than Tacitus: but this is not his peculiar glory. All the persons who
occupy a large space in his works have an individuality of character which seems to pervade all their words and actions. We
know them as if we had lived with them. Claudius, Nero, Otho,
both the Agrippinas, are master-pieces. But Tiberius is a still
higher miracle of art. The historian undertook to make us
intimately acquainted with a man singularly dark and inscrutable, — with a man whose real disposition long remained swathed
up in intricate folds of factitious virtues; and over whose actions
the hypocrisy of his youth, and the seclusion of his old age,

threw a singular mystery. He was to exhibit the specious qualities of the tyrant in a light which might render them transparent, and enable us at once to perceive the covering and the
vices which it concealed. He was to trace the gradations by
which the first magistrate of a republic, a senator mingling
freely in debate, a noble associating with his brother nobles, was
transformed into an Asiatic sultan ; he was to exhibit a character distinguished by courage, self-command, and profound
policy, yet defiled by all

> " th' extravagancy,
> And crazy ribaldry of fancy."

He was to mark the gradual effect of advancing age and
approaching death on this strange compound of strength and
weakness ; to exhibit the old sovereign of the world sinking into
a dotage which, though it rendered his appetites eccentric, and
his temper savage, never impaired the powers of his stern and
penetrating mind — conscious of failing strength, raging with
capricious sensuality, yet to the last the keenest of observers,
the most artful of dissemblers, and the most terrible of masters.
The task was one of extreme difficulty. The execution is almost
perfect.

The talent which is required to write history thus, bears a
considerable affinity to the talent of a great dramatist. There
is one obvious distinction. The dramatist creates, the historian
only disposes. The difference is not in the mode of execution,
but in the mode of conception. Shakespeare is guided by a
model which exists in his imagination ; Tacitus, by a model
furnished from without. Hamlet is to Tiberius what the Laoc-
oön is to the Newton of Roubilliac.

In this part of his art Tacitus certainly had neither equal nor second among the ancient historians. Herodotus, though he wrote in a dramatic form, had little of dramatic genius. The frequent dialogues which he introduces give vivacity and movement to the narrative; but are not strikingly characteristic. Xenophon is fond of telling his readers, at considerable length, what he thought of the persons whose adventures he relates. But he does not show them the men, and enable them to judge for themselves. The heroes of Livy are the most insipid of all beings, real or imaginary, the heroes of Plutarch always excepted. Indeed, the manner of Plutarch in this respect reminds us of the cookery of those continental inns, the horror of English travellers, in which a certain nondescript broth is kept constantly boiling, and copiously poured, without distinction, over every dish as it comes up to table. Thucydides, though at a wide interval, comes next to Tacitus. His Pericles, his Nicias, his Cleon, his Brasidas, are happily discriminated. The lines are few, the coloring faint; but the general air and expression are caught.

We begin, like the priest in Don Quixote's library, to be tired with taking down books one after another for separate judgment, and feel inclined to pass sentence on them in masses. We shall, therefore, instead of pointing out the defects and merits of the different modern historians, state generally in what particulars they have surpassed their predecessors, and in what we conceive them to have failed.

They have certainly been, in one sense, far more strict in their adherence to truth, than most of the Greek and Roman writers. They do not think themselves entitled to render their narrative interesting by introducing descriptions, conversations and harangues, which have no existence but in their own imagination. This improvement was gradually introduced. History commenced among the modern nations of Europe, as it had commenced among the Greeks, in romance. Froissart was our Herodotus. Italy was to Europe what Athens was to Greece. In Italy, therefore, a more accurate and manly mode of narration was early introduced. Machiavelli and Guicciardini, in imitation of Livy and Thucydides, composed speeches for their historical personages. But as the classical enthusiasm which distinguished the age of Lorenzo and Leo gradually subsided, this absurd practice was abandoned. In France, we fear, it still, in some degree, keeps its ground. In our own country, a writer who should venture on it would be laughed to scorn. Whether the historians of the last two centuries tell more truth than those of antiquity, may perhaps be doubted. But it is quite certain that they tell fewer falsehoods.

In the philosophy of history, the moderns have very far surpassed the ancients. It is not, indeed, strange that the Greeks and Romans should not have carried the science of government, or any other experimental science, so far as it has been carried in our time; for the experimental sciences are generally in a state of progression. They were better understood in the seventeenth century than in the sixteenth, and in the eighteenth century than in the seventeenth. But this constant improvement, this natural growth of knowledge, will not altogether account for the immense superiority of the modern writers. The difference is a difference not in degree but of kind. It is not merely that new principles have been discovered, but that new faculties seem to be exerted. It is not that at one time the human intellect should have made but small progress, and at another time have advanced far; but that at one time it should have been stationary, and at another time constantly proceeding. In taste and imagination, in the graces of style, in the arts of persuasion, in the magnificence of public works, the ancients were at least our equals. They reasoned as justly as ourselves on subjects which required pure demonstration. But in the moral sciences they made scarcely any advance. During the long period which elapsed between the fifth century before the Christian era, and the fifth century after it, little perceptible progress was made. All the metaphysical discoveries of all the philosophers, from the time of Socrates to the northern invasion, are not to be compared in importance with those which have been made in England every fifty years since the time of Elizabeth. There is not the least reason to believe that the principles of government, legislation, and political economy were better understood in the time of Augustus Cæsar, than in the time of Pericles. In our own country, the sound doctrines of trade and jurisprudence have been, within the lifetime of a single generation, dimly hinted, boldly propounded, defended, systematized, adopted by all reflecting men of all parties, quoted in legislative assemblies, incorporated into laws and treaties.

To what is this change to be attributed? Partly, no doubt, to the discovery of printing, a discovery which has not only diffused knowledge widely, but, as we have already observed, has also introduced into reasoning a precision unknown in those ancient communities, in which information was for the most part conveyed orally. There was, we suspect, another cause, less obvious, but still more powerful.

The spirit of the two most famous nations of antiquity was remarkably exclusive. In the time of Homer, the Greeks had not begun to consider themselves as a distinct race. They still looked with something of childish wonder and awe on the riches and wisdom of Sidon and Egypt. From what causes, and by what gradations, their feelings underwent a change, it is not easy to determine. Their history from the Trojan to the Persian war, is covered with an obscurity broken only by dim and scattered gleams of truth. But it is certain that a great alteration took place. They regarded themselves as a separate people. They had common religious rites, and common principles of public law, in which foreigners had no part. In all their political systems, monarchical, aristocratical, and democratical, there was a strong family likeness. After the retreat of Xerxes and the fall of Mardonius, national pride rendered the separation between the Greeks and the barbarians complete. The conquerors considered themselves men of a superior breed, men who, in their intercourse with neighboring nations, were to teach, and not to learn. They looked for nothing out of themselves. They borrowed nothing. They translated nothing. We cannot call to mind a single expression of any Greek writer earlier than the age of Augustus, indicating an opinion, that anything worth reading could be written in any language except his own. The feelings which sprung from national glory were not altogether extinguished by national degradation. They were fondly cherished through ages of slavery and shame. The literature of Rome herself was regarded with contempt by those who had

fled before her arms, and who bowed beneath her fasces. Voltaire says, in one of his six thousand pamphlets, that he was the
first person who told the French that England had produced
eminent men besides the Duke of Marlborough. Down to a
very late period the Greeks seem to have stood in need of
similar information with respect to their masters. With Paulus
Æmilius, Sylla, and Cæsar they were well acquainted. But the
notions which they entertained respecting Cicero and Virgil
were, probably, not unlike those which Boileau may have
formed about Shakespeare. Dionysius lived in the most splendid age of Latin poetry and eloquence. He was a critic, and,
after the manner of his age, an able critic. He studied the
language of Rome, associated with its learned men, and com-
piled its history. Yet he seems to have thought its literature
valuable only for the purpose of illustrating its antiquities. His
reading appears to have been confined to its public records, and
to a few old annalists. Once and but once, if we remember
rightly, he quotes Ennius, to solve a question of Etymology.
He has written much on the art of oratory : yet he has not mentioned the name of Cicero.

The Romans submitted to the pretensions of a race which
they despised. Their epic poet, while he claimed for them preeminence in the arts of government and war, acknowledged
their inferiority in taste, eloquence, and science. Men of letters
affected to understand the Greek language better than their
own. Pomponius preferred the honor of becoming an Athenian,
by intellectual naturalization, to all the distinctions which were
to be acquired in the political contests of Rome. His great
friend composed Greek poems and memoirs. It is well known

that Petrarch considered that beautiful language in which his sonnets are written, as a barbarous jargon, and entrusted his fame to those wretched Latin hexameters, which, during the last four centuries, have scarcely found four readers. Many eminent Romans appear to have felt the same contempt for their native tongue as compared with the Greek. The prejudice continued to a very late period. Julian was as partial to the Greek language as Frederic the Great to the French; and it seems that he could not express himself with elegance in the dialect of the state which he ruled.

Even those Latin writers who did not carry this affectation so far, looked on Greece as the only fount of knowledge. From Greece they derived the measures of their poetry, and indeed, all of poetry that can be imported. From Greece they borrowed the principles and the vocabulary of their philosophy. To the literature of other nations they do not seem to have paid the slightest attention. The sacred books of the Hebrews, for example, books which, considered merely as human compositions, are invaluable, to the critic, the antiquarian, and the philosopher, seem to have been utterly unnoticed by them. The peculiarities of Judaism, and the rapid growth of Christianity, attracted their notice. They made war against the Jews. They made laws against the Christians. But they never opened the books of Moses. Juvenal quotes the Pentateuch with censure. The author of the treatise on "the Sublime" quotes it with praise: but both of them quote it erroneously. When we consider what sublime poetry, what curious history, what striking and peculiar views of the Divine nature, and of the social duties of men, are to be found in the Jewish scriptures; when we consider that two sects on which the attention of the government was constantly fixed, appealed to those scriptures as the rule of their faith and practice, this indifference is astonishing. The fact seems to be, that the Greeks admired only themselves, and that the Romans admired only themselves and the Greeks. Literary men turned away with disgust from modes of thought and expression so widely different from all that they had been accustomed to admire. The effect was narrowness and sameness of thought. Their minds, if we may so express ourselves, bred in and in, and were accordingly cursed with barrenness, and degeneracy. No extraneous beauty or vigor was engrafted on the decaying stock. By an exclusive attention to one class of phenomena, by an exclusive taste for one species of excellence, the human intellect was stunted. Occasional coincidences were turned into general rules. Prejudices were confounded with instincts. On man, as he was found in a particular state of society — on government, as it had existed in a particular corner of the world, many just observations were made ; but of man as man, or government as government, little was known. Philosophy remained stationary. Slight changes, sometimes for the worse and sometimes for the better, were made in the superstructure. But nobody thought of examining the foundations.

. . The vast despotism of the Cæsars, gradually effacing all national peculiarities, and assimilating the remotest provinces of the Empire to each other, augmented the evil. At the close of the third century after Christ the prospects of mankind were fearfully dreary. A system of etiquette, as pompously frivolous as that of the Escurial, had been established. A sovereign almost invisible ; a crowd of dignitaries minutely distinguished by badges and titles; rhetoricians who said nothing but what had been said ten thousand times; schools in which nothing was taught but what had been known for ages, — such was the machinery provided for the government and instruction of the most enlightened part of the human race. That great community was then in danger of experiencing a calamity far more terrible than any of the quick, inflammatory, destroying maladies, to which nations are liable, — a tottering, drivelling, paralytic longevity, the immortality of the Struldbrugs, a Chinese civilization. It would be easy to indicate many points of resemblance between the subjects of Diocletian and the people of that Celestial Empire where, during many centuries, nothing has been learned or unlearned; where government, where education, where the whole system of life is a ceremony; where knowledge forgets to increase and multiply, and, like the talent buried in the earth, or the pound wrapped up in the napkin, experiences neither waste nor augmentation.

The torpor was broken by two great revolutions : the one moral, the other political; the one from within, the other from without. The victory of Christianity over Paganism, considered with relation to this subject only, was of great importance. It overthrew the old system of morals; and with it much of the old system of metaphysics. It furnished the orator with new topics of declamation, and the logician with new points of controversy. Above all, it introduced a new principle, of which the operation was constantly felt in every part of society. It stirred the stagnant mass from the inmost depths. It excited all the passions of a stormy democracy in the quiet and listless population of an overgrown empire. The fear of heresy did what the sense of oppression could not do: it changed men, accustomed to be turned over like sheep from tyrant to tyrant, into devoted partizans and obstinate rebels. The tones of an eloquence which had been silent for ages, resounded from the pulpit of Gregory. A spirit which had been extinguished on the plains of Philippi, revived in Athanasius and Ambrose.

Yet even this remedy was not sufficiently violent for the disease. It did not prevent the empire of Constantinople from relapsing, after a short paroxysm of excitement, into a state of stupefaction, to which history furnishes scarcely any parallel. We there find that a polished society, a society in which a most intricate and elaborate system of jurisprudence was established, in which the arts of luxury were well understood, in which the works of the great ancient writers were preserved and studied, existed for nearly a thousand years without making one great discovery in science, or producing one book which is read by any but curious inquirers. There were tumults, too, and controversies, and wars, in abundance: and these things, bad as they are in themselves, have generally been favorable to the progress of the intellect. But here they tormented without stimulating. The waters were troubled, but no healing influence descended. The agitations resembled the grinnings and writhings of a galvanized corpse, not the struggles of an athletic man.

From this miserable state the Western Empire was saved by the fiercest and most destroying visitation with which God has ever chastened his creatures — the invasion of the Northern nations. Such a cure was required for such a distemper. The Fire of London, it has been observed, was a blessing. It burned down the city, but it burned out the plague. The same may be said of the tremendous devastations of the Roman dominions. It annihilated the noisome recesses in which lurked the seeds of great moral maladies; it cleared an atmosphere fatal to the health and vigor of the human mind. It cost Europe a thousand years of barbarism to escape the fate of China.

At length the terrible purification was accomplished; and the second civilization of mankind commenced, under the circumstances which afforded a strong security that it would never retrograde and never pause. Europe was now a great federal community: her numerous states were united by the easy ties of international law and a common religion. Their institutions, their languages, their manners, their tastes in literature, their modes of education, were widely different. Their connection was close enough to allow of mutual observation and improvement, yet not so close as to destroy the idioms of national opinion and feeling.

The balance of moral and intellectual influence thus established between the nations of Europe, is far more important than the balance of political power. Indeed, we are inclined to think that the latter is valuable principally because it tends to maintain the former. The civilized world has thus been preserved from a uniformity of character fatal to all improvement. Every part of it has been illuminated with light reflected from every other. Competition has produced activity where monopoly would have produced sluggishness. The number of experiments in moral science which the speculator has an opportunity of witnessing, has been increased beyond all calculation. Society and human nature, instead of being seen in a single point of view, are presented to him under ten thousand different aspects.

By observing the manners of surrounding nations, by studying their literature, by comparing it with that of his own country and of the ancient republics, he is enabled to correct those errors into which the most acute men must fall when they reason from a single species to a genus. He learns to distinguish what is local from what is universal; what is transitory from what is eternal; to discriminate between exceptions and rules; to trace the operation of disturbing causes; to separate those general principles, which are always true and everywhere applicable, from the accidental circumstances with which, in every community, they are blended, and with which, in an isolated community, they are confounded by the most philosophical mind.

Hence it is, that, in generalization, the writers of modern times have far surpassed those of antiquity. The historians of our own country are unequalled in depth and precision of reason; and even in the works of our mere compilers, we often meet with speculations beyond the reach of Thucydides or Tacitus.

But it must, at the same time, be admitted that they have characteristic faults, so closely connected with their characteristic merits, and of such magnitude, that it may well be doubted whether, on the whole, this department of literature has gained or lost during the last two-and-twenty centuries.

The best historians of later times have been seduced from truth, not by their imagination, but by their reason. They far excel their predecessors in the art of deducing general principles from facts. But unhappily they have fallen into the error of distorting facts to suit general principles. They arrive at a theory from looking at some of the phenomena, and the remaining phenomena they strain or curtail to suit the theory. For this purpose it is not necessary that they should assert what is absolutely false, for all questions in morals and politics are questions of comparison and degree. Any proposition which does not involve a contradiction in terms, may, by possibility, be true; and if all the circumstances which raise a probability in its favor be stated and enforced, and those which lead to an opposite conclusion be omitted or lightly passed over, it may appear to be demonstrated. In every human character and transaction there is a mixture of good and evil — a little exaggeration, a little suppression, a judicious use of epithets, a watchful and searching scepticism with respect to the evidence on one side, a convenient credulity with respect to every report or tradition on the other, may easily make a saint of Laud, or a tyrant of Henry the Fourth.

This species of misrepresentation abounds in the most valuable works of modern historians. Herodotus tells his story like a slovenly witness, who, heated by partialities and prejudices, unacquainted with the established rules of evidence, and uninstructed as to the obligations of his oath, confounds what he imagines with what he has seen and heard, and brings out facts, reports, conjectures, and fancies, in one mass. Hume is an accomplished advocate : without positively asserting much more than he can prove, he gives prominence to all the circumstances which support his case; he glides lightly over those which are unfavorable to it; his own witnesses are applauded and encouraged; the statements which seem to throw discredit on them are controverted; the contradictions into which they fall are explained away; a clear and connected abstract of their evidence

is given. Every thing that is offered on the other side is scruti-
nized with the utmost severity; — every suspicious circumstance
is a ground for comment and invective; what cannot be denied
is extenuated, or passed by without notice; concessions even
are sometimes made — but this insidious candor only increases
the effect of the vast mass of sophistry.

We have mentioned Hume, as the ablest and most popular
writer of his class; but the charge which we have brought
against him is one to which all our most distinguished historians
are in some degree obnoxious. Gibbon, in particular, deserves
very severe censure. Of all the numerous culprits, however,
none is more deeply guilty than Mr. Mitford. We willingly
acknowledge the obligations which are due to his talents and
industry. The modern historians of Greece had been in the
habit of writing as if the world had learned nothing new during
the last sixteen hundred years. Instead of illustrating the
events which they narrated, by the philosophy of a more enlightened age, they judged of antiquity by itself alone. They seemed
to think that notions, long driven from every other corner of
literature, had a prescriptive right to occupy this last fastness.
They considered all the ancient historians as equally authentic.
They scarcely made any distinction between him who related
events at which he had himself been present, and him who five
hundred years after composed a philosophic romance for a society which had in the interval undergone a complete change. It
was all Greek, and all true! The centuries which separated
Plutarch from Thucydides seemed as nothing to men who lived
in an age so remote. The distance of time produced an error
similar to that which is sometimes produced by distance of

place. There are many good ladies who think that all the people in India live together, and who charge a friend setting out for Calcutta with kind messages to Bombay. To Rollin and Barthelemi, in the same manner, all the classics were contemporaries.

Mr. Mitford certainly introduced great improvements; he showed us that men who wrote in Greek and Latin sometimes told lies; he showed us that ancient history might be related in such a manner as to furnish not only allusions to school-boys, but important lessons to statesmen. From that love of theatrical effect and high-flown sentiment which had poisoned almost every other work on the same subject, his book is perfectly free. But his passion for a theory as false, and far more ungenerous, led him substantially to violate truth in every page. Statements unfavorable to democracy are made with unhesitating confidence, and with the utmost bitterness of language. Every charge brought against a monarch, or an aristocracy, is sifted with the utmost care. If it cannot be denied, some palliating supposition is suggested, or we are at least reminded that some circumstances now unknown *may* have justified what at present appears unjustifiable. Two events are reported by the same author in the same sentence; their truth rests on the same testimony; but the one supports the darling hypothesis, and the other seems inconsistent with it. The one is taken and the other is left.

The practice of distorting narrative into a conformity with theory, is a vice not so unfavorable as at first sight it may appear, to the interests of political science. We have compared the writers who indulge in it to advocates; and we may add, that their conflicting fallacies, like those of advocates, correct each other. It has always been held, in the most enlightened nations, that a tribunal will decide a judicial question most fairly, when it has heard two able men argue, as unfairly as possible, on the two opposite sides of it; and we are inclined to think that this opinion is just. Sometimes, it is true, superior eloquence and dexterity will make the worse appear the better reason; but it is at least certain that the judge will be compelled to contemplate the case under two different aspects. It is certain that no important consideration will altogether escape notice.

This is at present the state of history. The Poet-laureate appears for the Church of England, Lingard for the Church of Rome. Brodie has moved to set aside the verdicts obtained by Hume; and the cause in which Mitford succeeded, is, we understand, about to be reheard. In the midst of these disputes, however, history proper, if we may use the term, is disappearing. The high, grave, impartial summing up of Thucydides is nowhere to be found.

While our historians are practising all the arts of controversy, they miserably neglect the art of narration, the art of interesting the affections, and presenting pictures to the imagination. That a writer may produce these effects without violating truth, is sufficiently proved by many excellent biographical works. The immense popularity which well-written books of this kind have acquired, deserves the serious consideration of historians. Voltaire's "Charles the Twelfth," Marmontel's "Memoirs," Boswell's "Life of Johnson," Southey's account of Nelson, are perused with delight by the most frivolous and indolent.

Whenever any tolerable book of the same description makes its appearance, the circulating libraries are mobbed ; the book societies are in commotion; the new novel lies uncut; the magazines and newspapers fill their columns with extracts. In the meantime histories of great empires, written by men of eminent ability, lie unread on the ˇshelves of ostentatious libraries.

The writers of history seem to entertain an aristocratical contempt for the writers of memoirs. They think it beneath the dignity of men who describe the revolutions of nations, to dwell on the details which constitute the· charm of biography. They have imposed on themselves a code of conventional decencies, as absurd as that which has been the bane of the French drama. The most characteristic and interesting circumstances are omitted or softened down, because, as we are told, they are too trivial for the majesty of history. . The majesty of history seems to resemble the majesty of the poor King of Spain,. who died a martyr to ceremony, because the proper dignitaries were not at hand to render him assistance.

That history would be more amusing if this etiquette were relaxed, will, we suppose, be acknowledged. But would it be less dignified, or less useful ? What do we mean, when we say that one past event is important, and another insignificant? No past event has any intrinsic importance.· The knowledge of it is valuable only as it leads us to form just calculations with respect to the future. A history which does not serve this purpose, though it may be filled with battles, treaties, and commotions, is as useless as the series of turnpike-tickets collected by Sir Matthew Mite.

Let us suppose that Lord Clarendon, instead of filling hundreds of folio pages with copies of state papers, in which the same assertions and contradictions are repeated, till the reader is overpowered with weariness, had condescended to be the Boswell of the Long Parliament. Let us suppose that he had exhibited to us the wise and lofty self-government of Hampden, leading while he seemed to follow, and propounding unanswerable arguments in the strongest forms, with the modest air of an inquirer anxious for information; the delusions which misled the noble spirit of Vane; the coarse fanaticism which concealed the yet loftier genius of Cromwell, destined to control a mutinous army and a factious people, to abase the flag of Holland, to arrest the victorious arms of Sweden, and to hold the balance firm between the rival monarchies of France and Spain. Let us suppose that he had made his Cavaliers and Roundheads talk in their own style; that he had reported some of the ribaldry of Rupert's pages, and some of the cant of Harrison and Fleetwood. Would not his work in that case have been more interesting? Would it not have been more accurate?

A history in which every particular incident may be true, may on the whole be false. The circumstances which have most influence on the happiness of mankind, the changes of manners and morals, the transition of communities from poverty to wealth, from knowledge to ignorance, from ferocity to humanity, — these are, for the most part, noiseless revolutions. Their progress is rarely indicated by what historians are pleased to call important events. They are not achieved by armies, or enacted by senates. They are sanctioned by no treaties, and recorded in no archives. They are carried on in every school, in every church, behind ten thousand counters, at ten thousand firesides. The upper-current of society presents no certain criterion by which we can judge of the direction in which the undercurrent flows. We read of defeats and victories. But we know that nations may be miserable amidst victories, and prosperous amidst defeats. We read of the fall of wise ministers, and of the rise of profligate favorites. But we must remember how small a proportion the good or evil effected by a single statesman can bear to the good or evil of a great social system.

Bishop Watson compares a geologist to a gnat mounted on an elephant, and laying down theories as to the whole internal structure of the vast animal, from the phenomena of the hide. The comparison is unjust to the geologists ; but it is very applicable to those historians who write as if the body politic were homogeneous, who look only on the surface of affairs, and never think of the mighty and various organization which lies deep below.

In the works of such writers as these, England, at the close of the Seven Years' War, is in the highest state of prosperity. At the close of the American war she is in a miserable and degraded condition ; as if the people were not on the whole as rich, as well governed, and as well educated, at the latter period as at the former. We have read books called Histories of England, under the reign of George the Second, in which the rise of Methodism is not even mentioned. A hundred years hence this breed of authors will, we hope, be extinct. If it should still exist, the late ministerial interregnum will be described in terms which will seem to imply that all government was at an end ; that the social contract was annulled, and that

the hand of every man was against his neighbor, until the wisdom
and virtue of the new Cabinet educed order out of the chaos of
anarchy. We are quite certain that misconceptions as gross,
prevail at this moment, respecting many important parts of our
annals.

The effect of historical reading is analogous, in many respects,
to that produced by foreign travel. The student, like the tourist,
is transported into a new state of society. He sees new fashions.
He hears new modes of expression. His mind is enlarged by
contemplating the wide diversities of laws, of morals, and of
manners. But men may travel far, and return with minds as
contracted as if they had never stirred from their own market-
town. In the same manner, men may know the dates of many
battles, and the genealogies of many royal houses, and yet be
no wiser. Most people look at past times, as princes look at
foreign countries. More than one illustrious stranger has landed
on our island amidst the shouts of a mob, has dined with the
king, has hunted with the master of the stag-hounds, has seen
the Guards reviewed, and a knight of the garter installed; has
cantered along Regent Street; has visited St. Paul's, and noted
down its dimensions, and has then departed, thinking that he
has seen England. He has, in fact, seen a few public buildings,
public men, and public ceremonies. But of the vast and complex
system of society, of the fine shades of national character, of the
practical operation of government and laws, he knows nothing.
He who would understand these things rightly, must not confine
his observations to palaces and solemn days. He must see
ordinary men as they appear in their ordinary business and in
their ordinary pleasures. He must mingle in the crowds of the

exchange and the coffee-house. He must obtain admittance to the convivial table and the domestic hearth. He must bear with vulgar expressions. He must not shrink from exploring even the retreats of misery. He who wishes to understand the condition of mankind in former ages, must proceed on the same principle. If he attends only to public transactions, to wars, congresses, and debates, his studies will be as unprofitable as the travels of those imperial, royal, and serene sovereigns, who form their judgment of our island from having gone in state to a few fine sights, and from having held formal conference with a few great officers.

The perfect historian is he in whose work the character and spirit of an age are exhibited in miniature. He relates no fact, he attributes no expression to his characters, which is not authenticated by sufficient testimony. But by judicious selection, rejection, and arrangement, he gives to truth those attractions which have been usurped by fiction. In his narrative a due subordination is observed; some transactions are prominent, others retire. But the scale on which he represents them is increased or diminished, not according to the dignity of the persons concerned in them, but according to the degree in which they elucidate the condition of society and the nature of man. He shows us the court, the camp, and the senate. But he shows us also the nation. He considers no anecdote, no peculiarity of manner, no familiar saying, as too insignificant for his notice, which is not too insignificant to illustrate the operation of laws, of religion, and of education, and to mark the progress of the human mind. Men will not merely be described, but will be made intimately known to us. The changes of manners will be indicated, not merely by a few general phrases, or a few extracts from statistical documents, but by appropriate images presented in every line.

If a man, such as we are supposing, should write the history of England, he would assuredly not omit the battles, the sieges, the negotiations, the seditions, the ministerial changes. But with these he would intersperse the details which are the charm of historical romances. At Lincoln Cathedral there is a beautiful painted window, which was made by an apprentice out of the pieces of glass which had been rejected by his master. It is so far superior to every other in the church, that, according to the tradition, the vanquished artist killed himself from mortification. Sir Walter Scott, in the same manner, has used those fragments of truth which historians have scornfully thrown behind them, in a manner which may well excite their envy. He has constructed out of their gleanings works which, even considered as histories, are scarcely less valuable than theirs. But a truly great historian would reclaim those materials which the novelist has appropriated. The history of the government, and the history of the people, would be exhibited in that mode in which alone they can be exhibited justly, in inseparable conjunction and intermixture. We should not then have to look for the wars and votes of the Puritans in Clarendon, and for their phraseology in "Old Mortality;" for one half of King James in Hume, and for the other half in the "Fortunes of Nigel."

The early part of our imaginary history would be rich with coloring from romance, ballad, and chronicle. We should find ourselves in the company of knights such as those of Froissart, and of pilgrims such as those who rode with Chaucer from the Tabard. Society would be shown from the highest to the lowest, — from the royal cloth of state to the den of the outlaw; from the throne of the legate to the chimney-corner where the begging friar regaled himself. Palmers, minstrels, crusaders, — the stately monastery, with the good cheer in its refectory, and the high-mass in its chapel, — the manor-house, with its hunting and hawking, — the tournament, with its heralds and ladies, the trumpets and the cloth of gold, — would give truth and life to the representation. We should perceive, in a thousand slight touches, the importance of the privileged burgher, and the fierce and haughty spirit which swelled under the collar of the degraded villain. The revival of letters would not merely be described in a few magnificent periods. We should discern, in innumerable particulars, the fermentation of mind, the eager appetite for knowledge, which distinguished the sixteenth from the fifteenth century. In the Reformation we should see, not merely a schism which changed the ecclesiastical constitution of England, and the mutual relations of the European powers, but a moral war which raged in every family, which set the father against the son, and the son against the father, the mother against the daughter, and the daughter against the mother. Henry would be painted with the skill of Tacitus. We should have the change of his character from his profuse and joyous youth, to his savage and imperious old age. We should perceive the gradual progress of selfish and tyrannical passions, in a mind not naturally insensible or ungenerous; and to the last we should detect some remains of that open and noble temper which endeared him to a people whom he oppressed, struggling with the hardness of despotism, and the irritability of disease. We should see Elizabeth in all her weakness, and in all her strength, surrounded by the handsome favorites whom she never trusted, and the wise old statesmen, whom she never dismissed, uniting in herself the most contradictory qualities of both her parents, — the coquetry, the caprice, the petty malice of Anne, — the haughty and resolute spirit of Henry. We have no hesitation in saying, that a great artist might produce a portrait of this remarkable woman, at least as striking as that in the novel of "Kenilworth," without employing a single trait not authenticated by ample testimony. In the meantime, we should see arts cultivated, wealth accumulated, the conveniences of life improved. We should see the keeps, where nobles, insecure themselves, spread insecurity around them, gradually giving place to the halls of peaceful opulence, to the oriels of Longleat, and the stately pinnacles of Burleigh. We should see towns extended, deserts cultivated, the hamlets of fishermen turned into wealthy havens, the meal of the peasant improved, and his hut more commodiously furnished. We should see those opinions and feelings which produced the great struggle against the house of Stuart slowly growing up in the bosoms of private families, before they manifested themselves in parliamentary debates. Then would come the Civil War. Those skirmishes, on which Clarendon dwelt so minutely, would be told, as Thucydides would have told them, with perspicuous conciseness. They are merely connecting links. But the great characteristics of the age, the loyal enthusiasm of the brave English gentry, the fierce licentiousness of the swearing, dicing, drunken reprobates, whose excesses disgraced the royal cause, — the austerity of the

Presbyterian Sabbaths in the city, the extravagance of the independent preachers in the camp, the precise garb, the severe countenance, the petty scruples, the affected accent, the absurd names and phrases which marked the Puritans, — the valor, the policy, the public spirit, which lurked beneath these ungraceful disguises, the dreams of the raving Fifth-monarchy-man, the dreams, scarcely less wild, of the philosophic republican, — all these would enter into the representation, and render it at once more exact and more striking.

The instruction derived from history thus written would be of a vivid and practical character. It would be received by the imagination as well as by the reason. It would be not merely traced on the mind, but branded into it. Many truths, too, would be learned, which can be learned in no other manner. As the history of states is generally written, the greatest and most momentous revolutions seem to come upon them like supernatural inflictions, without warning or cause. But the fact is that such revolutions are almost always the consequences of moral changes, which have gradually passed on the mass of the community, and which ordinarily proceeded far, before their progress is indicated by any public measure. An intimate knowledge of the domestic history of nations is therefore abso-- lutely necessary to the prognosis of political events. A narrative defective in this respect is as useless as a medical treatise which should pass by all the symptoms attendant on the early stage of a disease, and mention only what occurs when the patient is beyond the reach of remedies.

A historian, such as we are attempting to describe, would indeed be an intellectual prodigy. In his mind, powers, scarcely compatible with each other, must be tempered into an exquisite harmony. We shall sooner see another Shakespeare or another Homer. The highest excellence to which any single faculty can be brought, would be less surprising than such a happy and delicate combination of qualities. Yet the contemplation of imaginary models is not an unpleasant or useless employment of the mind. It cannot, indeed, produce perfection, but it produces improvement, and nourishes that generous and liberal fastidiousness, which is not inconsistent with the strongest sensibility to merit, and which, while it exalts our conceptions of the art, does not render us unjust to the artist.

THE SCIENCE OF HISTORY.

A Lecture Delivered by James Anthony Froude at the Royal
Institution February 5, 1864.

(Born 1818.)

ADIES AND GENTLEMEN, — I have undertaken to
speak to you this evening on what is called the Science
of History. I fear it is a dry subject; and there
seems, indeed, something incongruous in the very connection of such words as Science and History. It is as if we
were to talk of the color of sound, or the longitude of the Rule-
of-three. Where it is so difficult to make out the truth on the
commonest disputed fact in matters passing under our very eyes,
how can we talk of a science in things long past, which come to
us only through books? It often seems to me as if History was
like a child's box of letters, with which we can spell any word
we please. We have only to pick out such letters as we want,
arrange them as we like, and say nothing about those which do
not suit our purpose.

   I will try to make the thing intelligible, and I will try not to weary you ; but I am doubtful of my success either way. First, however, I wish to say a word or two about the eminent person whose name is connected with this way of looking at History, and whose premature death struck us all with such a sudden sorrow. Many of you, perhaps, recollect Mr. Buckle as he ,stood not so long ago in this place. He spoke more than an hour without a note, — never repeating himself, never wasting words ; laying out his matter as easily and as pleasantly as if he had been talking to us at his own fireside. We might think what we pleased of Mr. Buckle's views, but it was plain enough that he was a man of uncommon power; and he had qualities also — qualities to which he, perhaps, himself attached little value — as rare as they were admirable.

Most of us, when we have hit on something which we are pleased to think important and original, feel as if we should burst with it. We come out into the book-market with our wares in hand, and ask for thanks and recognition. Mr. Buckle, at an early age, conceived the thought which made him famous, but he took the measure of his abilities. He knew that whenever he pleased he could command personal distinction, but he cared more for his subject than for himself. He was contented to work with patient reticence, unknown and unheard-of, for twenty years; and then, at middle life, he produced a work which was translated at once into French and German, and, of all places in the world, fluttered the dovecots of the Imperial Academy of St. Petersburg.

Goethe says somewhere, that as soon as a man has done any thing remarkable, there seems to be a general conspiracy to prevent him from doing it again. He is feasted, fêted, caressed ;

his time is stolen from him by breakfasts, dinners, societies, idle businesses of a thousand kinds. Mr. Buckle had his share of all this; but there are also more dangerous enemies that wait upon success like his. He had scarcely won for himself the place which he deserved, than his health was found shattered by his labors. He had but time to show us how large a man he was, time just to sketch the outlines of his philosophy, and he passed away as suddenly as he appeared. He went abroad to recover strength for his work, but his work was done with and over. He died of a fever at Damascus, vexed only that he was compelled to leave it uncompleted. Almost his last conscious words were: "My book, my book! I shall never finish my book!" He went away as he had lived, nobly careless of himself, and thinking only of the thing which he had undertaken to do.

But his labor had not been thrown away. Disagree with him as we might, the effect which he had already produced was unmistakable, and it is not likely to pass away. What he said was not essentially new. Some such interpretation of human things is as early as the beginning of thought. But Mr. Buckle, on the one hand, had the art which belongs to men of genius: he could present his opinions with peculiar distinctness; and, on the other hand, there is much in the mode of speculation at present current among us for which those opinions have an unusual fascination. They do not please us, but they excite and irritate us. We are angry with them; and we betray, in being so, an uneasy misgiving that there may be more truth in those opinions than we like to allow.

Mr. Buckle's general theory was something of this kind:

When human creatures began first to look about them in the world they lived in, there seemed to be no order in any thing. Days and nights were not the same length. The air was sometimes hot and sometimes cold. Some of the stars rose and set like the sun; some were almost motionless in the sky; some described circles round a central star above the north horizon. The planets went on principles of their own; and in the elements there seemed nothing but caprice. Sun and moon would at times go out in eclipse. Sometimes the earth itself would shake under men's feet; and they could only suppose that earth and air and sky and water were inhabited and managed by creatures as wayward as themselves.

Time went on, and the disorder began to arrange itself. Certain influences seemed beneficent to men, others malignant and destructive; and the world was supposed to be animated by good spirits and evil spirits, who were continually fighting against each other, in outward nature and in human creatures themselves. Finally, as men observed more and imagined less, these interpretations gave way also. Phenomena the most opposite in effect were seen to be the result of the same natural law. The fire did not burn the house down if the owners of it were careful, but remained on the hearth and boiled the pot; nor did it seem more inclined to burn a bad man's house down than a good man's, provided the badness did not take the form of negligence. The phenomena of nature were found for the most part to proceed in an orderly, regular way, and their variations to be such as could be counted upon. From observing the order of things, the step was easy to cause and effect. An eclipse, instead of being a sign of the anger of Heaven, was found to be the necessary and innocent result of the relative position of sun, moon, and earth. The comets became bodies in space, unrelated to the beings who had imagined that all creation was watching them and their doings. By degrees caprice, volition, all symptoms of arbitrary action, disappeared out of the universe; and almost every phenomenon in earth or heaven was found attributable to some law, either understood or perceived to exist. Thus nature was reclaimed from the imagination. The first fantastic conception of things gave way before the moral; the moral in turn gave way before the natural; and at last there was left but one small tract of jungle where the theory of law had failed to penetrate, — the doings and characters of human creatures themselves.

There, and only there, amidst the conflicts of reason and emotion, conscience and desire, spiritual forces were still conceived to exist. Cause and effect were not traceable when there was a free volition to disturb the connection. In all other things, from a given set of conditions the consequences necessarily followed. With man, the word "law" changed its meaning; and instead of a fixed order, which he could not choose but follow, it became a moral precept, which he might disobey if he dared.

This it was which Mr. Buckle disbelieved. The economy which prevailed throughout nature, he thought it very unlikely should admit of this exception. He considered that human beings acted necessarily from the impulse of outward circumstances upon their mental and bodily condition at any given moment. Every man, he said, acted from a motive; and his conduct was determined by the motive which affected him most powerfully. Every man naturally desires what he supposes to be good for him; but, to do well, he must know well. He will eat poison, so long as he does not know that it is poison. Let him see that it will kill him, and he will not touch it. The question was not of moral right and wrong. Once let him be thoroughly made to feel that the thing is destructive, and he will leave it alone by the law of his nature. His virtues are the result of knowledge; his faults, the necessary consequence of the want of it. A boy desires to draw. He knows nothing about it: he draws men like trees or houses, with their centre of gravity anywhere. He makes mistakes because he knows no better. We do not blame him. Till he is better taught, he cannot help it. But his instruction begins. He arrives at straight lines; then at solids; then at curves. He learns perspective, and light and shade. He observes more accurately the forms which he wishes to represent. He perceives effects, and he perceives the means by which they are produced. He has learned what to do; and, in part, he has learned how to do it. His after-progress will depend on the amount of force which his nature possesses; but all this is as natural as the growth of an acorn. You do not preach to the acorn that it is its duty to become a large tree; you do not preach to the art-pupil that it is his duty to become a Holbein. You plant your acorn in favorable soil, where it can have light and air, and be sheltered from the wind; you remove the superfluous branches, you train the strength into the leading shoots. The acorn will then become as fine a tree as it has vital force to become. The difference between men and other things is only in the largeness and variety of man's capacities; and in this special capacity, that he alone has the power of observing the circumstances favorable to his own growth, and can apply them for himself, yet, again, with this condition, — that he is not, as is commonly supposed, free to choose whether he will make use of these appliances or not. When he knows what is good for him, he will choose it; and he will judge what is good for him by the circumstances which have made him what he is.

And what he would do, Mr. Buckle supposed that he always had done. His history had been a natural growth as much as the growth of the acorn. His improvement had followed the progress of his knowledge; and, by a comparison of his outward circumstances with the condition of his mind, his whole proceedings on this planet, his creeds and constitutions, his good deeds and his bad, his arts and his sciences, his empires and his revolutions, would be found all to arrange themselves into clear relations of cause and effect.

If, when Mr. Buckle pressed his conclusions, we objected the difficulty of finding what the truth about past times really was, he would admit it candidly as far as concerned individuals; but there was not the same difficulty, he said, with masses of men. We might disagree about the character of Julius or Tiberius Cæsar, but we could know well enough the Romans of the Empire. We had their literature to tell us how they thought; we had their laws to tell us how they governed; we had the broad face of the world, the huge mountainous outline of their general doings upon it, to tell us how they acted. He believed it was all reducible to laws, and could be made as intelligible as the growth of the chalk cliffs or the coal measures.

And thus consistently Mr. Buckle cared little for individuals.

He did not believe (as some one has said) that the history of mankind is the history of its great men. Great men with him were but larger atoms, obeying the same impulses with the rest, only perhaps a trifle more erratic. With them or without them, the course of things would have been much the same.

As an illustration of the truth of his view, he would point to the new science of Political Economy. Here already was a large area of human activity in which natural laws were found to act unerringly. Men had gone on for centuries trying to regulate trade on moral principles. They would fix wages according to some imaginary rule of fairness; they would fix prices by what they considered things ought to cost; they encouraged one trade or discouraged another, for moral reasons. They might as well have tried to work a steam-engine on moral reasons. The great statesmen whose names were connected with these enterprises might have as well legislated that water should run uphill. There were natural laws, fixed in the conditions of things; and to contend against them was the old battle of the Titans against the gods.

As it was with political economy, so it was with all other forms of human activity; and as the true laws of political economy explained the troubles which people fell into in old times because they were ignorant of them, so the true laws of human nature, as soon as we knew them, would explain their mistakes in more serious matters, and enable us to manage better for the future. Geographical position, climate, air, soil, and the like, had their several influences. The northern nations are hardy and industrious, because they must till the earth if they would eat the fruits of it, and because the temperature is too low to make an idle life enjoyable.   In the south, the soil is more productive, while less food is wanted and fewer clothes; and, in the exquisite air, exertion is not needed to make the sense of existence delightful.   Therefore, in the south we find men lazy and indolent.

True, there are difficulties in these views; the home of the languid Italian was the home also of the sternest race of whom the story of mankind retains a record.   And again, when we are told that the Spaniards are superstitious because Spain is a country of earthquakes, we remember Japan, the spot in all the world where earthquakes are most frequent, and where at the same time there is the most serene disbelief in any supernatural agency whatsoever.

Moreover, if men grow into what they are by natural laws, they cannot help being what they are; and if they cannot help being what they are, a good deal will have to be altered in our general view of human obligations and responsibilities.

That, however, in these theories there is a great deal of truth, is quite certain, were there but a hope that those who maintain them would be contented with that admission.   A man born in a Mahometan country grows up a Mahometan; in a Catholic country, a Catholic; in a Protestant country, a Protestant.   His opinions are like his language : he learns to think as he learns to speak; and it is absurd to suppose him responsible for being what nature makes him.   We take pains to educate children. There is a good education and a bad education; there are rules well ascertained by which characters are influenced; and, clearly enough, it is no mere matter for a boy's free will whether he turns out well or ill.   We try to train him into good habits; we keep him out of the way of temptations; we see that he is well taught; we mix kindness and strictness; we surround him with every good influence we can command. These are what are termed the advantages of a good education; and if we fail to provide those under our care with it, and if they go wrong, the responsibility we feel is as much ours as theirs. This is at once an admission of the power over us of outward circumstances.

In the same way, we allow for the strength of temptations, and the like.

In general, it is perfectly obvious that men do necessarily absorb, out of the influences in which they grow up, something which gives a complexion to their whole after-character.

When historians have to relate great social or speculative changes, the overthrow of a monarchy, or the establishment of a creed, they do but half their duty if they merely relate the events. In an account, for instance, of the rise of Mahometanism, it is not enough to describe the character of the Prophet, the ends which he set before him, the means which he made use of, and the effect which he produced; the historian must show what there was in the condition of the Eastern races which enabled Mahomet to act upon them so powerfully; their existing beliefs, their existing moral and political condition.

In our estimate of the past, and in our calculations of the future, in the judgments which we pass upon one another, we measure responsibility, not by the thing done, but by the opportunities which people have had of knowing better or worse. In the efforts which we make to keep our children from bad associations or friends, we admit that external circumstances have a powerful effect in making men what they are.

But are circumstances every thing? That is the whole question. A science of history, if it is more than a misleading name, implies that the relation between cause and effect holds in human things as completely as in all others; that the origin of human actions is not to be looked for in mysterious properties of the mind, but in influences which are palpable and ponder-able.

When natural causes are liable to be set aside and neutralized by what is called volition, the word Science is out of place. If it is free to man to choose what he will do or not do, there is no adequate science of him. If there is a science of him, there is no free choice, and the praise or blame with which we regard one another are impertinent and out of place.

I am trespassing upon these ethical grounds because, unless I do, the subject cannot be made intelligible. Mankind are but an aggregate of individuals; History is but the record of in-dividual action : and what is true of the part is true of the whole.

We feel keenly about such things, and, when the logic becomes perplexing, we are apt to grow rhetorical about them. But rhetoric is only misleading. Whatever the truth may be, it is best that we should know it; and for truth of any kind we should keep our heads and hearts as cool as we can.

I will say at once, that, if we had the whole case before us; if we were taken, like Leibnitz's Tarquin, into the council-chamber of Nature, and were shown what we really were, where we came from, and where we were going, however unpleasant it might be for some of us to find ourselves, like Tarquin, made into villains, from the subtle necessities of "the best of all possible worlds," — nevertheless, some such theory as Mr. Buckle's might possibly turn out to be true. Likely enough, there is some great "equation of the universe" where the value of the unknown quantities can be determined. But we must treat things in relation to our own powers and positions, and the question is, whether the sweep of those vast curves can be measured by the intellect of creatures of a day like ourselves. ∠

The "Faust" of Goethe, tired of the barren round of earthly knowledge, calls magic to his aid. He desires, first, to see the spirit of the Macrocosmos, but his heart fails him before he ventures that tremendous experiment, and he summons before him, instead, the spirit of his own race. There he feels himself at home. The stream of life and the storm of action, the everlasting ocean of existence, the web and the woof, and the roaring loom of Time, — he gazes upon them all, and in passionate exultation claims fellowship with the awful thing before him. But the majestic vision fades, and a voice comes to him, — "Thou art fellow with the spirits which thy mind can grasp, not with me."

Had Mr. Buckle tried to follow his principles into detail, it might have fared no better with him than with "Faust."

What are the conditions of a science? and when may any subject be said to enter the scientific stage? I suppose when the facts begin to resolve themselves into groups; when phenomena are no longer isolated experiences, but appear in connection and order; when, after certain antecedents, certain consequences are uniformly seen to follow; when facts enough have been collected to furnish a basis for conjectural explanation; and when conjectures have so far ceased to be utterly vague that it is possible in some degree to foresee the future by the help of them.

Till a subject has advanced as far as this, to speak of a science of it is an abuse of language. It is not enough to say that there must be a science of human things because there is a science of all other things. This is like saying the planets must be inhabited because the only planet of which we have any experience is inhabited. It may or may not be true, but it is not a practical question; it does not affect the practical treatment of the matter in hand.

Let us look at the history of Astronomy.

So long as sun, moon, and planets were supposed to be gods or angels; so long as the sword of Orion was not a metaphor, but a fact; and the groups of stars which inlaid the floor of heaven were the glittering trophies of the loves and wars of the Pantheon, — so long there was no science of Astronomy. There was fancy, imagination, poetry, perhaps reverence, but no science. As soon, however, as it was observed that the stars retained their relative places; that the times of their rising and setting varied with the seasons; that sun, moon, and planets moved among them in a plane, and the belt of the Zodiac was marked out and divided, — then a new order of things began. Traces of the earlier stage remained in the names of the signs and constellations, just as the Scandinavian mythology survives now in the names of the days of the week; but, for all that, the understanding was now at work on the thing; science had begun, and the first triumph of it was the power of foretelling the future. Eclipses were perceived to recur in cycles of nineteen years, and philosophers were able to say when an eclipse was to be looked for. The periods of the planets were determined. Theories were invented to account for their eccentricities; and, false as those theories might be, the position of the planets could be calculated with moderate certainty by them. The very first result of the science, in its most imperfect stage, was a power of foresight; and this was possible before any one true astronomical law had been discovered.

We should not therefore question the possibility of a science of history because the explanations of its phenomena were rudimentary or imperfect: that they might be, and long continue to be, and yet enough might be done to show that there was such a thing, and that it was not entirely without use. But how was it that in those rude days, with small knowledge of mathematics, and with no better instruments than flat walls and dial-plates, those first astronomers made progress so considerable? Because, I suppose, the phenomena which they were observing recurred, for the most part, within moderate intervals; so that they could collect large experience within the compass of their natural lives; because days and months and years were measurable periods, and within them the more simple phenomena perpetually repeated themselves.

But how would it have been if, instead of turning on its axis once in twenty-four hours, the earth had taken a year about it; if the year had been nearly four hundred years; if man's life had been no longer than it is, and for the initial steps of astronomy there had been nothing to depend upon except observations recorded in history? How many ages would have passed, had this been our condition, before it would have occurred to any one that, in what they saw night after night, there was any kind of order at all?

We can see to some extent how it would have been, by the

present state of those parts of the science which in fact depend on remote recorded observations. The movements of the comets are still extremely uncertain. The times of their return can be calculated only with the greatest vagueness.

And yet such a hypothesis as I have suggested would but inadequately express the position in which we are in fact placed toward history. There the phenomena never repeat themselves. There we are dependent wholly on the record of things said to have happened once, but which never happen or can happen a second time. There no experiment is possible ; we can watch for no recurring fact to test the worth of our conjectures. It has been suggested fancifully, that, if we consider the universe to be infinite, time is the same as eternity, and the past is per-petually present. Light takes nine years to come to us from Sirius : those rays which we may see to-night, when we leave this place, left Sirius nine years ago; and could the inhabitants of Sirius see the earth at this moment, they would see the English army in the trenches before Sebastopol, Florence Nightingale watching at Scutari over the wounded at Inkermann, and the peace of England undisturbed by " Essays and Re-views."

As the stars recede into distance, so time recedes with them ; and there may be, and probably are, stars from which Noah might be seen stepping into the ark, Eve listening to the tempta-tion of the serpent, or that older race, eating the oysters and leaving the shell-heaps behind them, when the Baltic was an open sea.

Could we but compare notes, something might be done ; but of this there is no present hope, and without it there will be no science of history. Eclipses, recorded in ancient books, can be verified* by calculations, and lost dates can be recovered by them; and we can foresee, by the laws which they follow, when there will be eclipses again. Will a time ever be when the lost secret of the foundation of Rome can be recovered by historic laws? If not, where is our science? It may be said that this is a particular fact, that we can deal satisfactorily with general phenomena affecting eras and cycles. Well, then, let us take some general phenomenon; Mahometanism, for instance, or Buddhism. Those are large enough. Can you imagine a science which would have[1] *foretold* such movements as those? The state of things out of which they rose is obscure; but, suppose it not obscure, can you conceive that, with any amount of historical insight into the old Oriental beliefs, you could have seen that they were about to transform themselves into those particular forms and no other?

It is not enough to say, that, after the fact, you can understand partially how Mahometanism came to be. All historians worth the name have told us something about that. But when we talk of science, we mean something with more ambitious pretences, we mean something which can foresee as well as explain; and, thus looked at, to state the problem is to show its absurdity. As little could the wisest man have foreseen this mighty revolution, as thirty years ago such a thing as Mormonism could have been anticipated in America; as little as it could

---

[1] It is objected that geology is a science: yet that geology cannot foretell the future changes of the earth's surface. Geology is not a century old, and its periods are measured by millions of years. Yet, if geology cannot foretell future facts, it enabled Sir Roderick Murchison to foretell the discovery of Australian gold.

have been foreseen that table-turning and spirit-rapping would have been an outcome of the scientific culture of England in the nineteenth century.

The greatest of Roman thinkers, gazing mournfully at the seething mass of moral putrefaction round him, detected and deigned to notice among its elements a certain detestable super-stition, so he called it, rising up amidst the offscouring of the Jews, which was named Christianity. Could Tacitus have looked forward nine centuries to the Rome of Gregory VII, could he have beheld the representative of the majesty of the Cæsars holding the stirrup of the Pontiff of that vile and exe-crated sect, the spectacle would scarcely have appeared to him the fulfilment of a national expectation, or an intelligible result of the causes in operation round him. Tacitus, indeed, was born before the science of history; but would M. Comte have seen any more clearly?

Nor is the case much better if we are less hard upon our phil-osophy; if we content ourselves with the past, and require only a scientific explanation of that.

First, for the facts themselves. They come to us through the minds of those who recorded them, neither machines nor angels, but fallible creatures, with human passions and prejudices. Tacitus and Thucydides were perhaps the ablest men who ever gave themselves to writing history; the ablest, and also the most incapable of conscious falsehood. Yet even now, after all these centuries, the truth of what they relate is called in question. Good reasons can be given to show that neither of them can be confidently trusted. If we doubt with these, whom are we to believe?

Or, again, let the facts be granted. To revert to my simile of the box of letters, you have but to select such facts as suit you, you have but to leave alone those which do not suit you, and, let your theory of history be what it will, you can find no difficulty in providing facts to prove it.

You may have your Hegel's philosophy of history, or you may have your Schlegel's philosophy of history; you may prove from history that the world is governed in detail by a special Providence; you may prove that there is no sign of any moral agent in the universe, except man; you may believe, if you like it, in the old theory of the wisdom of antiquity; you may speak, as was the fashion in the fifteenth century, of " our fathers, who had more wit and wisdom than we; " or you may talk of " our barbarian ancestors," and describe their wars as the scuffling of kites and crows.

You may maintain that the evolution of humanity has been an unbroken progress toward perfection; you may maintain that there has been no progress at all, and that man remains the same poor creature that he ever was ; or, lastly, you may say, with the author of the " Contract Social," that men were purest and best in primeval simplicity, —

> " When wild in woods the noble savage ran."

In all or any of these views, history will stand your friend. History, in its passive · irony, will make no objection. Like Jarno, in Goethe's novel, it will not condesend to argue with you, and will provide you with abundant illustrations of any thing which you may wish to believe.

"What is history," said Napoleon, "but a fiction agreed '

upon?" "My friend," said Faust to the student, who was growing enthuiastic about the spirit of past ages, — "my friend, the times which are gone are a book with seven seals ; and what you call the spirit of past ages is but the spirit of this or that worthy gentleman in whose mind those ages are reflected."

One lesson, and only one, history may be said to repeat with distinctness : that the world is built somehow on moral foundations; that, in the long run, it is well with the good; in the long run, it is ill with the wicked. But this is no science; it is no more than the old doctrine taught long ago by the Hebrew prophets. The theories of M. Comte and his disciples advance us, after all, not a step beyond the trodden and familiar ground. If men are not entirely animals, they are at least half animals, and are subject in this aspect of them to the conditions of animals. So far as those parts of man's doings are concerned, which neither have, nor need have, any thing moral about them, so far the laws of him are calculable. There are laws for his digestion, and laws of the means by which his digestive organs are supplied with matter. But pass beyond them, and where are we ? In a world where it would be as easy to calculate men's actions by laws like those of positive philosophy as to measure the orbit of Neptune with a foot rule, or weigh Sirius in a grocer's scale.

And it is not difficult to see why this should be. The first principle, on which the theory of a science of history can be plausibly argued, is that all actions whatsoever arise from self-interest. It may be enlightened self-interest, it may be unenlightened; but it is assumed as an axiom, that every man, in whatever he does, is aiming at something which he considers will promote his happiness. His conduct is not determined by his will; it is determined by the object of his desire. Adam Smith, in laying the foundations of political economy, expressly eliminates every other motive. He does not say that men never act on other motives; still less, that they never ought to act on other motives. He asserts merely that, as far as the arts of production are concerned, and of buying and selling, the action of self-interest may be counted upon as uniform. What Adam Smith says of political economy, Mr. Buckle would extend over the whole circle of human activity.

Now, that which especially distinguishes a high order of man from a low order of man — that which constitutes human goodness, human greatness, human nobleness — is surely not the degree of enlightenment with which men pursue their own advantage: but it is self-forgetfulness, it is self-sacrifice; it is the disregard of personal pleasure, personal indulgence, personal advantages remote or present, because some other line of conduct is more right.

We are sometimes told that this is but another way of expressing the same thing; that, when a man prefers doing what is right, it is only because to do right gives him a higher satisfaction. It appears to me, on the contrary, to be a difference in the very heart and nature of things. The martyr goes to the stake, the patriot to the scaffold, not with a view to any future reward, to themselves, but because it is a glory to fling away their lives for truth and freedom. And so through all phases of existence, to the smallest details of common life, the beautiful character is the unselfish character. Those whom we most love and admire are those to whom the thought of self seems never to occur; who do simply and with no ulterior aim — with no thought whether it will be pleasant to themselves or unpleasant — that which is good and right and generous.

Is this still selfishness, only more enlightened? I do not think so. The essence of true nobility, is neglect of self. Let the thought of self pass in, and the beauty of a great action is gone, like the bloom from a soiled flower. Surely it is a paradox to speak of the self-interest of a martyr who dies for a cause, the triumph of which he will never enjoy; and the greatest of that great company in all ages would have done what they did, had their personal prospects closed with the grave. Nay, there have been those so zealous for some glorious principle as to wish themselves blotted out of the book of Heaven if the cause of Heaven could succeed.

And out of this mysterious quality, whatever it be, arise the higher relations of human life, the higher modes of human obligation. Kant, the philosopher, used to say that there were two things which overwhelmed him with awe as he thought of them. One was the star-sown deep of space, without limit and without end; the other was, right and wrong. Right, the sacrifice of self to good; wrong, the sacrifice of good to self, — not graduated objects of desire, to which we are determined by the degrees of our knowledge, but wide asunder as pole and pole, as light and darkness: one the object of infinite love; the other, the object of infinite detestation and scorn. It is in this marvellous power in men to do wrong (it is an old story, but none the less true for that), — it is in this power to do wrong — wrong or right, as it lies somehow with ourselves to choose — that the impossibility stands of forming scientific calculations of what men will do before the fact, or scientific explanations of what they have done after the fact. If men were consistently selfish, you might analyze their motives; if they were consistently noble they would express in their conduct the laws of the highest perfection. But so long as two natures are mixed together, and the strange creature which results from the combination is now under one influence and now under another, so long you will make nothing of him except from the old-fashioned moral — or, if you please, imaginative — point of view.

Even the laws of political economy itself cease to guide us when they touch moral government. So long as labor is a chattel to be bought and sold, so long, like other commodities, it follows the condition of supply and demand. But if, for his misfortune, an employer considers that he stands in human relations toward his workmen; if he believes, rightly or wrongly, that he is responsible for them; that in return for their labor he is bound to see that their children are decently taught, and they and their families decently fed and clothed and lodged; that he ought to care for them in sickness and in old age, — then political economy will no longer direct him, and the relations between himself and his dependents will have to be arranged on quite other principles.

So long as he considers only his own material profit, so long supply and demand will settle every difficulty ; but the introduction of a new factor spoils the equation.

And it is precisely in this debatable ground of low motives and noble emotions; in the struggle, ever failing yet ever renewed, to carry truth and justice into the administration of human society ; in the establishment of states and in the overthrow of tyrannies; in the rise and fall of creeds; in the world of ideas; in the character and deeds of the great actors in the drama of life, where good and evil fight out their everlasting battle, now ranged in opposite camps, now and more often in the heart, both of them, of each living man, — that the true human interest of history resides. The progress of industries, the growth of material and mechanical civilization, are interesting; but they are not the most interesting. They have their reward in the increase of material comforts; but, unless we are mistaken about our nature, they do not highly concern us after all.

Once more: not only is there in men this baffling duality of principle, but there is something else in us which still more defies scientific analysis.

Mr. Buckle would deliver himself from the eccentricities of this and that individual by a doctrine of averages. Though he cannot tell whether A, B, or C will cut his throat, he may assure himself that one man in every fifty thousand, or thereabout (I forget the exact proportion), will cut his throat, and with this he consoles himself. No doubt it is a comforting discovery. Unfortunately, the average of one generation need not be the average of the next. We may be converted by the Japanese, for all that we know, and the Japanese methods of taking leave of life may become fashionable among us. Nay, did not Novalis suggest that the whole race of men would at last become so disgusted with their impotence, that they would extinguish themselves by a simultaneous act of suicide, and make room for a better order of beings? Anyhow, the fountain out of which the race is flowing perpetually changes; no two generations are alike. Whether there is a change in the organization itself we cannot tell; but this is certain, — that as the planet varies with the atmosphere which surrounds it, so each new generation varies from the last, because it inhales as its atmosphere the accumulated experience and knowledge of the whole past of the world. These things form the spiritual air which we breathe as we grow; and, in the infinite multiplicity of elements of which that air now is composed, it is forever a matter of conjecture what the minds will be like which expand under its influence.

From the England of Fielding and Richardson to the England of Miss Austen, from the England of Miss Austen to the England of Railways and Free Trade, how vast the change! Yet perhaps Sir Charles Grandison would not seem so strange to us now as one of ourselves will seem to our great-grandchildren. The world moves faster and faster; and the difference will probably be considerably greater.

The temper of each new generation is a continual surprise. The Fates delight to contradict our most confident expectations. Gibbon believed that the era of conquerors was at an end. Had he lived out the full life of man, he would have seen Europe at the feet of Napoleon. But a few years ago we believed the world had grown too civilized for war, and the Crystal Palace in Hyde Park was to be the inauguration of a new era. Battles bloody as Napoleon's are now the familiar tale of every day; and the arts which have made greatest progress are the arts of destruction. What next? We may strain our eyes into the future which lies beyond this waning century; but never was conjecture more at fault. It is blank darkness, which even the imagination fails to people.

What, then, is the use of History, and what are its lessons?
If it can tell us little of the past, and nothing of the future, why
waste our time over so barren a study?

First, it is a voice forever sounding across the centuries the
laws of right and wrong. Opinions alter, manners change,
creeds rise and fall, but the moral law is written on the tablets
of eternity. For every false word or unrighteous deed, for cruelty
and oppression, for lust or vanity, the price has to be paid at
last; not always by the chief offenders, but paid by some one.
Justice and truth alone endure and live. Injustice and falsehood may be long-lived, but doomsday comes at last to them, in
French revolutions and other terrible ways.

That is one lesson of history. Another is, that we should
draw no horoscopes; that we should expect little, for what we
expect will not come to pass. Revolutions, reformations,—
those vast movements into which heroes and saints have flung
themselves, in the belief that they were the dawn of the
millennium,— have not borne the fruit which they looked for.
Millenniums are still far away. These great convulsions leave
the world changed,—perhaps improved, but not improved as
the actors in them hoped it would be. Luther would have gone
to work with less heart, could he have foreseen the Thirty Years'
War, and in the distance the theology of Tubingen. Washington might have hesitated to draw the sword against England,
could he have seen the country which he made as we see it
now.[1]

The most remarkable anticipations fail us, antecedents the

---

[1] February, 1864.

most apposite mislead us, because the conditions of human problems never repeat themselves. Some new feature alters everything, — some element which we detect only in its after-operation.

But this, it may be said, is but a meagre outcome. Can the long records of humanity, with all its joys and sorrows, its sufferings and its conquests, teach us more than this? Let us approach the subject from another side.

If you were asked to point out the special features in which Shakespeare's plays are so transcendently excellent, you would mention perhaps, among others, this — that his stories are not put together, and his characters are not conceived, to illustrate any particular law or principle. They teach many lessons, but not any one prominent above another; and when we have drawn from them all the direct instruction which they contain, there remains still something unresolved, — something which the artist gives, and which the philosopher cannot give.

It is in this characteristic that we are accustomed to say Shakespeare's supreme *truth* lies. He represents real life. His drama teaches as life teaches, — neither less nor more. He builds his fabrics, as Nature does, on right and wrong; but he does not struggle to make Nature more systematic than she is. In the subtle interflow of good and evil; in the unmerited sufferings of innocence; in the disproportion of penalties to desert; in the seeming blindness with which justice, in attempting to assert itself, overwhelms innocent and guilty in a common ruin, — Shakespeare is tr ⁴ real experience. The mystery of life he leaves as he finds it; and, in his most tremendous positions, he is addressing rather the intellectual emotions than the understanding, — knowing well that the understanding in such things is at fault, and the sage as ignorant as the child.

. Only the highest order of genius can represent Nature thus. An inferior artist produces either something entirely immoral, where good and evil are names, and nobility of disposition is supposed to show itself in the absolute disregard of them, or else, if he is a better kind of man, he will force on Nature a didactic purpose; he composes what are called moral tales, which may edify the conscience, but only mislead the intellect.

The finest work of this kind produced in modern times is Lessing's play of " Nathan the Wise." The object of it is to teach religious toleration. The doctrine is admirable, the mode ' in which it is enforced is interesting ; but it has the fatal fault that it is not true. Nature does not teach religious toleration by . any such direct method ; and the result is — no one knew it better than Lessing himself — that the play is not poetry, but only splendid manufacture. Shakespeare is eternal ; Lessing's " Nathan " will pass away with the mode of thought which gave it birth. One is based on fact ; the other, on human theory about fact. The theory seems at first sight to contain the most immediate instruction ; but it is not really so.

Cibber and others, as you know, wanted to alter Shakespeare. The French king, in " Lear," was to be got rid of ; Cordelia was to marry Edgar, and Lear himself was to be rewarded for his sufferings by a golden old age. They could not bear that Hamlet should suffer for the sins of Claudius. The wicked king was to die, and the wicked mother ; and Hamlet and Ophelia were to make a match of it, and live happily ever after. A common novelist would have arranged it thus; and you would have had your comfortable moral that wickedness was fitly punished, and virtue had its due reward, and all would have been well. But Shakespeare would not have it so. Shakespeare knew that crime was not so simple in its consequences, or Providence so paternal. He was contented to take the truth from life ; and the effect upon the mind of the most correct theory of what life ought to be, compared to the effect of the life itself, is infinitesimal in comparison.

Again, let us compare the popular historical treatment of remarkable incidents with Shakespeare's treatment of them. Look at "Macbeth." You may derive abundant instruction from it, — instruction of many kinds. There is a moral lesson of profound interest in the steps by which a noble nature glides to perdition. In more modern fashion you may speculate, if you like, on the political conditions represented there, and the temptation presented in absolute monarchies to unscrupulous ambition ; you may say, like Doctor Slop, these things could not have happened under a constitutional government : or, again, you may take up your parable against superstition ; you may dilate on the frightful consequences of a belief in witches, and reflect on the superior advantages of an age of schools and newspapers. If the bare facts of the story had come down to us from a chronicler, and an ordinary writer of the nineteenth century had undertaken to relate them, his account, we may depend upon it, would have been put together upon one or other of these principles. Yet, by the side of that unfolding of the secrets of the prison-house of the soul, what lean and shrivelled anatomies the best of such descriptions would seem !

Shakespeare himself, I suppose, could not have given us a theory of what he meant; he gave us the thing itself, on which we might make whatever theories we pleased.

Or, again, look at Homer.

The " Iliad" is from two to three thousand years older than " Macbeth," and yet it is as fresh as if it had been written yesterday. We have there no lessons save in the emotions which rise in us as we read. Homer had no philosophy; he never struggles to press upon us his views about this or that; you can scarcely tell, indeed, whether his sympathies are Greek or Trojan : but he represents to us faithfully the men and women among whom he lived. He sang the tale of Troy, he touched his lyre, he drained the golden beaker in the halls of men like those on whom he was conferring immortality. And thus, although no Agamemnon, king of men, ever led a Grecian fleet to Ilium; though no Priam sought the midnight tent of Achilles ; though Ulysses and Diomed and Nestor were but names, and Helen but a dream, yet, through Homer's power of representing men and women, those old Greeks will still stand out from amidst the darkness of the ancient world with a sharpness of outline which belongs to no period of history except the most recent. For the mere hard purposes of history, the " Iliad " and " Odyssey " are the most effective books which ever were written. We see the hall of Menelaus, we see the garden of Alcinous, we see Nausicaa among her maidens on the shore, we see the mellow monarch sitting with ivory sceptre in the market-place dealing out genial justice. Or, again, when the wild mood is on, we can hear the crash of the spears, the rattle of the armor as the heroes fall, and the plunging of the horses among the slain. Could we enter the palace of an old Ionian lord, we know what we should see there; we know the words in which he would address us. We could meet Hector as a friend. If we could choose a companion to spend an evening with over a fireside, it would be the man of many counsels, the husband of Penelope.

I am not going into the vexed question whether history or poetry is the more true. It has been sometimes said that poetry is the more true, because it can make things more like what our moral sense would prefer they should be. We hear of poetic justice and the like, as if nature and fact were not just enough.

I entirely dissent from that view. So far as poetry attempts to improve on truth in that way, so far it abandons truth, and is false to itself. Even literal facts, exactly as they were, a great poet will prefer whenever he can get them. Shakespeare in the historical plays is studious, wherever possible, to give the very words which he finds to have been used; and it shows how wisely he was guided in this, that those magnificent speeches of Wolsey are taken exactly, with no more change than the metre makes necessary, from Cavendish's Life. Marlborough read Shakespeare for English history, and read nothing else. The poet only is not bound, when it is inconvenient, to what may be called the accidents of facts. It was enough for Shakespeare to know that Prince Hal in his youth had lived among loose companions, and the tavern in Eastcheap came in to fill out his picture; although Mrs. Quickly and Falstaff and Poins and Bardolph were more likely to have been fallen in with by Shakespeare himself at the Mermaid, than to have been comrades of the true Prince Henry. It was enough for Shakespeare to draw

real men, and the situation, whatever it might be, would sit easy
on them. In this sense only it is that poetry is truer than
History,— that it can make a picture more complete. It may
take liberties with time and space, and give the action distinctness by throwing it into more manageable compass. But it may
not alter the real conditions of things, or represent life as other
than it is. The greatness of the poet depends on his being true
to Nature, without insisting that Nature shall theorize with him,
without making her more just, more philosophical, more moral
than reality ; and, in difficult matters, leaving much to reflection
which cannot be explained.

And if this be true of poetry — if Homer and Shakespeare
are what they are from the absence of every thing didactic
about them — may we not thus learn something of what history
should be, and in what sense it should aspire to teach ?

If poetry must not theorize, much less should the historian
theorize, whose obligations to be true to fact are even greater
than the poet's. If the drama is grandest when the action is
least explicable by laws, because then it best resembles life,
then history will be grandest also under the same conditions.
" Macbeth," were it literally true, would be perfect history; and
so far as the historian can approach to that kind of model, so
far as he can let his story tell itself in the deeds and words of
those who act it out, so far is he most successful. His work is
no longer the vapor of his own brain, which a breath will scatter ;
it is the thing itself, which will have interest for all time. A
thousand theories may be formed about it, — spiritual theories.
Pantheistic theories, cause and effect theories? but each age
will have its own philosophy of history, and all these in turn will

fail and die. Hegel falls out of date, Schlegel falls out of date, and Comte in good time will fall out of date; the thought about the thing must change as we change; but the thing itself can never change; and a history is durable or perishable as it contains more or least of the writer's own speculations. The splendid intellect of Gibbon for the most part kept him true to the right course in this; yet the philosophical chapters for which he has been most admired or censured may hereafter be thought the least interesting in his work. The time has been when they would not have been comprehended; the time may come when they will seem commonplace.

It may be said, that in requiring history to be written like a drama, we require an impossibility.

For history to be written with the complete form of a drama, doubtless is impossible; but there are periods, and these the periods, for the most part, of greatest interest to mankind, the history of which may be so written that the actors shall reveal their characters in their own words; where mind can be seen matched against mind, and the great passions of the epoch not simply be described as existing, but be exhibited at their white heat in the souls and hearts possessed by them. There are all the elements of drama—drama of the highest order—where the huge forces of the times are as the Grecian destiny, and the power of the man is seen either stemming the stream till it overwhelms him, or ruling while he seems to yield to it.

It is Nature's drama, — not Shakespeare's, but a drama none the less.

So at least it seems to me. Wherever possible, let us not be told *about* this man or that. Let us hear the man himself speak, let us see him act, and let us be left to form our own opinions about him. The historian, we are told, must not leave his readers to themselves. He must not only lay the facts before them : he must tell them what he himself thinks about those facts. In my opinion, this is precisely what he ought not to do. Bishop Butler says somewhere, that the best book which could be written would be a book consisting only of premises, from which the readers should draw conclusions for themselves. The highest poetry is the very thing which Butler requires, and the highest history ought to be. We should no more ask for a theory of this or that period of history, than we should ask for a theory of " Macbeth " or " Hamlet." Philosophies of history, sciences of history, — all these there will continue to be : the fashions of them will change, as our habits of thought will change , each new philosopher will find his chief employment in showing that before him no one understood any thing ; but the drama of history is imperishable, and the lessons of it will be like what we learn from Homer or Shakespeare, — lessons for which we have no words.

The address of history is less to the understanding than to the higher emotions. We learn in it to sympathize with what is great and good ; we learn to hate what is base. In the anomalies of fortune we feel the mystery of our mortal existence ; and in the companionship of the illustrious natures who have shaped the fortunes of the world, we escape from the littlenesses which cling to the round of common life, and our minds are tuned in a higher and nobler key.

For the rest, and for those large questions which I touched in connection with Mr. Buckle, we live in times of disintegration, and none can tell what will be after us. What opinions, what convictions, the infant of to-day will find prevailing on the earth, if he and it live out together to the middle of another century, only a very bold man would undertake to conjecture. "The time will come," said Lichtenberg, in scorn at the materializing tendencies of modern thought, — " the time will come when the belief in God will be as the tales with which old women frighten children ; when the world will be a machine, the ether a gas, and God will be a force." Mankind, if they last long enough on the earth, may develop strange things out of themselves ; and the growth of what is called the Positive Philosophy is a curious commentary on Lichtenberg's prophecy. But whether the end be seventy years hence, or seven hundred, — be the close of the mortal history of humanity as far distant in the future as its shadowy beginnings seem now to lie behind us, — this only we may foretell with confidence, — that the riddle of man's nature will remain unsolved. There will be that in him yet which phys- ical laws will fail to explain, — that something, whatever it be, in himself and in the world, which science cannot fathom, and which suggests the unknown possibilities of his origin and his destiny. There will remain yet

> " Those obstinate questionings
> Of sense and outward things ;
> Falling from us, vanishing ;
> Blank misgivings of a creature
> Moving about in worlds not realized ;
> High instincts, before which our mortal nature
> Doth tremble like a guilty thing surprised."

There will remain
> " Those first affections,
> Those shadowy recollections,

Which, be they what they may,
Are yet the fountain-light of all our day, —
Are yet the master-light of all our seeing, —
Uphold us, cherish, and have power to make
Our noisy years seem moments in the being
　　Of the Eternal Silence."

RACE AND LANGUAGE.

BY EDWARD A. FREEMAN.
(Born 1823.)

T is no very great time since the readers of the English newspapers were, perhaps a little amused, perhaps a little startled, at the story of a deputation of Hungarian students going to Constantinople to present a sword of honor to an Ottoman general. The address and the answer enlarged on the ancient kindred of Turks and Magyars, on the long alienation of the dissevered kinsfolk, on the return of both in these later times to a remembrance of the ancient kindred and to the friendly feelings to which such kindred gave birth. The discourse has a strange sound when we remember the reigns of Sigismund and Wladislaus, when we think of the dark days of Nikopolis and Varna, when we think of Huniades encamped at the foot of Hæmus, and of Belgrade beating back Mahomet the Conqueror from her gates. The Magyar and the Ottoman embracing with the joy of reunited kinsfolk is a sight which certainly no man would have looked forward to in the fourteenth or fifteenth century. At an earlier time the ceremony might have seemed a degree less wonderful. If a man whose ideas are drawn wholly from the modern map should sit down to study the writings of Constantine Porphyrogennêtos, he would perhaps be startled at finding Turks and Franks spoken of as neighbors, at finding *Turcia* and *Francia* — we must not translate Τουϱϰία and Φϱαγγία by *Turkey* and *France*—spoken of as border-lands. A little study will perhaps show him that the change lies almost wholly in the names and not in the boundaries. The lands are there still, and the frontier between them has shifted much less than one might have looked for in nine hundred years. Nor has there been any great change in the population of the two countries. The Turks and the Franks of the Imperial geographer are there still, in the lands which he calls Turcia and Francia; only we no longer speak of them as Turks and Franks. The Turks of Constantine are Magyars; the Franks of Constantine are Germans. The ·Magyar students may not unlikely have turned over the Imperial pages, and they may have seen how their forefathers stand described there. We can hardly fancy that the Ottoman general is likely to have given much time to lore of such a kind. Yet the Ottoman answer was as brim full of ethnological and antiquarian sympathy as the Magyar address. It is hardly to be believed that a Turk, left to himself, would by his own efforts have found out the primeval kindred between Turk and Magyar. He might remember that Magyar exiles had found a safe shelter on Ottoman territory; he might look deep enough into the politics of the present moment to see that the rule of Turk and Magyar alike is threatened by the growth of Slavonic national life. But the idea that Magyar and Turk owe each other any love or any duty, directly on the ground of primeval kindred, is certainly not likely to have presented itself to the untutored Ottoman mind. In short, it sounds, as some one said at the time, rather like the dream of a professor who has run wild with an ethnological craze, than like the serious thought of a practical man of any nation. Yet the Magyar students seem to have meant their address quite seriously. And the Turkish general, if he did not take it seriously, at least thought it wise to shape his answer as if he did. As a piece of practical politics, it sounds like Frederick Barbarossa threaten-ing to avenge the defeat of Crassus upon Saladin, or like the French of the revolutionary wars making the Pope Pius of those days answerable for the wrongs of Vercingetorix. The thing sounds like comedy, almost like conscious comedy. But it is a kind of comedy which may become tragedy, if the idea from which it springs get so deeply rooted in men's minds as to lead to any practical consequences. As long as talk of this kind does not get beyond the world of shot-headed students, it may pass for a craze. It would be more than a craze, if it should be so widely taken up on either side that the statesmen on either side find it expedient to profess to take it up also.

To allege the real or supposed primeval kindred between Magyars and Ottomans as a ground for political action, or at least for political sympathy, in the affairs of the present mo ment, is an extreme case — some may be inclined to call it a *reductio ad absurdum* — of a whole range of doctrines and senti-ments which have in modern days gained a great power over men's minds. They have gained so great a power that those who may regret their influence cannot afford to despise it. To

make any practical inference from the primeval kindred of
Magyar and Turk is indeed pushing the doctrine of race, and
of sympathies arising from race, as far as it well can be pushed.
Without plunging into any very deep mysteries, without committing ourselves to any dangerous theories in the darker regions
of ethnological inquiry, we may perhaps be allowed at starting
to doubt whether there is any real primeval kindred between the
Ottoman and the Finnish Magyar. It is for those who have
gone specially deep into the antiquities of the non-Aryan races to
say whether there is or is not. At all events, as far as the great
facts of history go, the kindred is of the vaguest and most
shadowy kind. It comes to little more than the fact that Magyars and Ottomans are alike non-Aryan invaders who have
made their way into Europe within recorded times, and that
both have, rightly or wrongly, been called by the name of
Turks These do seem rather slender grounds on which to
build up a fabric of national sympathy between two nations,
when several centuries of living practical history all pull the
other way. It is hard to believe that the kindred of Turk and
Magyar was thought of when a Turkish Pasha ruled at Buda.
Doubtless Hungarian Protestants often deemed, and not unrea-
sonably deemed, that the contemptuous toleration of the Moslem
Sultan was a lighter yoke than the persecution of the Catholic
Emperor. But it was hardly on grounds of primeval kindred
that they made the choice. The ethnological dialogue held at
Constantinople does indeed sound like ethnological theory run
mad. But it is the very wildness of the thing which gives it its
importance. The doctrine of race, and of sympathies springing
from race, must have taken very firm hold indeed of men's

minds before it could be carried out in a shape which we are tempted to call so grotesque as this.

The plain fact is that the new lines of scientific and historical inquiry which have been opened in modern times have had a distinct and deep effect upon the politics of the age. The fact may be estimated in many ways, but its existence as a fact cannot be denied. Not in a merely scientific or literary point of view, but in one strictly practical, the world is not the same world as it was when men had not yet dreamed of the kindred between Sanscrit, Greek, and English, when it was looked on as something of a paradox to hint that there was a distinction between Celtic and Teutonic tongues and nations. Ethological and philological researches — I do not forget the distinction between the two, but for the present I must group them together — have opened the way for new national sympathies, new national antipathies, such as would have been unintelligible a hundred years ago. A hundred years ago a man's political likes and dislikes seldom went beyond the range which was suggested by the place of his birth or immediate descent. Such birth or descent made him a member of this or that political community, a subject of this or that prince, a citizen — perhaps a subject — of this or that commonwealth. The political community of which he was a member had its traditional alliances and traditional enmities, and by those alliances and enmities the likes and dislikes of the members of that community were guided. But those traditional alliances and enmities were seldom determined by theories about language or race. The people of this or that place might be discontented under a foreign government; but, as a rule, they were discontented only if subjection to that foreign government

brought with it personal oppression, or at least political degradation. Regard or disregard of some purely local privilege or
local feeling went for more than the fact of a government being
native or foreign. What we now call the sentiment of nationality did not go for much; what we call the sentiment of race
went for nothing at all. Only a few men here and there would
have understood the feelings which have led to those two great
events of our own time, the political reunion of the German and
Italian nations after their long political dissolution. Not a soul
would have understood the feelings which have allowed Panslavism to be a great practical agent in the affairs of Europe, and
which have made talk about "the Latin race," if not practical,
at least possible. Least of all, would it have been possible to
give any touch of political importance to what would have then
seemed so wild a dream as a primeval kindred between Magyar
and Ottoman.

That feelings such as these, and the practical consequences
which have flowed from them, are distinctly due to scientific and
historical teaching there can, I think, be no doubt. Religious
sympathy and purely national sympathy are both feelings of
much simpler growth, which need no deep knowledge nor any
special teaching. The cry which resounded through Christendom when the Holy City was taken by the Mussulmans, the cry
which resounded through Islam when the same city was taken
by the Christians, the spirit which armed England to support
French Huguenots and which armed Spain to support French
Leaguers, all spring from motives which lie on the surface. Nor
need we seek for any explanation but such as lies on the surface
for the natural wish for closer union which arose among Germans

or Italians who found themselves parted off by purely dynastic arrangements from men who were their countrymen in everything else. Such a feeling has to strive with the counter-feeling which springs from local jealousies and local dislikes; but it is a perfectly simple feeling, which needs no subtle research either to arouse or to understand it. So, if we draw our illustrations from the events of our own time, there is nothing but what is perfectly simple in the feeling which calls Russia, as the most powerful of Orthodox states, to the help of her Orthodox brethren everywhere, and which calls the members of the Orthodox Church everywhere to look to Russia as their protector. The feeling may have to strive against a crowd of purely political considerations, and by those purely political considerations it may be outweighed. But the feeling is in itself altogether simple and natural. So again, the people of Montenegro and of the neighboring lands in Herzegovina and by the *Bocche* of Cattaro feel themselves countrymen in every sense but the political accident which keeps them asunder. They are drawn together by a tie which every one can understand, by the same tie which would draw together the people of three adjoining English counties, if any strange political action should part them asunder in like manner. The feeling here is that of nationality in the strictest sense, nationality in a purely local or geographical sense. It would exist all the same if Panslavism had never been heard of; it might exist though those who feel it had never heard of the Slavonic race at all. It is altogether another thing when we come to the doctrine of race, and of sympathies founded on race, in the wider sense. Here we have a feeling which professes to bind together, and which as a matter of fact has had a real effect in binding together, men whose kindred to one another is not so obvious at first sight as the kindred of Germans, Italians, or Serbs who are kept asunder by nothing but a purely artificial political boundary. It is a feeling at whose bidding the call to union goes forth to men whose dwellings are geographically far apart, to men who may have had no direct dealings with one another for years or for ages, to men whose languages, though the scholar may at once see that they are closely akin, may not be so closely akin as to be mutually intelligible for common purposes. A hundred years back the Servian might have cried for help to the Russian on the ground of common Orthodox faith ; he would hardly have called for help on the ground of common Slavonic speech and origin. If he had done so, it would have been rather by way of grasping at any chance, however desperate or far-fetched, than as putting forward a serious and well understood claim which he might expect to find accepted and acted on by large masses of men. He might have received help, either out of genuine sympathy springing from community of faith or from the baser thought that he could be made use of as a convenient political tool. He would have got but little help purely on the ground of a community of blood and speech which had had no practical result for ages. When Russia in earlier days interfered between the Turk and his Christian subjects, there is no sign of any sympathy felt or possessed for Slavs as Slavs. Russia dealt with Montenegro, not, as far as one can see, out of any Slavonic brotherhood, but because an independent Orthodox state at enmity with the Turk could not fail to be a useful ally. The earlier dealings of Russia with the subject nations were far more busy among the Greeks than among the Slavs. In fact, till quite lately, all the Orthodox subjects of the Turk were in most European eyes looked on as alike Greeks. The Orthodox Church has been commonly known as the Greek Church; and it has often been very hard to make people understand that the vast mass of the members of that so-called Greek Church are not Greek in any other sense. In truth we may doubt whether, till comparatively lately, the subject nations themselves were fully alive to the differences of race and speech among them. A man must in all times and places know whether he speaks the same language as another man; but he does not always go on to put his consciousness of difference into the shape of a sharply drawn formula. Still less does he always make the difference the ground of any practical course of action. The Englishman in the first days of the Norman Conquest felt the hardships of foreign rule, and he knew that those hardships were owing to foreign rule. But he had not learned to put his sense of hardship into any formula about an oppressed nationality. So, when the policy of the Turk found that the subtle intellect of the Greek could be made use of as an instrument of dominion over the other subject nations, the Bulgarian felt the hardship of the state of things in which, as it was proverbially said, his body was in bondage to the Turk and his soul in bondage to the Greek. But we may suspect that this neatly turned proverb dates only from the awakening of a distinctly national Bulgarian feeling in modern times. The Turk was felt to be an intruder and an enemy, because his rule was that of an open oppressor belonging to another creed. The Greek, on the other hand, though his spiritual dominion brought undoubted practical evils with it, was not felt to be an intruder and an enemy in the same sense. His quicker intellect and superior refinement made him a model. The Bulgarian imitated the Greek tongue and Greek manners; he was willing in other lands to be himself looked on as a Greek. It is only in quite modern times, under the direct influence of the preaching of the doctrine of race, that a hard and fast line has been drawn between Greeks and Bulgarians. That doctrine has cut two ways. It has given both nations, Greek and Bulgarian alike, a renewed national life, national strength, national hopes, such as neither of them had felt for ages. In so doing, it has done one of the best and most hopeful works of the age. But in so doing, it has created one of the most dangerous of immediate political difficulties. In calling two nations into a renewed being, it has arrayed them in enmity against each other, and that in the face of a common enemy in whose presence all lesser differences and jealousies ought to be hushed into silence.

There is then a distinct doctrine of race, and of sympathies founded on race, distinct from the feeling of community of religion, and distinct from the feeling of nationality in the narrower sense. It is not so simple or easy a feeling as either of those two. It does not in the same way lie on the surface; it is not in the same way grounded on obvious facts which are plain to every man's understanding. The doctrine of race is essentially an artificial doctrine, a learned doctrine. It is an inference from facts which the mass of mankind could never have found out for themselves; facts which, without a distinctly learned teaching, could never be brought home to them in any intelligible shape. Now what is the value of such a doctrine?

Does it follow that, because it is confessedly artificial, because it springs, not from a spontaneous impulse, but from a learned teaching, it is therefore necessarily foolish, mischievous, perhaps unnatural? It may perhaps be safer to hold that, like many other doctrines, many other sentiments, it is neither universally good nor universally bad, neither inherently wise nor inherently foolish. It may be safer to hold that it may, like other doctrines and sentiments, have a range within which it may work for good, while in some other range it may work for evil. It may in short be a doctrine which is neither to be rashly accepted, nor rashly cast aside, but one which may need to be guided, regulated, modified, according to time, place, and circumstance. I am not now called on so much to estimate the practical good and evil of the doctrine as to work out what the doctrine itself is, and to try to explain some difficulties about it, but I must emphatically say that nothing can be more shallow, nothing more foolish, nothing more purely sentimental, than the talk of those who think that they can simply laugh down or shriek down any doctrine or sentiment which they themselves do not understand. A belief or a feeling which has a practical effect on the conduct of great masses of men, sometimes on the conduct of whole nations, may be very false and very mischievous; but it is in every case a great and serious fact, to be looked gravely in the face. Men who sit at their ease and think that all wisdom is confined to themselves and their own clique may think themselves vastly superior to the great emotions which stir our times, as they would doubtless have thought themselves vastly superior to the emotions which stirred the first Saracens or the first Crusaders. But the emotions are there all the same, and they do their work all the same. The most highly educated man in the most highly educated society cannot sneer them out of being.

But it is time to pass to the more strictly scientific aspect of the subject. The doctrine of race, in its popular form, is the direct offspring of the study of scientific philology; and yet it is just now, in its popular form at least, somewhat under the ban of scientific philologers. There is nothing very wonderful in this. It is in fact the natural course of things which might almost have been reckoned on beforehand. When the popular mind gets hold of a truth, it seldom gets hold of it with strict scientific precision. It commonly gets hold of one side of the truth ; it puts forth that side of the truth only. It puts that side forth in a form which may not be in itself distorted or exaggerated, but which practically becomes distorted and exaggerated, because other sides of the same truth are not brought into their due relation with it. The popular idea thus takes a shape which is naturally offensive to men of strict precision, and which men of strict scientific precision have naturally, and from their own point of view quite rightly, risen up to rebuke. Yet it may often happen that, while the scientific statement is the only true one for scientific purposes, the popular version may also have a kind of practical truth for the somewhat rough and ready purposes of a popular version. In our present case scientific philologers are beginning to complain, with perfect truth and perfect justice from their own point of view, that the popular doctrine of race confounds race and language. They tell us, and they do right to tell us, that language is no certain test of race, that men who speak the same tongue are not therefore necessarily men of the same blood. And they tell us further, that from whatever quarter the alleged popular confusion came, it certainly did not come from any teaching of scientific philologers. The truth of all this cannot be called in question. We have too many instances in recorded history of nations laying aside the use of one language and taking to the use of another, for any one who cares for accuracy to set down language as any sure test of race. In fact, the studies of the philologer and those of the ethnologer strictly so called are quite distinct, and they deal with two wholly different sets of phenomena. The science of the ethnologer is strictly a physical science. He has to deal with purely physical phenomena; his business lies with the different varieties of the human body, and specially, to take that branch of his inquiries which most impresses the unlearned, with the various conformations of the human skull. His researches differ in nothing from those of the zoölogist or the palæontologist, except that he has to deal with the physical phenomena of man, while they deal with the physical phenomena of other animals. He groups the different races of men, exactly as the others group the genera and species of living or extinct mammals or reptiles. The student of ethnology as a physical science may indeed strengthen his conclusions by evidence of other kinds, evidence from arms, ornaments, pottery, modes of burial. But all these are secondary; the primary ground of classification is the physical conformation of man himself. As to language, the ethnological method, left to itself, can find out nothing whatever. The science of the ethnologer then is primarily physical; it is historical only in that secondary sense in which palæontology, and geology itself, may fairly be called historical. It arranges the varieties of mankind according to a strictly physical classification; what the language of each variety may have been, it leaves to the professors of another branch of study to find out.

The science of the philologer, on the other hand, is strictly historical. There is doubtless a secondary sense in which purely philological science may be fairly called physical, just as there is a secondary sense in which pure ethnology may be called historical. That is to say, philology has to deal with physical phenomena, so far as it has to deal with the physical aspect of the sounds of which human language is made up. Its primary business, like the primary business of any other historical science, is to deal with phenomena which do not depend on physical laws, but which do depend on the human will. The science of language is, in this respect, like the science of human institutions or of human beliefs. Its subject-matter is not, like that of pure ethnology, what man is, but, like that of any other historical science, what man does. It is plain that no man's will can have any direct influence on the shape of his skull. I say no direct influence, because it is not for me to rule how far habits, places of abode, modes of life, a thousand things which do come under the control of the human will, may indirectly affect the physical conformation of a man himself or of his descendants. Some observers have made the remark that men of civilized nations who live in a degraded social state do actually approach to the physical type of inferior races. However this may be, it is quite certain, that as no man can by taking thought add a cubit to his stature, so no man can by taking thought make his skull brachycephalic or dolichocephalic. But the language which a man speaks does depend upon his will; he can by taking thought make his speech Romance or Teutonic. No doubt he has in most cases practically no choice in the matter. The language which he speaks is practically determined for him by fashion, habit, early teaching, a crowd of things over which he has practically no control. But still the control is not physical and inevitable, as it is in the case of the shape of his skull. If we say that he cannot help speaking in a particular way; that is, that he cannot help speaking a particular language, this simply means that his circumstances are such that no other way of speaking presents itself to his mind. And in many cases, he has a real choice between two or more ways of speaking; that is, between two or more languages. Every word that a man speaks is the result of a real, though doubtless unconscious, act of his free will. We are apt to speak of gradual changes in language, as in institutions or anything else, as if they were the result of a physical law, acting upon beings who had no choice in the matter. Yet every change of the kind is simply the aggregate of various acts of the will on the part of all concerned. Every change in speech, every introduction of a new sound or a new word, was really the result of an act of the will of some one or other. The choice may have been unconscious; circumstances may have been such as practically to give him but one choice; still he did choose; he spoke in one way, when there was no physical hindrance to his speaking in another way, when there was no physical compulsion to speak at all. The Gauls need not have changed their own language for Latin; the change was not the result of a physical necessity, but of a number of acts of the will on the part of this and that Gaul. Moral causes directed their choice, and determined that Gaul should become a Latin-speaking land. But whether the skulls of the Gauls should be long or short, whether their hair should be black or yellow, those were points over which the Gauls themselves had no direct control whatever.

The study of men's skulls then is a study which is strictly physical, a study of facts over which the will of man has no direct control. The study of men's languages is strictly an historical study, a study of facts over which the will of man has a direct control. It follows therefore from the very nature of the two studies that language cannot be an absolutely certain test of physical descent. A man cannot, under any circumstances, choose his own skull; he may, under some circumstances, choose his own language. He must keep the skull which has been given him by his parents; he cannot, by any process of taking thought, determine what kind of skull he will hand on to his own children. But he may give up the use of the language which he has learned from his parents, and he may determine what language he will teach to his children. The physical characteristics of a race are unchangeable, or are changed only by influences over which the race itself has no direct control. The language which the race speaks may be changed, either by a conscious act of the will or by that power of fashion which is in truth the aggregate of countless unconscious acts of the will. And, as the very nature of the case thus shows that language is no sure test of race, so the facts of recorded history equally prove the same truth. Both individuals and whole nations do in fact often exchange the language of their forefathers for some other language. A man settles in a foreign country. He learns the language of that country; sometimes he forgets the use of his own language. His children may perhaps speak both tongues; if they speak one tongue only, it will be the tongue of the country where they live. In a generation or two all trace of foreign origin will have passed away. Here then language is no test of race. If the great-grandchildren speak the language of their great-grandfathers, it will simply be as they may speak any other foreign language. Here are men who by speech belong to one nation, by actual descent to another. If they lose the physical characteristics of the race to which the original settler belonged, it will be due to intermarriage, to climate, to some cause altogether independent of language. Every nation will have some adopted children of this kind, more or fewer; men who belong to it by speech, but who do not belong to it by race. And what happens in the case of individuals happens in the case of whole nations. The pages of history are crowded with cases in which nations have cast aside the tongue of their forefathers, and have taken instead the tongue of some other people. Greek in the East, Latin in the West, became the familiar speech of millions who had not a drop of Greek or Italian blood in their veins. The same has been the case in later times with Arabic, Persian, Spanish, German, English. Each of those tongues has become the familiar speech of vast regions where the mass of the people are not Arabian, Spanish, or English, otherwise than by adoption. The Briton of Cornwall has, slowly but in the end thoroughly, adopted the speech of England. In the American continent full-blooded Indians preside over commonwealths which speak the tongue of Cortes and Pizarro. In the lands to which all eyes are now turned, the Greek, who has been busily assimilating strangers ever since he first planted his colonies in Asia and Sicily, goes on busily assimilating his Albanian neighbors. And between renegades, janissaries, and mothers of all nations, the blood of many a Turk must be physically anything rather than Turkish. The inherent nature of the case, and the witness of recorded history, join together to prove that language is no certain test of race, and that the scientific philologers are doing good service to accuracy of expression and accuracy of thought by emphatically calling attention to the fact that language is no such test.

But, on the other hand, it is quite possible that the truth to which our attention is just now most fittingly called may, if put forth too broadly and without certain qualifications, lead to error quite as great as the error at which it is aimed. I do not suppose that any one ever thought that language was, necessarily and in all cases, an absolute and certain test. If anybody does think so, he has put himself altogether out of court by shutting his eyes to the most manifest facts of the case. But there can be no doubt that many people have given too much importance to language as a test of race. Though they have not wholly forgotten the facts which tell the other way, they have not brought them out with enough prominence. But I can also believe that many people have written and spoken on the subject in a way which cannot be justified from a strictly scientific point of view, but which may have been fully justified from the point of view of the writers and speakers themselves. It may often happen that a way of speaking may not be scientifically accurate, but may yet be quite near enough to the truth for the

purposes of the matter in hand. It may, for some practical or
even historical purpose, be really more true than the statement
which is scientifically more exact. Language is no certain test
of race; but if a man, struck by this wholesome warning, should
run off into the belief that language and race have absolutely
nothing to do with one another, he had better have gone without
the warning. For in such a case the last error would be worse
than the first. The natural instinct of mankind connects race
and language. It does not assume that language is an infallible
test of race; but it does assume that language and race have
something to do with one another. It assumes, that though
language is not an accurately scientific test of race, yet it is a
rough and ready test which does for many practical purposes.
To make something more of an exact definition, one might say,
that though language is not a test of race, it is, in the absence
of evidence to the contrary, a presumption of race; that though
it is not a test of race, yet it is a test of something which, for
many practical purposes, is the same as race.

Professor Max Müller warned us long ago that we must not
speak of a Celtic skull. Mr. Sayce has more lately warned us
that we must not infer from community of Aryan speech that
there is any kindred in blood between this or that Englishman
and this or that Hindoo. And both warnings are scientifically
true. Yet any one who begins his studies on these matters with
Professor Müller's famous Oxford Essay will practically come to
another way of looking at things. He will fill his mind with a
vivid picture of the great Aryan family, as yet one, dwelling in
one place, speaking one tongue, having already taken the first
steps toward settled society, recognizing the domestic relations,

possessing the first rudiments of government and religion, and calling all these first elements of culture by names of which traces still abide here and there among the many nations of the common stock. He will go on to draw pictures equally vivid of the several branches of the family parting off from the primeval home. One great branch he will see going to the south-east, to become the forefathers of the vast, yet isolated colony in the Asiatic lands of Persia and India. He watches the remaining mass sending off wave after wave, to become the forefathers of the nations of historical Europe. He traces out how each branch starts with its own share of the common stock — how the language, the creed, the institutions, once common to all, grow up into different, yet kindred, shapes, among the many parted branches which grew up, each with an independent life and strength of its own. This is what our instructors set before us as the true origin of nations and their languages. And, in drawing out the picture, we cannot avoid, our teachers themselves do not avoid, the use of words which imply that the strictly family relation, the relation of community of blood, is at the root of the whole matter. We cannot help talking about the family and its branches, about parents, children, brothers, sisters, cousins. The nomenclature of natural kindred exactly fits the case; it fits it so exactly that no other nomenclature could enable us to set forth the case with any clearness. Yet we cannot be absolutely certain that there was any real community of blood in the whole story. We really know nothing of the origin of language or the origin of society. We may make a thousand ingenious guesses; but we cannot prove any of them. It may be that the group which came together, and which formed the primeval society which spoke the primeval Aryan tongue, were not brought together by community of blood, but by some other cause which threw them in one another's way. If we accept the Hebrew genealogies, they need not have had any community of blood nearer than common descent from Adam and Noah. That is, they need not have been all children of Shem, of Ham, or of Japheth; some children of Shem, some of Ham, and some of Japheth may have been led by some cause to settle together. Or if we believe in independent creations of men, or in the development of men out of mollusks, the whole of the original society need not have been descendants of the same man or the same mollusk. In short, there is no theory of the origin of man which requires us to believe that the primeval Aryans were a natural family; they may have been more like an accidental party of fellow-travellers. And if we accept them as a natural family, it does not follow that the various branches which grew into separate races and nations, speaking separate though kindred languages, were necessarily marked off by more immediate kindred. It may be that there is no nearer kindred in blood between this or that Persian, this or that Greek, this or that Teuton, than the general kindred of all Aryans. For, when this or that party marched off from the common home, it does follow that those who marched off together were necessarily immediate brothers or cousins. The party which grew into Hindoos or Teutons may not have been made up exclusively of one set of .near kinsfolk. Some of the children of the same parents or forefathers may have marched one way, while others marched another way, or stayed behind. We may, if we please, indulge our fancy by conceiving that there may actually be family distinctions older than distinctions of nation and race. It may be that the Gothic *Amali* and the Roman *Æmilii* — I throw out the idea as a mere illustration — were branches of a family which had taken a name before the division of Teuton and Italian. Some of the members of that family may have joined the band of which came the Goths, while other members joined the band of which came the Romans. There is no difference but the length of time to distinguish such a supposed case from the case of an English family, one branch of which settled in the seventeenth century at Boston in Massachusetts, while another branch stayed behind at Boston in Holland. Mr. Sayce says truly that the use of a kindred language does not prove that the Englishman and the Hindoo are really akin in race; for, as he adds, many Hindoos are men of non-Aryan race who have simply learned to speak tongues of Sanscrit origin. He might have gone on to say, with equal truth, that there is no positive certainty that there was any community in blood among the original Aryan group itself, and that if we admit such community of blood in the original Aryan group, it does not follow that there is any further special kindred between Hindoo and Hindoo or between Englishman and Englishman. The original group may not have been a family, but an artificial union. And if it was a family, those of its members who marched together east or west or north or south may have had no tie of kindred beyond the common cousinship of all.

Now the tendency of this kind of argument is to lead to something a good deal more startling than the doctrine that language is no certain test of race. Its tendency is to go on further, and to show that race is no certain test of community of blood.

And this comes pretty nearly to saying that there is no such thing as race at all. For our whole conception of race starts from the idea of community of blood. If the word."race" does not mean community of blood, it is hard to see what it does mean. Yet it is certain that there can be no positive proof of real community of blood, even among those groups of mankind which we instinctively speak of as families and races. It is not merely that the blood has been mingled in after-times; there is no positive proof that there was any community of blood in the beginning. No living Englishman can prove with absolute certainty that he comes in the male line of any of the Teutonic settlers in Britain in the fifth or sixth centuries. I say in the male line, because any one who is descended from any English king can prove such descent, though he can prove it only through a long and complicated web of female successions. But we may be sure that in no other case can such a pedigree be proved by the kind of proof which lawyers would require to make out the title to an estate or a peerage. The actual forefathers of the modern Englishman may chance to have been, not true-born Angles or Saxons, but Britons, Scots, in later days Frenchmen, Flemings, men of any other nation who learned to speak English and took to themselves English names. But supposing that a man could make out such a pedigree, supposing that he could prove that he came in the male line of some follower of Hengest or Cerdic, he would be no nearer to proving original community of blood either in the particular Teutonic race or in the general Aryan family. If direct evidence is demanded, we must give up the whole doctrine of families and races, as far as we take language, manners, institutions, any thing but physical conformation, as the distinguishing marks of races and families. That is to say, if we wish never to use any word of whose accuracy we cannot be perfectly certain, we must leave off speaking of races and families at all from any but the purely physical side. We must content ourselves with saying that certain groups of mankind have a common history, that they have languages, creeds, and institutions in common, but that we have no evidence whatever to show how they came to have languages, creeds, and institutions in common. We cannot say for certain what was the tie which brought the members of the original group together, any more than we can name the exact time and the exact place when and where they came together.

We may thus seem to be landed in a howling wilderness of scientific uncertainty. The result of pushing our inquiries so far may seem to be to show that we really know nothing at all. But in truth the uncertainty is no greater than the uncertainty which attends all inquiries in the historical sciences. Though a historical fact may be recorded in the most trustworthy documents, though it may have happened in our own times, though we may have seen it happen with our own eyes, yet we cannot have the same certainty about it as the mathematician has about the proposition which he proves to absolute demonstration. We cannot have even that lower degree of certainty which the geologist has with regard to the order of succession between this and that *stratum*. For in all historical inquiries we are dealing with facts which themselves come within the control of human will and human caprice, and the evidence for which depends on the trustworthiness of human informants, who may either purposely deceive or unwittingly mislead. A man may

lie ; he may err. The triangles and the rocks can neither lie
nor err. I may with my own eyes see a certain man do a
certain act ; he may tell me himself, or some one else may tell
me that he is the same man who did some other act; but
as to his statement I cannot have absolute certainty, and no
one but myself can have absolute certainty as to the statement
which I make as to the facts which I saw with my own eyes.
Historical evidence may range through every degree, from the
barest likelihood to that undoubted moral certainty on which
every man acts without hesitation in practical affairs. But it
cannot get beyond this last standard. If, then, we are ever to
use words like race, family, or even nation, to denote groups of
mankind marked off by any kind of historical, as distinguished
from physical, characteristics, we must be content to use those
words, as we use many other words, without being able to prove
that our use of them is accurate, as mathematicians judge of
accuracy. I cannot be quite sure that William the Conqueror
landed at Pevensey, though I have strong reasons for believing
that he did so. And I have strong reasons for believing many
facts about race and language about which I am much further
from being quite sure than I am about William's landing at
Pevensey. In short, in all these matters, we must be satisfied to
let presumption very largely take the place of actual proof ; and,
if we only let presumption in, most of our difficulties at once fly
away. Language is no certain test of race; but it is a presumption of race. Community of race, as we commonly understand
race, is no certain proof of original community of blood ; but it
is a presumption of original community of blood. The presumption amounts to moral proof, if only we do not insist on

proving such physical community of blood as would satisfy a genealogist. It amounts to moral proof, if all that we seek is to establish a relation in which the community of blood is the leading idea, and in which, where natural community of blood does not exist, its place is supplied by something which by a legal fiction is looked upon as its equivalent.

If, then, we do not ask for scientific, for what we may call physical, accuracy, but if we are satisfied with the kind of proof which is all that we can ever get in the historical sciences — if we are satisfied to speak in a way which is true for popular and practical purposes — then we may say that language has a great deal to do with race, as race is commonly understood, and that race has a great deal to do with community of blood. If we once admit the Roman doctrine of adoption, our whole course is clear. The natural family is the starting-point of every thing; but we must give the natural family the power of artificially enlarging itself by admitting adoptive members. A group of mankind is thus formed, in which it does not follow that all the members have any natural community of blood, but in which community of blood is the starting-point, in which those who are connected by natural community of blood form the original body within whose circle the artificial members are admitted. A group of mankind thus formed is something quite different from a fortuitous concurrence of atoms. Three or four brothers by blood, with a fourth or fifth man whom they agree to look on as filling in every thing the same place as a brother by blood, form a group which is quite unlike a union of four or five men, none of whom is bound by any tie of blood to any of the others. In the latter kind of union the notion of kindred does not come in

at all. In the former kind the notion of kindred is the groundwork of every thing; it determines the character of every relation and every action, even though the kindred between some
members of the society and others may be owing to a legal fiction
and not to natural descent. All that we know of the growth of
tribes, races, nations, leads us to believe that they grew in this
way. Natural kindred was the groundwork, the leading and
determining idea; but, by one of those legal fictions which have
had such an influence on all institutions, adoption was in certain
cases allowed to count as natural kindred.[1]

The usage of all languages shows that community of blood
was the leading idea in forming the greater and smaller groups
of mankind. Words like φῦλον, γένος, *gens, natio, kin,* all point
to the natural family as the origin of all society. The family in
the narrower sense, the children of one father in one house,
grew into a more extended family, the *gens.* Such were the
Alkmaiônidai, the Julii, or the Scyldingas, the real or artificial
descendants of a real or supposed forefather. The nature of
the *gens* has been set forth often enough. If it is a mistake to
fancy that every Julius or Cornelius was the natural kinsman of
every other Julius or Cornelius, it is equally a mistake to think
that the *gens Julia* or *Cornelia* was in its origin a mere artificial
association, into which the idea of natural kindred did not enter.
It is indeed possible that really artificial *gentes,* groups of men

---

[1] I am here applying to this particular purpose a line of thought which both myself
and others have often applied to other purposes. See, above all, Sir Henry Maine's
lecture on " Kinship as the Basis of Society " in the lectures on the " Early History
of Institutions; " I would refer also to my own lecture on " The State" in "Comparative Politics."

of whom it might chance that none were natural kinsmen, were formed in later times after the model of the original *gentes*. Still such imitation would bear witness to the original conception of the *gens*. It would be the doctrine of adoption turned the other way; instead of a father adopting a son, a number of men would agree to adopt a common father. The family then grew into the *gens;* the union of *gentes* formed the state, the political community, which in its first form was commonly a tribe. Then came the nation, formed of a union of tribes. Kindred, real or artificial, is the one basis on which all society and all government has grown up.

Now it is plain, that as soon as we admit the doctrine of artificial kindred — that is, as soon as we allow the exercise of the law of adoption, physical purity of race is at an end. Adoption treats a man as if he were the son of a certain father; it cannot really make him the son of that father. If a brachycephalic father adopts a dolichocephalic son, the legal act cannot change the shape of the adopted son's skull. I will not undertake to say whether, not indeed the rite of adoption, but the influences and circumstances which would spring from it, might not, in the course of generations, affect even the skull of the man who entered a certain *gens*, tribe, or nation by artificial adoption only. If by any chance the adopted son spoke a different language from the adopted father, the rite of adoption itself would not of itself change his language. But it would bring him under influences which would make him adopt the language of his new *gens* by a conscious act of the will, and which would make his children adopt it by the same unconscious act of the will by which each child adopts the language of his parents. The adopted son, still more the son of the adopted son, became, in speech, in feelings, in worship, in every thing but physical descent, one with the *gens* into which he was adopted. He became one of that *gens* for all practical, political, historical, purposes. It is only the physiologist who could deny his right to his new position. The nature of the process is well expressed by a phrase of our own law. When the nation — the word itself keeps about it the remembrance of birth as the groundwork of every thing — adopts a new citizen, that is, a new child of the state, he is said to be *naturalized*. That is, a legal process puts him in the same position, and gives him the same rights, as a man who is a citizen and a son by birth. It is assumed that the rights of citizenship come by nature — that is, by birth. The stranger is admitted to them only by a kind of artificial birth; he is naturalized by law; his children are in a generation or two naturalized in fact. There is now no practical distinction between the Englishman whose forefathers landed with William, or even between the Englishman whose forefathers sought shelter from Alva or from Louis the Fourteenth, and the Englishman whose forefathers landed with Hengest. It is for the physiologist to say whether any difference can be traced in their several skulls; for all practical purposes, historical or political, all distinction between these several classes has passed away.

We may, in short, say that the law of adoption runs through every thing, and that it may be practised on every scale. What adoption is at the hands of the family, naturalization is at the hands of the state. And the same process extends itself from adopted or naturalized individuals to large classes of men, indeed to whole nations. When the process takes place on this scale, we may best call it assimilation. Thus Rome assimilated the continental nations of Western Europe to that degree that, allowing for a few survivals here and there, not only Italy, but Gaul and Spain, became Roman. The people of those lands, admitted step by step to the Roman franchise, adopted the name and tongue of Romans. It must soon have been hard to distinguish the Roman colonist in Gaul or Spain from the native Gaul or Spaniard who had, as far as in him lay, put on the guise of a Roman. This process of assimilation has gone on everywhere and at all times. When two nations come in this way into close contact with one another, it depends on a crowd of circumstances which shall assimilate the other, or whether they shall remain distinct without assimilation either way. Sometimes the conquerors assimilate their subjects; sometimes they are assimilated by their subjects; sometimes conquerors and subjects remain distinct forever. When assimilation either way does take place, the direction which it takes in each particular case will depend, partly on their respective numbers, partly on their degrees of civilization. A small number of less civilized conquerors will easily be lost among a greater number of more civilized subjects, and that even though they give their name to the land and people which they conquer. The modern Frenchman represents, not the conquering Frank, but the conquered Gaul, or, as he called himself, the conquered Roman. The modern Bulgarian represents, not the Finnish conqueror, but the conquered Slav. The modern Russian represents, not the Scandinavian ruler, but the Slav who sent for the Scandinavian to rule over him. And so we might go on with endless other cases. The point is that the process of adoption, naturalization, assimilation, has gone on everywhere. No nation can boast of absolute purity of blood, though no doubt some nations come much nearer to it than others. When I speak of purity of blood, I leave out of sight the darker questions which I have already raised with regard to the groups of mankind in days before recorded history. I assume great groups like Celtic, Teutonic, Slavonic, as having what we may call a real corporate existence, however we may hold that that corporate existence began. My present point is that no existing nation is, in the physiologist's sense of purity, purely Celtic, Teutonic, Slavonic, or any thing else. All races have assimilated a greater or less amount of foreign elements. Taking this standard, one which comes more nearly within the range of our actual knowledge than the possibilities of unrecorded times, we may again say that, from the purely scientific or physiological point of view, not only is language no test of race, but that, at all events, among the great nations of the world, there is no such thing as purity of race at all.

But, while we admit this truth, while we even insist upon it from the strictly scientific point of view, we must be allowed to look at it with different eyes from a more practical standing point. This is the standing point, whether of history which is the politics of the past, or of politics which are the history of the present. From this point of view, we may say unhesitatingly that there are such things as races and nations, and that to the grouping of those races and nations language is the best guide. We cannot undertake to define with any philosophical precision the exact distinction between race and race, between nation and nation. Nor can we undertake to define with the like precision in what way the distinctions between race and race, between nation and nation, began. But all analogy leads us to believe that tribes, nations, races, were all formed according to the original model of the family, the family which starts from the idea of the community of blood, but which allows artificial adoption to be its legal equivalent. In all cases of adoption, naturalization, assimilation, whether of individuals or of large classes of men, the adopted person or class is adopted into an existing community. Their adoption undoubtedly influences the community into which they are adopted. It at once destroys any claim on the part of that community to purity of blood, and it influences the adopting community in many ways, physical and moral. A family, a tribe, or a nation, which has largely recruited itself by adopted members, cannot be the same as one which has never practised adoption at all, but all whose members come of the original stock. But the influence which the adopting community exercises upon its adopted members is far greater than any influence which they exercise upon it. It cannot change their blood; it cannot give them new natural forefathers; but it may do every thing short of this; it may make them, in speech, in feeling, in thought, and in habit, genuine members of the community which has artificially made them its own. While there is not in any nation, in any race, any such thing as strict purity of blood, yet there is in each nation, in each race, a dominant element — or rather something more than an element — something which is the true essence of the race or nation, something which sets its standard and determines its character, something which draws to itself and assimilates to itself all other elements. It so works that all other elements are not co-equal elements with itself, but mere infusions poured into an already existing body. Doubtless these infusions do in some measure influence the body which assimilates them; but the influence which they exercise is as nothing compared to the influence which they undergo. We may say that they modify the character of the body into which they are assimilated; they do not affect its personality. Thus, assuming the great groups of mankind as primary facts, the origin of which lies beyond our certain knowledge, we may speak of families and races, of the great Aryan family and of the races into which it parted, as groups which have a real, practical existence, as groups founded on the ruling primeval idea of kindred, even though in many cases the kindred may not be by natural descent, but only by law of adoption. The Celtic, Teutonic, Slavonic races of man are real living and abiding groups, the distinction between which we must accept among the primary facts of history. And they go on as living and abiding groups, even though we know that each of them has assimilated many adopted members, sometimes from other branches of the Aryan family, sometimes from races of men alien to the whole Aryan stock. These races which, in a strictly physiological point of view, have no existence at all, have a real existence from the more practical point of view of history and politics. The Bulgarian calls to the Russian for help, and the Russian answers to his call for help, on the ground of their being alike members of the one Slavonic race. It may be that, if we could trace out the actual pedigree of this or that Bulgarian, of this or that Russian, we might either find that there was no real kindred between them, or we might find that there was a real kindred, but a kindred which must be traced up to another stock than that of the Slav. In point of actual blood, instead of both being Slavs, it may be that one of them comes, it may be that both of them come, of a stock which is not Slavonic or even Aryan. The Bulgarian may chance to be a Bulgarian in a truer sense than he thinks for; he may come of the blood of those original Finnish conquerors who gave the Bulgarian name to the Slavs among whom they were merged. And if this or that Bulgarian may chance to come of the stock of Finnish conquerors assimilated by their Slavonic subjects, this or that Russian may chance to come of the stock of Finnish subjects assimilated by their Slavonic conquerors. It may then so happen that the cry for help goes up and is answered on a ground of kindred which in the eye of the physiologist has no existence. Or it may happen that the kindred is real in a way which neither the suppliant nor his helper thinks of. But in either case, for the practical purposes of human life, the plea is a good plea; the kindred on which it is founded is a real kindred. It is good by the law of adoption. It is good by the law the force of which we all admit whenever we count a man as an Englishman whose forefathers, two generations or twenty generations back, came to our shores as strangers. For all practical purposes, for all the purposes which guide men's actions, public or private, the Russian and the Bulgarian, kinsmen so long parted, perhaps in very truth no natural kinsmen at all, are members of the same race, bound together by the common sentiment of race. They belong to the same race, exactly as an Englishman whose forefathers came into Britain fourteen hundred years back, and an Englishman whose forefathers came only one or two hundred years back, are alike members of the same nation, bound together by a tie of common nationality.⁊

And now, having ruled that races and nations, though largely formed by the working of an artificial law, are still rèal and living things, groups in which the idea of kindred is the idea around which every thing has grown, how are we to define our races and our nations? How are we to mark them off one from the other? Bearing in mind the cautions and qualifications which have been already given, bearing in mind large classes of exceptions which will presently be spoken of, I say unhesitatingly that for practical purposes there is one test, and one only, and that that test is language. It is hardly needful to show that races and nations cannot be defined by the merely political arrangements which group men under various governments. For some purposes of ordinary language, for some purposes of ordinary politics, we are tempted, sometimes driven, to take this standard. And in some parts of the world, in our own Western Europe for instance, nations and governments do, in a rough way, fairly answer to one another. And, in any case, political divisions are not without their influence on the formation of national divisions, while national divisions ought to have the greatest influence on political divisions. That is to say, *primâ facie* a nation and government should coincide. I say only *primâ facie;* for this is assuredly no inflexible rule; there are often good reasons why it should be otherwise; only, whenever it is otherwise, there should be some good reason forthcoming. It might even be true that in no case did a government and a nation exactly coincide, and yet it would none the less be the rule that a government and a nation should coincide. That is

to say, so far as a nation and a government coincide, we accept
it as the natural state of things, and ask no question as to the
cause.   So far as they do not coincide, we mark the case as
exceptional, by asking what is the cause.   And by saying that a
government and a nation should coincide we mean that, as far
as possible, the boundaries of governments should be so laid out
as to agree with the boundaries of nations.   That is, we assume
the nation as something already existing, something primary, to
which the secondary arrangements of government should, as far
as possible, conform.   How then do we define the nation, which
is, if there is no especial reason to the contrary, to fix the
limits of a government?   Primarily, I say, as a rule, but a
rule subject to exceptions, — as a *primâ facie* standard, subject
to special reasons to the contrary, — we define the nation by
language.   We may at least apply the test negatively.   It would
be unsafe to rule that all speakers of the same language must
have a common nationality ; but we may safely say that where
there is not community of language, there is no common nationality in the highest sense.   It is true that without community of
language there may be an artificial nationality, a nationality
which may be good for all political purposes, and which may
engender a common national feeling.   Still this is not quite the
same thing as that fuller national unity which is felt where there
is community of language.   In fact mankind instinctively takes
language as the badge of nationality.   We so far take it as the
badge, that we instinctively assume community of language as a
nation as the rule, and we set down any thing that departs from
that rule as an exception.   The first idea suggested by the word
Frenchman or German or any other national name, is that he is

a man who speaks French or German as his mother-tongue. We take for granted, in the absence of any thing to make us think otherwise, that a Frenchman is a speaker of French and that a speaker of French is a Frenchman. Where in any case it is otherwise, we mark that case as an exception, and we ask the special cause. Again, the rule is none the less the rule, nor the exceptions the exceptions, because the exceptions may easily outnumber the instances which conform to the rule. The rule is still the rule, because we take the instances which conform to it as a matter of course, while in every case which does not conform to it we ask for the explanation. All the larger countries of Europe provide us with exceptions; but we treat them all as exceptions. We do not ask why a native of France speaks French. But when a native of France speaks as his mother-tongue some other tongue than French, when French, or something which popularly passes for French, is spoken as his mother-tongue by some one who is not a native of France, we at once ask the reason. And the reason will be found in each case in some special historical cause which withdraws that case from the operation of the general law. A very good reason can be given why French, or something which popularly passes for French, is spoken in parts of Belgium and Switzerland whose inhabitants are certainly not Frenchmen. But the reason has to be given, and it may fairly be asked. ↳

In the like sort, if we turn to our own country, whenever within the bounds of Great Britain we find any tongue spoken other than English, we at once ask the reason and we learn the special historic cause.. In a part of France and a part of Great Britain we find tongues spoken which differ alike from English and from French, but which are strongly akin to one another. We find that these are the survivals of a group of tongues once common to Gaul and Britain, but which the settlement of other nations, the introduction and the growth of other tongues, have brought down to the level of survivals. So again we find islands which both speech and geographical position seem to mark as French, but which are dependencies, and loyal dependencies, of the English crown. We soon learn the cause of the phenomenon which seems so strange. Those islands are the remains of a state and a people which adopted the French tongue, but which, while it remained one, did not become a part of the French state. That people brought England by force of arms under the rule of their own sovereigns. The greater part of that people were afterward conquered by France, and gradually became French in feeling as well as in language. But a remnant clave to their connection with the land which their forefathers had conquered, and that remnant, while keeping the French tongue, never became French in feeling. This last case, that of the Norman islands, is a specially instructive one. Normandy and England were politically connected, while language and geography pointed rather to a union between Normandy and France. In the case of continental Normandy, where the geographical tie was strongest, language and geography together could carry the day, and the continental Norman became a Frenchman. In the islands, where the geographical tie was less strong, political traditions and manifest interest carried the day against language and a weaker geographical tie. The insular Norman did not become a Frenchman. But neither did he become an Englishman. He alone remained Norman, keeping

his own tongue and his own laws, but attached to the English
crown by a tie a once of tradition and of advantage. Between
states of the relative size of England and the Norman islands,
the relation naturally becomes a relation of dependence on the
part of the smaller members of the union. But it is well to
remember that our forefathers never conquered the forefathers
of the men of the Norman islands, but that their forefathers
did once conquer ours.

These instances, and countless others, bear out the position
that, while community of language is the most obvious sign of
common nationality, while it is the main element, or something
more than an element, in the formation of nationality, the rule
is open to exceptions of all kinds, and that the influence of
language is at all times liable to be overruled by other influences. But all the exceptions confirm the rule, because we
specially ,remark those cases which contradict the rule, and
we do not specially remark those cases which do not conform to it.

In the cases which we have just spoken of, the growth of the
nation as marked out by language, and the growth of the
exceptions to the rule of language, have both come through the
gradual, unconscious working of historical causes. Union under
the same government, or separation under separate governments, have been among the foremost of those historical causes.
The French nation consists of the people of all that extent of
continuous territory which has been brought under the rule of
the French kings. But the working of the cause has been
gradual and unconscious. There was no moment when any one
deliberately proposed to form a French nation by joining

together all the separate duchies and counties which spoke the
French tongue. Since the French nation has been formed,
men have proposed to annex this or that land on the ground
that its people spoke the French tongue, or perhaps only some
tongue akin to the French tongue. But the formation of the
French nation itself was the work of historical causes, the work
doubtless of a settled policy acting through many generations,
but not the work of any conscious theory about races and languages. It is a special mark of our time, a special mark of the
influence which doctrines about race and language have had on
men's minds, that we have seen great nations united by processes
in which theories of race and language really have had much to
do with bringing about their union. If statesmen have not been
themselves moved by such theories, they have at least found that
it suited their purpose to make use of such theories as a means
of working on the minds of others. In the reunion of the severed German and Italian nations, the conscious feeling of nationality, and the acceptance of a common language as the outward
badge of nationality, had no small share. Poets sang of language as the badge of national union; statesmen made it the
badge, so far as political considerations did not lead them to do
anything else. The revived kingdom of Italy is very far from
taking in all the speakers of the Italian tongue. Lugano, Trent,
Aquileia—to take places which are clearly Italian, and not
to bring in places of more doubtful nationality, like the cities of
Istria and Dalmatia—form no part of the Italian political body,
and Corsica is not under the same rule as the other two great
neighboring islands. But the fact that all these places do not
belong to the Italian body at once suggests the twofold ques-

tion, why they do not belong to it, and whether they ought not to belong to it. History easily answers the first question; it may perhaps also answer the second question in a way which will say Yes as regards one place and No as regards another. Ticino must not lose her higher freedom; Trieste must remain the needful mouth for southern Germany; Dalmatia must not be cut off from the Slavonic mainland; Corsica would seem to have sacrificed national feeling to personal hero-worship. But it is certainly hard to see why Trent and Aquileia should be kept apart from the Italian body. On the other hand, the revived Italian kingdom contains very little which is not Italian in speech. It is perhaps by a somewhat elastic view of language that the dialect of Piedmont and the dialect of Sicily are classed under one head; still, as a matter of fact, they have a single classical standard, and they are universally accepted as varieties of the same tongue. But it is only in a few Alpine valleys that languages are spoken which, whether Romance or Teutonic, are in any case not Italian. The reunion of Italy, in short, took in all that was Italian, save when some political cause hindered the rule of language from being followed. Of any thing not Italian by speech so little has been taken in that the non-Italian parts of Italy, Burgundian Aosta and the Seven German Communes — if these last still keep their Teutonic language, — fall under the rule that there are some things too small for laws to pay heed to.

But it must not be forgotten that all this simply means that in the lands of which we have just been speaking the process of adoption has been carried out on the largest scale. Nations, with languages as their rough practical test, have been formed;

but they have been formed with very little regard to physical
purity of blood.　In short, throughout Western Europe assimilation has been the rule.　That is to say, in any of the great
divisions of Western Europe, though the land may have been
settled and conquered over and over again, yet the mass of the
people of the land have been drawn to some one national type.
Either some one among the races inhabiting the land has taught
the others to put on its likeness, or else a new national type has
arisen which has elements drawn from several of those races.
Thus the modern Frenchman may be defined as produced by
the union of blood which is mainly Celtic with a speech which
is mainly Latin, and with an historical polity which is mainly
Teutonic.　That is, he is neither Gaul, Roman, nor Frank, but
a fourth type which has drawn important elements from all
three.　Within modern France this new national type has so
far assimilated all others as to make everthing else merely
exceptional.　The Fleming of one corner, the Basque of another,
even the far more important Breton of a third corner, have all in
this way become mere exceptions to the general type of the
country.　If we pass into our own islands, we shall find that the
same process has been at work.　If we look to Great Britain
only, we shall find that, though the means have not been the
same, yet the end has been gained hardly less thoroughly than
in France.　For all real political purposes, for every thing which
concerns a nation in the face of other nations, Great Britain is
as thoroughly united as France is.　Englishmen, Scotchmen,
Welshmen, feel themselves one people in the general affairs of
the world.　A secession of Scotland or Wales is as unlikely as a
secession of Normandy or Languedoc.　The part of the island

which is not thoroughly assimilated in language, that part which still speaks Welsh or Gaelic, is larger in proportion than the non-French part of modern France. But however much either the northern or the western Briton may, in a fit of antiquarian politics, declaim against the Saxon, for all practical political purposes he and the Saxon are one. The distinction between the southern and the northern English — for the men of Lothian and Fife must allow me to call them by this last name — is, speaking politically and without ethnological or linguistic precision, much as if France and Aquitaine had been two kingdoms united on equal terms, instead of Aquitaine being merged in France. When we cross into Ireland, we indeed find another state of things, and one which comes nearer to some of the phenomena which we shall come to in other parts of the world. Ireland is, most unhappily, not so firmly united to Great Britain as the different parts of Great Britain are to one another. Still even here the division arises quite as much from geographical and historical causes as from distinctions of race strictly so called. If Ireland had had no wrongs, still two great islands can never be so thoroughly united as a continuous territory can be. On the other hand, in point of language, the discontented part of the United Kingdom is much less strongly marked off than that fraction of the contented part which is not thoroughly assimilated. Irish is certainly not the language of Ireland in at all the same degree in which Welsh is the language of Wales. The Saxon has commonly to be denounced in the Saxon tongue.

In some other parts of Western Europe, as in the Spanish and Scandinavian peninsulas, the coincidence of language and nationality is stronger then it is in France, Britain, or even Italy. No one speaks Spanish except in Spain or in the colonies of Spain. And within Spain the proportion of those who do not speak Spanish, namely the Basque remnant, is smaller than the non-assimilated element in Britain and France. Here two things are to be marked : First, the modern Spanish nation has been formed, like the French, by a great process of assimilation ; secondly, the actual national arrangements of the Spanish peninsula are wholly due to historical causes, we might almost say historical accidents, and those of very recent date. Spain and Portugal are separate kingdoms, and we look on their inhabitants as forming separate nations. But this is simply because a Queen of Castile in the fifteenth century married a King of Aragon. Had Isabel married a King of Portugal, we should now talk of Spain and Aragon as we now talk of Spain and Portugal, and we should count Portugal for part of Spain. In language, in history, in every thing else, Aragon was really more distinct from Castile than Portugal was. The King of Castile was already spoken of as King of Spain, and Portugal would have merged in the Spanish kingdom at last as easily as Aragon did. In Scandinavia, on the other hand, there must have been less assimilation than anywhere else. In the present kingdoms of Norway and Sweden, there must be a nearer approach to actual purity of blood than in any other part of Europe. One cannot fancy that much Finnish blood has been assimilated, and there have been no conquests or settlements later than that of the Northmen themselves.

When we pass into Central Europe we shall find a somewhat different state of things. The distinctions of race seem to be more lasting. While the national unity of the German Empire is greater than that of either France or Great Britain, it has not only subjects of other languages, but actually discontented subjects, in three corners, on its French, its Danish, and its Polish frontiers. We ask the reason, and it will be at once answered that the discontent of all three is the result of recent conquest, in two cases of very recent conquest indeed. But this is one of the very points to be marked; the strong national unity of the German Empire. has been largely the result of assimilation; and these three parts, where recent conquest has not yet been followed by assimilation, are chiefly important because, in all three cases, the discontented territory is geographically continuous with a territory of its own speech outside the Empire. This does not prove that assimilation can never take place; but it will undoubtedly make the process longer and harder.

So again, wherever German-speaking people dwell outside the bounds of the revived German state, as well as when that revived German state contains other than German-speaking people, we ask the reason and we can find it. Political reasons forbade the immediate annexation of Austria, Tyrol, and Salzburg. Combined political and geographical reasons, and, if we look a little deeper, ethnological reasons too, forbade the annexation of Courland, Livonia, and Esthonia. Some reason or other will, it may be hoped, always be found to hinder the annexation of lands which, like Zürich and Berne, have reached a higher political level. Outlying brethren in Transylvania or at Saratof again come under the rule " De minimis non curat lex." In all these cases the rule that nationality and language should go together, yields to unavoidable circumstances. But, on the other hand, where French or Danish or Slavonic or Lithuanian is spoken within the bounds of. the new Empire, the principle that language is the badge of nationality, that without community of language nationality is imperfect, shows itself in another shape. One main object of modern policy is to bring these exceptional districts under the general rule by spreading the German language in them. Everywhere, in short, wherever a power is supposed to be founded on nationality, the common feeling of mankind instinctively takes language as the test of nationality. We assume language as the test of a nation, without going into any minute questions as to the physical purity of blood in that nation. A continuous territory, living under the same government and speaking the same tongue, forms a nation for all practical purposes. If some of its inhabitants do not belong to the original stock by blood, they at least belong to it by adoption.

The question may now fairly be asked, What is the case in those parts of the world where people who are confessedly of different races and languages inhabit a continuous territory and live under the same government? How do we define nationality in such cases as these? The answer will be very different in different cases, according to the means by which the different national elements in such a territory have been brought together. They may form what I have already called an artificial nation, united by an act of its own free will. Or it may be simply a case where distinct nations, distinct in every thing which can be looked on as forming a nation, except the possession of an independent government, are brought together, by whatever causes, under a common ruler. The former case is very distinctly an exception which proves the rule, and the latter is, though in quite another way, an exception which proves the rule also. Both cases may need somewhat more in the way of definition. We will begin with the first, the case of a nation which has been formed out of elements which differ in language, but which still have been brought together so as to form an artificial nation. In the growth of the chief nations of Western Europe, the principle which was consciously or unconsciously followed has been that the nation should be marked out by language, and the use of any tongue other than the dominant tongue of the nation should be at least exceptional. But there is one nation in Europe, one which has a full right to be called a nation in a political sense, which has been formed on the directly opposite principle. The Swiss Confederation has been formed by the union of certain detached fragments of the German, Italian, and Burgundian nations. It may indeed be said that the process has been in some sort a process of adoption, that the Italian and Burgundian elements have been incorporated into an already existing German body ; that, as those elements were once subjects or dependents or protected allies, the case is one of clients or freedmen who have been admitted to the full privileges of the *gens*. This is undoubtedly true, and it is equally true of a large part of the German element itself. Throughout the Confederation, allies and subjects have been raised to the rank of confederates. But the former position of the component elements does not matter for our purpose. As a matter of fact, the foreign dependencies have all been admitted into the Confederation on equal terms. German is undoubtedly the language of a great majority of the Confederation; but the two recognized Romance languages are each the speech, not of a mere fragment or survival, like Welsh in Britain or Breton in France, but of a large minority forming a visible element in the general body. The three languages are all of them alike recognized as national languages, though, as if to keep up the universal rule that there should be some exceptions to all rules, a fourth language still lives on within the bounds of the Confederation, which is not admitted to the rights of the other three, but is left in the state of a fragment or a survival.[1] Is such an artificial body as this to be called a nation? It is plainly not a nation by blood or by speech. It can hardly be called a nation by adoption. For, if we choose to say that the three elements have all agreed to adopt one another as brethren, yet it has been adoption without assimilation. Yet surely the Swiss Confederation is a nation. It is not a mere power, in which various nations are brought together, whether willingly or unwillingly, under a common ruler, but without any further tie of union. For all political purposes, the Swiss Confederation is a nation, a nation capable of as strong and true national feeling as any other nation. Yet it is a nation purely artificial, one in no way defined by blood or speech. It thus proves the rule in two ways. We at once feel that this artificially formed nation, which has no common language, but each

---

[1] While the Swiss Confederation recognizes German, French, and Italian as all alike national languages, the independent Romance language, which is still used in some parts of the Canton of Graubünden, that which is known specially as *Romansch*, is not recognized. It is left in the same position in which Welsh and Gaelic are left in Great Britain, in which Basque, Breton, Provençal, Walloon, and Flemish are left within the borders of that French kingdom which has grown so as to take them all in.

of whose elements speaks a language common to itself with some other nation, is something different from those nations which are defined by a universal or at least a predominant language. We mark it as an exception, as something different from other cases. And when we see how nearly this artificial nation comes, in every point but that of language, to the likeness of those nations which are defined by language, we see that it is a nation defined by language which sets the standard, and after the model of which the artificial nation forms itself. The case of the Swiss Confederation and its claim to rank as a nation would be like the case of those *gentes*, if any such there were, which did not spring even from the expansion of an original family, but which were artificially formed in imitation of those which did, and which, instead of a real or traditional forefather, chose for themselves an adopted one.

In the Swiss Confederation, then, we have a case of a nation formed by an artificial process, but which still is undoubtedly a nation in the face of other nations. We now come to the other class, in which nationality and language keep the connection which they have elsewhere, but in which nations do not even in the roughest way answer to governments. We have only to go into the Eastern lands of Europe to find a state of things in which the notion of nationality, as marked out by language and national feeling, has altogether parted company from the notion of political government. It must be remembered that this state of things is not confined to the nations which are or have lately been under the yoke of the Turk. It extends also to the nations or fragments of nations which make up the

Austro-Hungarian monarchy. In all the lands held by these
two powers we come across phenomena of geography, race, and
language, which stand out in marked contrast with anything to
which we are used in Western Europe. We may perhaps better
understand what those phenomena are, if we suppose a state of
things which sounds absurd in the West, but which has its
exact parallel in many parts of the East. Let us suppose that
in a journey through England we came successively to districts,
towns, or villages, where we found, one after another, first,
Britons speaking Welsh; then Romans speaking Latin; then
Saxons or Angles speaking an older form of our own tongue;
then Scandinavians speaking Danish; then Normans speaking
Old-French; lastly perhaps a settlement of Flemings, Huguenots,
or Palatines, still remaining a distinct people and speaking their
own tongue. Or let us suppose a journey through Northern
France, in which we found at different stages, the original Gaul,
the Roman, the Frank, the Saxon of Bayeux, the Dane of
Coutances, each remaining a distinct people, each of them keeping the tongue which they first brought with them into the land.
Let us suppose further that, in many of these cases, a religious
distinction was added to a national distinction. Let us conceive one village Roman Catholic, another Anglican, others
Nonconformist of various types, even if we do not call up any
remnants of the worshippers of Jupiter or of Woden. All this
seems absurd in any Western country, and absurd enough it is.
But the absurdity of the West is the living reality of the East.
There we may still find all the chief races which have ever
occupied the country, still remaining distinct, still keeping separate tongues, and those for the most part, their own original

tongues. Within the present and late European dominions of the Turk, the original races, those whom we find there at the first beginnings of history, are all there still, and two of them keep their original tongues. They form three distinct nations. First of all there are the Greeks. We have not here to deal with them as the representatives of that branch of the Roman Empire which adopted their speech, but simply as one of the original elements in the population of the Eastern peninsula. Known almost down to our day by their historical name of Romans, they have now fallen back on the name of Hellênes. And to that name they have a perfectly good claim. If the modern Greeks are not all true Hellênes, they are an aggregate of adopted Hellênes gathered round and assimilated to a true Hellenic kernel. Here we see the oldest recorded inhabitants of a large part of the land abiding, and abiding in a very different case from the remnants of the Celt and the Iberian in Western Europe. The Greeks are no survival of a nation ; they are a true and living nation, a nation whose importance is quite out of its proportion to its extent in mere numbers. They still abide, the predominant race in their own ancient and again independent land, the predominant race in those provinces of the continental Turkish dominion which formed part of their ancient land, the predominant race through all the shores and islands of the Ægean and of part of the Euxine also. In near neighborhood to the Greeks still live another race of equal antiquity, the Skipetar or Albanians. These, as I believe is no longer doubted, represent the ancient Illyrians. The exact degree of their ethnical kindred with the Greeks is a scientific question which need not here be considered ; but the facts that

they are more largely intermingled with the Greeks'than any of
the other neighboring nations, that they show a special power of
identifying themselves with the Greeks, a power, so to speak, of
becoming Greeks and making part of the artificial Greek nation,
are matters of practical history. It must never be forgotten,
that among the worthies of the Greek War of Independence, some
of the noblest were not of Hellenic but Albanian blood. The
Orthodox Albanian easily turns into a Greek; and the Mahometan Albanian is something which is broadly distinguished from
a Turk. He has, as he well may have, a strong national feeling,
and that national feeling has sometimes got the better of religious
divisions. If Albania is among the most backward parts of the
peninsula, still it is, by all accounts, the part where there is
most hope of men of different religions joining together against
the common enemy.

Here then are two ancient races, the Greeks and another race,
not indeed so advanced, so important, or so widely spread, but
a race which equally keeps a real national being. There is also
a third ancient race which survives as a distinct people, though
they have for ages adopted a foreign language. These are the
Vlachs or Roumans, the surviving representatives of the great
race, call it Thracian or any other, which at the beginning of
history held the great inland mass of the Eastern peninsula,
with the Illyrians to the west of them and the Greeks to the
south. Every one knows, that in the modern principality of
Roumania and in the adjoining parts of the Austro-Hungarian
monarchy, there is to be seen that phenomenon so unique in the
East, a people who not only, as the Greeks did till lately, still
keep the Roman name, but who speak neither Greek nor Turkish,

neither Slav nor Skipetar, but a dialect of Latin, a tongue akin, not to the tongues of any of their neighbors, but to the tongues of Gaul, Italy, and Spain. And any one who has given any real attention to this matter knows that the same race is to be found, scattered here and there, if in some parts only as wandering shepherds, in the Slavonic, Albanian, and Greek lands south of the Danube. The assumption has commonly been that this outlying Romance people owe their Romance character to the Roman colonization of Dacia under Trajan. In this view, the modern Roumans would be the descendants of Trajan's colonists and of Dacians who had learned of them to adopt the speech and manners of Rome. But when we remember that Dacia was the first Roman province to be given up — that the modern Roumania was for ages the highway of every barbarian tribe on its way from the East to the West — that the land has been conquered and settled and forsaken over and over again, — it would be passing strange if this should be the one land, and its people the one race, to keep the Latin tongue when it has been forgotten in all the neighboring countries. In fact, this idea has been completely dispersed by modern research. The establishment of the Roumans in Dacia is of comparatively recent date, beginning only in the thirteenth century. The Roumans of Wallachia, Moldavia, and Transylvania, are isolated from the scattered Rouman remnant on Pindos and elsewhere. They represent that part of the inhabitants of the peninsula which became Latin, while the Greeks remained Greek, and the Illyrians remained barbarian. Their lands, Mœsia, Thrace specially so called, and Dacia, were added to the empire at various times from Augustus to Trajan. That they should gradually adopt the Latin language is in no sort wonderful. Their position with regard to Rome was exactly the same as that of Gaul and Spain. Where Greek civilization had been firmly established, Latin could nowhere displace it. Where Greek civilization was unknown, Latin overcame the barbarian tongue. It would naturally do so in this part of the East exactly as it did in the West.[1]

Here then we have in the Southeastern peninsula three nations which have all lived on to all appearances from the very beginnings of European history, three distinct nations, speaking three distinct languages. We have nothing answering to this in the West. It needs no proof that the speakers of Celtic and Basque in Gaul and in Spain do not hold the same position in Western Europe which the Greeks, Albanians, and Roumans do in Eastern Europe. In the East the most ancient inhabitants of the land are still there, not as scraps or survivals, not as fragments of nations lingering on in corners, but as nations in the strictest sense, nations whose national being forms an element in every modern and political question. They all have their memories, their grievances, and their hopes; and their memories, their grievances, and their hopes are all of a practical and political kind. Highlanders, Welshmen, Bretons, French Basques, whatever we say of the Spanish brethren, have doubtless memories, but they have hardly political grievances or hopes. Ireland may have political grievances; it certainly has political hopes; but they are not exactly of the same kind as the grievances or hopes of the Greek, the Albanian, and the Rouman. Let Home

---

[1] On Rouman history I have followed Roesler's *Romänische Studien* and Iireck's *Geschichte der Bulgaren.*

Rule succeed to the extent of setting up an independent king and parliament of Ireland, yet the language and civilization of that king and parliament would still be English. Ireland would form an English state, politically hostile, it may be, to Great Britain, but still an English state. No Greek, Albanian, or Rouman state would be in the same way either Turkish or Austrian.

On these primitive and abiding races came, as on other parts of Europe, the Roman conquest. That conquest planted Latin colonies on the Dalmatian coast, where the Latin tongue still remains in its Italian variety as the speech of literature and city life; it Romanized one great part of the earlier inhabitants; it had the great political effect of all, that of planting the Roman power in a Greek city, and thereby creating a state, and in the end a nation, which was Roman on one side, and Greek on the other. Then came the Wandering of the Nations, on which, as regards men of our own race, we need not dwell. The Goths marched at will through the Eastern Empire; but no Teutonic settlement was ever made within its bounds, no lasting Teutonic settlement was ever made even on its border. The part of the Teuton in the West was played, far less perfectly indeed, by the Slav in the East. He is there what the Teuton is here, the great representative of what we may call the modern European races, those whose part in history began after the establishment of the Rouman power. The differences between the position of the two races are chiefly these. The Slav in the East has præ-Roman races standing alongside of him in a way in which the Teuton has not in the West. On the Greeks and Albanians he has had but little influence; on the Rouman and his language

his influence has been far greater, but hardly so great as the Influence of the Teuton on the Romance nations and languages
of Western Europe. The Slav too stands alongside of races
which have come in since his own coming, in a way in which the
Teuton in the West is still further from doing. That is to say,
besides Greeks, Albanians, and Roumans, he stands alongside
of Bulgarians, Magyars, and Turks, who have nothing to answer
to them in the West. The Slav, in the time of his coming, in
the nature of his settlement, answers roughly to the Teuton; his
position is what that of the Teuton would be, if Western Europe
had been brought under the power of an alien race at some time
later than his own settlement. The Slavs undoubtedly form the
greatest element in the population of the Eastern peninsula, and
they once reached more widely still. Taking the Slavonic name
in its widest meaning, they occupy all the lands from the Danube
and its great tributaries southward to the strictly Greek border.
The exceptions are where earlier races remain, Greek or Italian
on the coast-line, Albanian in the mountains. The Slavs hold
the heart of the peninsula, and they hold more than the peninsula itself. The Slav lives equally on both sides of what is or was
the frontier of the Austrian and Ottoman empires; indeed, but
for another set of causes which have affected Eastern Europe,
the Slav might have reached uninterruptedly from the Baltic to
the Ægean.

This last set of causes are those which specially distinguish
the histories of Eastern and of Western Europe; a set of causes
which, though exactly twelve hundred years old,[1] are still fresh

---

[1] It should be remembered that, as the year 1879 saw the beginning of the liberated Bulgarian state, the year 679 saw the beginning of the first Bulgarian kingdom
south of the Danube.

and living, and which are the special causes which have aggravated the special difficulties of the last five hundred years. In
Western Europe, though we have had plenty of political conquests, we have had no national migrations since the days of the
Teutonic settlements — at least, if we may extend these last so
as to take in the Scandinavian settlements in Britain and Gaul.
The Teuton has pressed to the East at the expense of the Slav
and the Old-Prussian : the borders between the Romance and
the Teutonic nations in the West have fluctuated; but no third
set of nations has come in, strange alike to the Roman and the
Teuton and to the whole Aryan family. As the Huns of Attila
showed themselves in Western Europe as passing ravagers, so
did the Magyars at a later day; so did the Ottoman Turks in a
day later still, when they besieged Vienna and laid waste the
Venetian mainland. But all these Turanian invaders appeared
in Western Europe simply as passing invaders; in Eastern
Europe their part has been widely different. Besides the temporary dominion of Avars, Patzinaks, Chazars, Cumans, and a
crowd of others, three bodies of more abiding settlers, the Bulgarians, the Magyars, and the Mongol conquerors of Russia,
have come in by one path; a fourth, the Ottoman Turks, have
come in by another path. Among all these invasions we have
one case of thorough assimilation, and only one. The original
Finnish Bulgarians have, like Western conquerors, been lost
among Slavonic subjects and neighbors. The geographical
function of the Magyar has been to keep the two. great groups
of Slavonic nations apart. To his coming, more than to any
other cause, we may attribute the great historical gap which
separates the Slav of the Baltic from his southern kinsfolk. The

work of the Ottoman Turk we all know. These latter settlers remain alongside of the Slav, just as the Slav remains alongside of the earlier settlers. The Slavonized Bulgarians are the only instance of assimilation such as we are used to in the West. All the other races, old and new, from the Albanian to the Ottoman, are still there, each keeping its national being and its national speech. And in one part of the ancient Dacia we must add quite a distinct element, the element of Teutonic occupation in a form unlike any in which we see it in the West, in the shape of the Saxons of Transylvania.

We have thus worked out our point in detail. While in each Western country some one of the various races which have settled in it has, speaking roughly, assimilated the others, in the lands which are left under the rule of the Turk, or which have been lately delivered from his rule, all the races that have ever settled in the country still abide side by side. So when we pass into the lands which form the Austro-Hungarian monarchy, we find that that composite dominion is just as much opposed as the dominion of the Turk is to those ideas of nationality toward which Western Europe has been long feeling its way. We have seen by the example of Switzerland that it is possible to make an artificial nation out of fragments which have split off from three several nations. But the Austro-Hungarian monarchy is not a nation, not even an artificial nation of this kind. Its elements are not bound together in the same way as the three elements of the Swiss Confederation. It does indeed contain one whole nation in the form of the Magyars; we might say that it contains two, if we reckon the Czechs for a distinct nation. Of its other elements, we may for the moment set aside

those parts of Germany which are so strangely united with the
crowns of Hungary and Dalmatia. In those parts of the monarchy which come within the more strictly Eastern lands — the
Roman and the *Rouman*, — we may so distinguish the Romance-
speaking inhabitants of Dalmatia and the Romance-speaking
inhabitants of Transylvania. The Slav of the north and of the
south, the Magyar conqueror, the Saxon immigrant, all abide as
distinct races. That the Ottoman is not to be added to our list
in Hungary, while he is to be added in lands farther south, is
simply because he has been driven out of Hungary, while he is
allowed to abide in lands farther south. No point is more
important to insist on now than the fact that the Ottoman once
held the greater part of Hungary by exactly the same right, the
right of the strongest, as that by which he still holds Macedonia
and Epeiros. It is simply the result of a century of warfare,
from Sobieski to Joseph the Second, which fixed the boundary
which only yesterday seemed eternal to diplomatists, but which
now seems to have vanished. That boundary has advanced and
gone back over and over again. As Buda once was Turkish,
Belgrade has more than once been Austrian. The whole of the
southeastern lands, Austrian, Turkish, and independent, from
the Carpathian Mountains southward, present the same characteristic of permanence and distinctness among the several races
which occupy them. The several races may lie, here in large
continuous masses, there in small detached settlements; but
there they all are in their distinctness. There is among them
plenty of living and active national feeling; but while in the
West, political arrangements for the most part follow the great
lines of national feeling, in the East the only way in which

national feeling can show itself is by protesting, whether in arms or otherwise, against existing political arrangements. Save the Magyars alone, the ruling race in the Hungarian kingdom, there is no case in those lands in which the whole continuous territory inhabited by speakers of the same tongue is placed under a separate national government of its own. And, even in this case, the identity between nation and government is imperfect in two ways. It is imperfect, because, after all, though Hungary has a separate national government in internal matters, yet it is not the Hungarian kingdom, but the Austro-Hungarian monarchy of which it forms a part, which counts as a power among the other powers of Europe. And the national character of the Hungarian government is equally imperfect from the other side. It is national as regards the Magyar; it is not national as regards the Slav, the Saxon, and the Rouman. Since the liberation of part of Bulgaria, no whole European nation is under the rule of the Turk. No one nation of the Southeast peninsula forms a single national government. One fragment of a nation is free under a national government, another fragment is ruled by civilized strangers, a third is trampled down by barbarians. The existing states of Greece, Roumania, and Servia are far from taking in the whole of the Greek, Rouman, and Servian nations. In all these lands, Austrian, Turkish, and independent, there is no difficulty in marking off the several nations; only in no case do the nations answer to any existing political power.

In all these cases, where nationality and government are altogether divorced, language becomes yet more distinctly the test of nationality than it is in Western lands where nationality and government do to some extent coincide. And when nationality and language do not coincide in the East, it is owing to another cause, of which also we know nothing in the West. In many cases religion takes the place of nationality; or rather the ideas of religion and nationality can hardly be distinguished. In the West a man's nationality is in no way affected by the religion which he professes, or even by his change from one religion to another. In the East it is otherwise. The Christian renegade who embraces Islam becomes for most practical purposes a Turk. Even if, as in Crete and Bosnia, he keeps his Greek or Slavonic language, he remains Greek or Slav only in a secondary sense. For the first principle of the Mahometan religion, the lordship of the true believer over the infidel, cuts off the possibility of any true national fellowship between the true believer and the infidel. Even the Greek or Armenian who embraces the Latin creed goes far toward parting with his nationality as well as with his religion. For the adoption of the Latin creed implies what is in some sort the adoption of a new allegiance, the accepting of the authority of the Roman Bishop. In the Armenian indeed we are come very near to the phenomena of the further East, where names like Parsee and Hindoo, names in themselves as strictly ethnical as Englishman or Frenchman, have come to express distinctions in which religion and nationality are absolutely the same thing. Of this whole class of phenomena the Jew is of course the crowning example. But we speak of these matters here only as bringing in an element in the definition of nationality to which we are unused in the West. But it quite comes within our present subject to give one definition from the Southeastern lands. What is the Greek? Clearly he who is at once a Greek in speech and

Orthodox in faith. The Hellenic Mussulmans in Crete, even the Hellenic Latins in some of the other islands, are at the most imperfect members of the Hellenic body. The utmost that can be said is that they keep the power of again entering that body, either by their own return to the national faith, or by such a change in the state of things as shall make difference in religion no longer inconsistent with true national fellowship.

Thus, wherever we go, we find language to be the rough practical test of nationality. The exceptions are many; they may perhaps outnumber the instances which conform to the rule. Still they are exceptions. Community of language does not imply community of blood; it might be added that diversity of language does not imply diversity of blood. But community of language is, in the absence of any evidence to the contrary, a presumption of the community of blood, and it is proof of something which for practical purposes is the same as community of blood. To talk of "the Latin race," is in strictness absurd. We know that the so called race is simply made up of those nations which adopted the Latin language. The Celtic, Teutonic, and Slavonic races may conceivably have been formed by a like artificial process. But the presumption is the other way; and if such a process ever took place, it took place long before history began. The Celtic, Teutonic, and Slavonic races come before us as groups of mankind marked out by the test of language. Within those races separate nations are again marked out by a stricter application of the test of language. Within the race we may have languages which are clearly akin to each other, but which need not be mutually intelligible. Within the nation we have only dialects which are mutually intelligible, or which, at all events, gather round some one central dialect which is intelligible to all. We take this standard of races and nations, fully aware that it will not stand a physiological test, but holding that for all practical purposes adoption must pass as equivalent to natural descent. And, among the practical purposes which are affected by the facts of race and nationality, we must, as long as a man is what he is, as long as he has not been created afresh according to some new scientific pattern, not shrink from reckoning those generous emotions which, in the present state of European feeling, are beginning to bind together the greater as well as the lesser groups of mankind. The sympathies of men are beginning to reach wider than could have dreamed of a century ago. The feeling which was once confined to the mere household extended itself to the tribe or the city. From the tribe or city it extended itself to the nation; from the nation it is beginning to extend itself to the whole race. In some cases it can extend itself to the whole race far more easily than in others. In some cases historical causes have made nations of the same race bitter enemies, while they have made nations of different races friendly allies. The same thing happened in earlier days between tribes and cities of the same nation. But, when hindrances of this kind do not exist, the feeling of race, as something beyond the narrower feeling of nationality, is beginning to be a powerful agent in the feelings and actions of men and of nations. A long series of mutual wrongs, conquest, and oppression on one side, avenged by conquest and oppression on the other side, have made the Slav of Poland and the Slav of Russia the bitterest of enemies. No such hindrance exists to stop the flow of natural and generous feeling between the Slav of Russia and the Slav of the Southeastern lands. Those whose statesmanship consists in some hand-to-mouth shift for the moment, whose wisdom consists in refusing to look either back to the past or onward to the future, cannot understand this great fact of our times; and what they cannot understand they mock at. But the fact exists and does its work in spite of them. And it does its work none the less because in some cases the feeling of sympathy is awakened by a claim of kindred, where, in the sense of the physiologist or the genealogist, there is no kindred at all. The practical view, historical or political, will accept as members of this or that race or nation many members whom the physiologist would shut out, whom the English lawyer would shut out, but whom the Roman lawyer would gladly welcome to every privilege of the stock on which they were grafted. The line of the Scipios, of the Cæsars, and of the Antonines, was continued by adoption; and for all practical purposes the nations of the earth have agreed to follow the examples set them by their masters.

KIN BEYOND SEA.*

By WILLIAM EWART GLADSTONE.
(Born 1809.)

"When Love unites, wide space divides in vain,
And hands may clasp across the spreading main."

T is now nearly half a century since the works of De Tocqueville and De Beaumont, founded upon personal observation, brought the institutions of the United States effectually within the circle of European thought and interest. They were co-operators, but not upon an equal scale. De Beaumont belongs to the class of ordinary, though able, writers : De Tocqueville was the Burke of his age, and his treatise upon America may well be regarded as among the best books hitherto produced for the political student of all times and countries.

But higher and deeper than the concern of the Old World at large in the thirteen colonies, now grown into thirty-eight States, besides eight Territories, is the special interest of England in their condition and prospects.

---

* Published in the *North American Review* for September, 1878. Republished by permission.

I do not speak of political controversies between them and us, which are happily, as I trust, at an end. I do not speak of the vast contribution which, from year to year, through the operations of a colossal trade, each makes to the wealth and comfort of the other; nor of the friendly controversy, which in its own place it might be well to raise, between the leanings of America to Protectionism, and the more daring reliance of the old country upon free and unrestricted intercourse with all the world. Nor of the menace which, in the prospective development of her resources, America offers to the commercial preeminence of England.[1] On this subject I will only say that it is she alone who, at a coming time, can, and probably will, wrest from us that commercial primacy. We have no title, I have no inclination, to murmur at the prospect. If she acquires it, she will make the acquisition by the right of the strongest; but, in this instance, the strongest means the best. She will probably become what we are now, the head servant in the great household of the world, the employer of all employed; because her service will be the most and ablest. We have no more title against her, than Venice, or Genoa, or Holland has had against us. One great duty is entailed upon us, which we, unfortunately, neglect: the duty of preparing, by a resolute and sturdy effort, to reduce our public burdens, in preparation for a day when we

---

1 [This topic was much more largely handled by me in the Financial Statement which I delivered, as Chancellor of the Exchequer, on May 2, 1866. I recommend attention to the excellent article by Mr. Henderson, in the *Contemporary Review* for October, 1878: and I agree with the author in being disposed to think that the protective laws of America effectually bar the full development of her competing power. — W. E. G., Nov. 6, 1878.]

shall probably have less capacity than we have now to bear them.

Passing by all these subjects, with their varied attractions, I come to another, which lies within the tranquil domain of political philosophy. The students of the future, in this department, will have much to say in the way of comparison between American and British institutions. The relationship between these two is unique in history. It is always interesting to trace and to compare Constitutions, as it is to compare languages ; especially in such instances as those of the Greek States and the Italian Republics, or the diversified forms of the feudal system in the different countries of Europe. But there is no parallel in all the records of the world to the case of that prolific British mother, who has sent forth her innumerable children over all the earth to be the founders of half-a-dozen empires. She, with her progeny, may almost claim to constitute a kind of Universal Church in politics. But, among these children, there is one whose place in the world's eye and in history is superlative : it is the American Republic. She is the eldest born. She has, taking the capacity of her land into view as well as its mere measurement, a natural base for the greatest continuous empire ever established by man. And it may be well here to mention what has not always been sufficiently observed, that the distinction between continuous empire, and empire severed and dispersed over sea, is vital. The development, which the Republic has effected, has been unexampled in its rapidity and force. While other countries have doubled, or at most trebled, their population, she has risen, during one single century of freedom, in round numbers, from two millions to forty-five. As to riches, it is reasonable to establish, from the decennial stages of the progress thus far achieved, a series for the future; and, reckoning upon this basis, I suppose that the very next census, in the year 1880, will exhibit her to the world as certainly the wealthiest of all the nations. The huge figure of a thousand millions sterling, which may be taken roundly as the annual income of the United Kingdom, has been reached at a surprising rate; a rate which may perhaps be best expressed by saying, that if we could have started forty or fifty years ago from zero, at the rate of our recent annual increment, we should now have reached our present position. But while we have been advancing with this portentous rapidity, America is passing us by as if in a canter. Yet even now the work of searching the soil and the bowels of the territory, and opening out her enterprise throughout its vast expanse, is in its infancy. The England and the America of the present are probably the two strongest nations of the world. But there can hardly be a doubt, as between the America and the England of the future, that the daughter, at some no very distant time, will, whether fairer or less fair, be unquestionably yet stronger than the mother.

" O matre forti filia fortior."[1]

But all this pompous detail of material triumphs, whether for the one or for the other, is worse than idle, unless the men of the two countries shall remain, or shall become, greater than the mere things that they produce, and shall know how to regard those things simply as tools and materials for the attainments of the highest purposes of their being. Ascending, then, from the

---

[1] See Hor., Od. I., 16.

ground-floor of material industry toward the regions in which these purposes are to be wrought out, it is for each nation to consider how far its institutions have reached a state in which they can contribute their maximum to the store of human happiness and excellence. And for the political student all over the world, it will be beyond any thing curious as well as useful to examine with what diversities, as well as what resemblances, of apparatus the two greater branches of a race born to command have been minded, or induced, or constrained to work out, in their sea-severed seats, their political destinies according to the respective laws appointed for them.

No higher ambition can find vent in a paper such as this, than to suggest the position and claims of the subject, and slightly to indicate a few outlines, or, at least, fragments, of the working material.

In many and the most fundamental respects the two still carry in undiminished, perhaps in increasing, clearness, the notes of resemblance that beseem a parent and a child. .

Both wish for self-government; and, however grave the drawbacks under which in one or both it exists, the two have, among the great nations of the world, made the most effectual advances toward the true aim of rational politics.

They are similarly associated in their fixed idea that the force, in which all government takes effect, is to be constantly backed, and, as it were, illuminated, by thought in speech and writing. The ruler of St. Paul's time " bare the sword " (Rom. xiii : 4). Bare it, as the Apostle says, with a mission to do right ; but he says nothing of any duty, or any custom, to show by reason that he was doing right. Our two governments, whatsoever they do, have to give reasons for it; not reasons which will convince the unreasonable, but reasons which on the whole will convince the average mind, and carry it unitedly forward in a course of action, often, though not always, wise, and carrying within itself provisions, where it is unwise, for the correction or its own unwisdom before it grow into an intolerable rankness. They are governments, not of force only, but of persuasion.

Many more are the concords, and not less vital than these, of the two nations, as expressed in their institutions. They alike prefer the practical to the abstract. They tolerate opinion, with only a reserve on behalf of decency; and they desire to confine coercion to the province of action, and to leave thought, as such, entirely free. They set a high value on liberty for its own sake. They desire to give full scope to the principle of self-reliance in the people, and they deem self-help to be immeasurably superior to help in any other form; to be the only help, in short, which ought not to be continually, or periodically, put upon its trial, and required to make good its title. They mistrust and mislike the centralization of power; and they cherish municipal, local, even parochial liberties, as nursery grounds, not only for the production here and there of able men, but for the general training of public virtue and independent spirit. They regard publicity as the vital air of politics; through which alone, in its freest circulation, opinions can be thrown into common stock for the good of all, and the balance of relative rights and claims can be habitually and peaceably adjusted. It would be difficult in the case of any other pair of nations, to present an assemblage of traits at once so common and so distinctive, as has been given in this probably imperfect enumeration.

There were, however, the strongest reasons why America could not grow into a reflection or repetition of England. Passing from a narrow island to a continent almost without bounds, the colonists at once and vitally altered their conditions of thought as well as of existence, in relation to the most important and most operative of all social facts, the possession of the soil. In England, inequality lies embedded in the very base of the social structure; in America it is a late, incidental, unrecognized product, not of tradition, but of industry and wealth, as they advance with various and, of necessity, unequal steps. Heredity, seated as an idea in the heart's core of Englishmen, and sustaining far more than it is sustained by those of our institutions which express it, was as truly absent from the intellectual and moral store, with which the colonists traversed the Atlantic, as if it had been some forgotten article in the bills of lading that made up their cargoes. Equality combined with liberty, and renewable at each descent from one generation to another, like a lease with stipulated breaks, was the groundwork of their social creed. In vain was it sought, by arrangements such as those connected with the name of Baltimore or of Penn, to qualify the action of those overpowering forces which so determined the case. Slavery itself, strange as it now may seem, failed to impair the theory however it may have imported into the practice a hideous solecism. No hardier republicanism was generated in New England than in the Slave States of the South, which produced so many of the great statesmen of America.

It may be said that the North, and not the South, had the larger number of colonists; and was the centre of those commanding moral influences which gave to the country as a whole its political and moral atmosphere. The type and form of manhood for America was supplied neither by the Recusant in Maryland, nor by the Cavalier in Virginia, but by the Puritan of New England; and it would have been a form and type widely different could the colonization have taken place a couple of centuries, or a single century, sooner. Neither the Tudor, nor even the Plantagenet period, could have supplied its special form. The Reformation was a cardinal factor in its production; and this in more ways than one.

Before that great epoch, the political forces of the country were represented on the whole by the monarch on one side, and the people on the other. In the people, setting aside the latent vein of Lollardism, there was a general homogeneity with respect to all that concerned the relation of governors and governed. In the deposition of sovereigns, the resistance to abuses, the establishment of institutions for the defence of liberty, there were no two parties to divide the land. But, with the Reformation, a new dualism was sensibly developed among us. Not a dualism so violent as to break up the national unity, but yet one so marked and substantial, that thenceforward it was very difficult for any individual or body of men to represent the entire English character, and the old balance of its forces. The wrench which severed the Church and people from the Roman obedience left for domestic settlement thereafter a tremendous internal question, between the historical and the new, which in its milder form perplexes us to this day. Except during the short reign of Edward VI, the civil power, in various methods and degrees, took what may be termed the traditionary side, and favored the development of the historical more than the individual aspect of the national religion. These elements confronted one another during the reigns of the earlier Stuarts, not only with obstinacy but with fierceness. There had grown up with the Tudors, from a variety of causes, a great exaggeration of the idea of royal power; and this arrived, under James I and Charles I, at a rank maturity. Not less, but even more masculine and determined, was the converse development. Mr. Hallam saw, and has said, that at the outbreak of the Great Rebellion, the old British Constitution was in danger, not from one party but from both. In that mixed fabric had once been harmonized the ideas, both of religious duty, and of allegiance as related to it, which were now held in severance. The hardiest and dominating portion of the American colonists represented that severance in its extremest form, and had dropped out of the order of the ideas, which they carried across the water, all those elements of political Anglicism, which give to aristocracy in this country a position only second in strength to that of freedom. State and Church alike had frowned upon them; and their strong reaction was a reaction of their entire nature, alike of the spiritual and the secular man. All that was democratic in the policy of England, and all that was Protestant in her religion, they carried with them, in pronounced and exclusive forms, to a soil and a scene singularly suited for their growth.

It is to the honor of the British Monarchy that, upon the whole, it frankly recognized the facts, and did not pedantically endeavor to constrain by artificial and alien limitations the growth of the infant states. It is a thing to be remembered that the accusations of the colonies in 1776 were entirely levelled at the king actually on the throne, and that a general acquittal was thus given by them to every preceding reign. Their infancy had been upon the whole what their manhood was to be, self-governed and republican. Their Revolution, as we call it, was like ours in the main, a vindication of liberties inherited and possessed. It was a Conservative revolution ; and the happy result was that, notwithstanding the sharpness of the collision with the mother-country, and with domestic loyalism, the Thirteen Colonies made provision for their future in conformity, as to all that determined life and manners with the recollections of their past. The two Constitutions of the two countries express indeed rather the differences than the resemblances of the nations. The one is a thing grown, the other a thing made ; the one a *praxis*, the other a *poiesis :* the one the offspring of tendency and indeterminate time, the other of choice and of an epoch. But, as the British Constitution is the most subtle organism which has proceeded from the womb and the long gestation of progressive history, so the American Constitution is, so-far as I can see, the most wonderful work ever struck off at a given time by the brain and purpose of man. It has had a century of trial, under the pressure of exigencies caused by an expansion unexampled in point of rapidity and range : and its exemption from formal change, though not entire, has certainly proved the sagacity of the constructors, and the stubborn strength of the fabric.

One whose life has been greatly absorbed in working, with others, the institutions of his own country, has not had the opportunities necessary for the careful and searching scrutiny of institutions elsewhere. I should feel, in looking at those of

America, like one who attempts to scan the stars with the naked eye. My notices can only be few, faint, and superficial; they are but an introduction to what I have to say of the land of my birth. A few sentences will dispose of them.

₁∴ America, whose attitude toward England has always been masculine and real, has no longer to anticipate at our hands the frivolous and offensive criticisms which were once in vogue among us. But neither nation prefers (and it would be an ill sign if either did prefer) the institutions of the other; and we certainly do not contemplate the great Republic in the spirit of mere optimism. We see that it has a marvellous and unexampled adaptation for its peculiar vocation; that it must be judged, not in the abstract, but under the fore-ordered laws of its existence; that it has purged away the blot with which we brought it into the world; that it gravely and vigorously grapples with the problem of making a continent into a state; and that it treasures with fondness the traditions of British antiquity, which are in truth unconditionally its own, as well, and as much as they are ours. The thing that perhaps chiefly puzzles the inhabitants of the old country is why the American people should permit their entire existence to be continually disturbed by the business of the Presidential elections; and, still more, why they should raise to its maximum the intensity of this perturbation by providing, as we are told, for what is termed a clean sweep of the entire civil service, in all its ranks and departments, on each accession of a chief magistrate. We do not perceive why this arrangement is more rational than would be a corresponding usage in this country on each change of Ministry. Our practice is as different as possible. We limit to a few scores of persons the removals and appointments on these occasions; although our Ministries seem to us, not unfrequently, to be more sharply severed from one another in principle and tendency than are the successive Presidents of the great Union.

It would be out of place to discuss in this article occasional phenomena of local corruption in the United States, by which the nation at large can hardly be touched : or the mysterious manipulations of votes for the Presidency, which are now understood to be under examination ; or the very curious influences which are shaping the politics of the negroes and of the South. These last are corollaries to the great slave-question : and it seems very possible that after a few years we may see most of the laborers, both in the Southern States and in England, actively addicted to the political support of that section of their countrymen who to the last had resisted their emancipation.

But if there be those in this country who think that American democracy means public levity and intemperance, or a lack of skill and sagacity in politics, or the absence of self-command and self-denial, let them bear in mind a few of the most salient and recent facts of history which may profitably be recommended to their reflections. We emancipated a million of negroes by peaceful legislation ; America liberated four or five millions by a bloody civil war : yet the industry and exports of the Southern States are maintained, while those of our negro colonies have dwindled ; the South enjoys all its franchises, but we have, *proh pudor !* found no better method of providing for peace and order in Jamaica, the chief of our islands, than by the hard and vulgar, even where needful, expedient of abolishing entirely its representative institutions.

The Civil War compelled the States, both North and South, to train and embody a million and a half of men, and to present to view the greatest, instead of the smallest, armed forces in the world. Here there was supposed to arise a double danger. First, that on a sudden cessation of the war, military life and habits could not be shaken off, and, having become rudely and widely predominant, would bias the country toward an aggressive policy, or, still worse, would find vent in predatory or revolutionary operations. Secondly, that a military caste would grow up with its habits of exclusiveness and command, and would influence the tone of politics in a direction adverse to republican freedom. But both apprehensions proved to be wholly imaginary. The innumerable soldiery was at once dissolved. Cincinnatus, no longer an unique example, became the commonplace of every day, the type and mould of a nation. The whole enormous mass quietly resumed the habits of social life. The generals of yesterday were the editors, the secretaries, and the solicitors of to-day. The just jealousy of the State gave life to the now forgotten maxim of Judge Blackstone, who denounced as perilous the erection of a separate profession of arms in a free country. The standing army, expanded by the heat of civil contest to gigantic dimensions, settled down again into the framework of a miniature with the returning temperature of civil life, and became a power well-nigh invisible, from its minuteness, amidst the powers which sway the movements of a society exceeding forty millions.

More remarkable still was the financial sequel to the great conflict. The internal taxation for Federal purposes, which before its commencement had been unknown, was raised, in

obedience to an exigency of life and death, so as to exceed
every present and every past example. It pursued and worried
all the transactions of life. The interest of the American debt
grew to be the highest in the world, and the capital touched five
hundred and sixty millions sterling. Here was provided for the
faith and patience of the people a touchstone of extreme severity.
In England, at the close of the great French war, the propertied
classes, who were supreme in Parliament, at once rebelled
against the Tory Government, and refused to prolong the income
tax even for a single year. We talked big, both then and now,
about the payment of our national debt; but sixty-three years
have since elapsed, all of them except two called years of peace,
and we have reduced the huge total by about one ninth; that is
to say, by little over one hundred millions, or scarcely more than
one million and a half a year. This is the conduct of a State
elaborately digested into orders and degrees, famed for wisdom
and forethought, and consolidated by a long experience. But
America continued long to bear, on her unaccustomed and still
smarting shoulders, the burden of the war taxation. In twelve
years she has reduced her debt by one hundred and fifty-eight
millions sterling, or at the rate of thirteen millions for every
year. In each twelve months she has done what we did in eight
years; her self-command, self-denial, and wise forethought for
the future have been, to say the least, eightfold ours. These are
facts which redound greatly to her honor; and the historian will
record with surprise that an enfranchised nation tolerated burdens which in this country a selected class, possessed of the
representation, did not dare to face, and that the most unmiti-
gated democracy known to the annals of the world resolutely

reduced at its own cost prospective liabilities of the State, which the aristocratic, and plutocratic, and monarchical government of the United Kingdom has been contented ignobly to hand over to posterity. And such facts should be told out. It is our fashion so to tell them, against as well as for ourselves; and the record of them may some day be among the means of stirring us up to a policy more worthy of the name and fame of England.

It is true, indeed, that we lie under some heavy and, I fear, increasing disadvantages, which amount almost to disabilities. Not, however, any disadvantage respecting power, as power is commonly understood. But, while America has a nearly homogeneous country, and an admirable division of political labor between the States individually and the Federal Government, we are, in public affairs, an overcharged and overweighted people.[1] We have undertaken the cares of empire upon a scale, and with a diversity, unexampled in history; and, as it has not yet pleased Providence to endow us with brain-force and animal strength in an equally abnormal proportion, the consequence is that we perform the work of government, as to many among its more important departments, in a very superficial and slovenly manner. The affairs of the three associated kingdoms, with their great diversities of law, interest, and circumstance, make the government of them, even if they stood alone, a business more voluminous, so to speak, than that of any other thirty-three millions of civilized men. To lighten the cares of the central legislature by judicious devolution, it is probable that much

---

[1] [This subject has been more fully developed by me in an article on "England's Mission," contributed to *The Nineteenth Century* for September of the present year. — W. E. G., December, 1878.]

might be done; but nothing is done, or even attempted to be done. The greater colonies have happily attained to a virtual self-government; yet the aggregate mass of business connected with our colonial possessions continues to be very large. The Indian Empire is of itself a charge so vast, and demanding so much thought and care, that if it were the sole transmarine appendage to the crown, it would amply tax the best ordinary stock of human energies. Notoriously it obtains from the Parliament only a small fraction of the attention it deserves. Questions affecting individuals, again, or small interests, or classes, excite here a greater interest, and occupy a larger share of time, than, perhaps, in any other community. In no country, I may add, are the interests of persons or classes so favored when they compete with those of the public; and in none are they more exacting, or more wakeful to turn this advantage to the best account. With the vast extension of our enterprise and our trade, comes a breadth of liability not less large, to consider every thing that is critical in the affairs of foreign states; and the real responsibilities thus existing for us, are unnaturally inflated for us by fast-growing tendencies toward exaggeration of our concern in these matters, and even toward setting up fictitious interests in cases where none can discern them except ourselves, and such continental friends as practice upon our credulity and our fears for purposes of their own. Last of all, it is not to be denied that in what I have been saying, I do not represent the public sentiment. The nation is not at all conscious of being overdone. The people see that their House of Commons is the hardest-working legislative assembly in the world: and, this being so, they assume it is all right.

Nothing pays better, in point of popularity, than those gratui-
tous additions to obligations already beyond human strength,
which look like accessions or assertion of power; such as the
annexation of new territory, or the silly transaction known as
the purchase of shares in the Suez Canal.

All my life long I have seen this excess of work as compared
with the power to do it; but the evil has increased with the
surfeit of wealth, and there is no sign that the increase is near
its end. The people of this country are a very strong people;
but there is no strength that can permanently endure, without
provoking inconvenient consequences, this kind of political
debauch. It may be hoped, but it cannot be predicted, that the
mischief will be encountered and subdued at the point where it
will have become sensibly troublesome, but will not have grown
to be quite irremediable.

The main and central point of interest, however, in the institutions of a country is the manner in which it draws together
and compounds the public forces in the balanced action of the
State. It seems plain that the formal arrangements for this
purpose in America are very different from ours. It may even
be a question whether they are not, in certain respects, less
popular; whether our institutions do not give more rapid effect,
than those of the Union, to any formed opinion, and resolved
intention, of the nation.

In the formation of the Federal Government we seem to
perceive three stages of distinct advancement. First, the formation of the Confederation, under the pressure of the War of
Independence. Secondly, the Constitution, which placed the
Federal Government in defined and direct relation with the

people inhabiting the several States. Thirdly, the struggle with the South, which for the first time, and definitely, decided that to the Union, through its Federal organization, and not to the State governments, were reserved all the questions not decided and disposed of by the express provisions of the Constitution itself.[1] The great *arcanum imperii*, which with us belongs to the three branches of the Legislature, and which is expressed by the current phrase, "omnipotence of Parliament," thus became the acknowledged property of the three branches of the Federal Legislature; and the old and respectable doctrine of State independence is now no more than an archæological relic, a piece of historical antiquarianism. Yet the actual attributions of the State authorities cover by far the largest part of the province of government; and by this division of labor and authority, the problem of fixing for the nation a political centre of gravity is divested of a large part of its difficulty and danger, in some proportions to the limitations of the working precinct.

Within that precinct, the initiation as well as the final sanction in the great business of finance is made over to the popular branch of the Legislature, and a most interesting question arises upon the comparative merits of this arrangement, and of our

---

[1] [This is a proposition of great importance in a disputed subject-matter; and consequently I have not announced it in a dogmatic manner, but as a portion of what we "seem to perceive" in the progress of the American Constitution. It expresses an opinion formed by me upon an examination of the original documents, and with some attention to the history, which I have always considered, and have often recommended to others, as one of the most fruitful studies of modern politics. This is not the proper occasion to develop its grounds: but I may say that I am not at all disposed to surrender it in deference to one or two rather contemptuous critics. — W. E. G., December, 1868.]

own method, which theoretically throws upon the Crown the responsibility of initiating public charge, and under which, until a recent period, our practice was in actual and even close correspondence with this theory.

We next come to a difference still more marked. The Federal Executive is born anew of the nation at the end of each four years, and dies at the end. But, during the course of those years, it is independent, in the person both of the President and of his Ministers, alike of the people, of their representatives, and of that remarkable body, the most remarkable of all the inventions of modern politics, the Senate of the United States. In this important matter, whatever be the relative excellencies and defects of the British and American systems, it is most certain that nothing would induce the people of this country, or even the Tory portion of them, to exchange our own for theirs. It may, indeed, not be obvious to the foreign eye what is the exact difference of the two. Both the representative chambers hold the power of the purse. But in America its conditions are such that it does not operate in any way on behalf of the Chamber or of the nation, as against the Executive. In England, on the contrary, its efficiency has been such that it has worked out for itself channels of effective operation, such as to dispense with its direct use, and avoid the inconveniences which might be attendant upon that use. A vote of the House of Commons, declaring a withdrawal of its confidence, has always sufficed for the purpose of displacing a Ministry; nay, persistent obstruction of its measures, and even lighter causes, have conveyed the hint, which has been obediently taken. But the people, how is it with them? Do not the people in England part with their power, and make it over to the House of Commons, as completely as the American people part with it to the President? They give it over for four years : we for a period which on the average is somewhat more : they, to resume it at a fixed time ; we, on an unfixed contingency, and at a time which will finally be determined, not according to the popular will, but according to the views which a Ministry may entertain of its duty or convenience.

All this is true; but it is not the whole truth. In the United Kingdom, the people as such cannot commonly act upon the Ministry as such. But mediately, though not immediately, they gain the end : for they can work upon that which works upon the Ministry, namely, on the House of Commons. Firstly, they have not renounced, like the American people, the exercise of their power for a given time; and they are at all times free by speech, petition, public meeting, to endeavor to get it back in full by bringing about a dissolution. Secondly, in a Parliament with nearly 660 members, vacancies occur with tolerable frequency ; and, as they are commonly filled up forthwith, they continually modify the color of the Parliament, conformably, not to the past, but to the present feeling of the nation ; or, at least, of the constituency, which for practical purposes is different indeed, yet not very different. But, besides exercising a limited positive influence on the present, they supply a much less limited indication of the future. Of the members who at a given time sit in the House of Commons, the vast majority, probably more than nine-tenths, have the desire to sit there again, after a dissolution which may come at any moment. They therefore study political weather-wisdom, and in varying degrees adapt them-

selves to the indications of the sky. It will now be readily
perceived how the popular sentiment in England, so far as it is
awake, is not meanly provided with the ways of making itself
respected, whether for the purpose of displacing and replacing
a Ministry, or of constraining it (as sometimes happens) to alter
or reverse its policy sufficiently, at least, to conjure down the
gathering and muttering storm.

It is true, indeed, that every nation is of necessity, to a great
extent, in the condition of the sluggard with regard to public
policy ; hard to rouse, harder to keep aroused, sure after a little
while to sink back into his slumber : —

> " Pressitigue jacentem,
> Dulcis et alta quies, placidæque simillima morti."
> — *Æn.,* vi, 522.

The people have a vast, but an encumbered power; and, in
their struggles with overweaning authority, or with property, the
excess of force, which they undoubtedly possess, is more than
counterbalanced by the constant wakefulness of the adversary,
by his knowledge of their weakness, and by his command of
opportunity. But this is a fault lying rather in the conditions of
human life than in political institutions. There is no known
mode of making attention and inattention equal in their results.
It is enough to say that in England, when the nation can attend,
it can prevail. So we may say, then, that in the American
Union the Federal Executive is independent for each four years
both of the Congress and of the people. But the British Ministry is largely dependent on the people whenever the people
firmly will it; and is always dependent on the House of Commons, except of course when it can safely and effectually appeal
to the people.

So far, so good. But if we wish really to understand the manner in which the Queen's Government over the British Empire is carried on, we must now prepare to examine into some sharper contrasts than any which our path has yet brought into view. The power of the American Executive resides in the person of the actual President, and passes from him to his successor. His Ministers, grouped around him, are the servants, not only of his office, but of his mind. The intelligence, which carries on the Government, has its main seat in him. The responsibility of failures is understood to fall on him; and it is round his head that success sheds its halo. The American Government is described truly as a Government composed of three members, of three powers distinct from one another. The English Government is likewise so described, not truly, but conventionally. For in the English Government there has gradually formed itself a fourth power, entering into and sharing the vitality of each of the other three, and charged with the business of holding them in harmony as they march.

This Fourth Power is the Ministry, or more properly the Cabinet. For the rest of the Ministry is subordinate and ancillary; and, though it largely shares in many departments the labors of the Cabinet, yet it has only a secondary and derivative share in the higher responsibilities. No account of the present British Constitution is worth having which does not take this Fourth Power largely and carefully into view. And yet it is not a distinct power, made up of elements unknown to the other three; any more than a sphere contains elements other than those referable to the three co-ordinates, which determine the position of every point in space. The Fourth Power is parasitical to the three others; and lives upon their life, without any separate existence. One portion of it forms a part, which may be termed an integral part, of the House of Lords, another of the House of Commons; and the two conjointly, nestling within the precinct of Royalty, form the inner Council of the Crown, assuming the whole of its responsibilities, and in consequence wielding, as a rule, its powers. The Cabinet is the threefold hinge that connects together for action the British Constitution of King or Queen, Lords and Commons. Upon it is concentrated the whole strain of the Government, and it constitutes from day to day the true centre of gravity for the working system of the State, although the ultimate superiority of force resides in the representative chamber.

There is no statute or legal usage of this country which requires that the Ministers of the Crown should hold seats in the one or the other House of Parliament. It is perhaps on this account that, while most of my countrymen would, as I suppose, declare it to be a becoming and convenient custom, yet comparatively few are aware how near the seat of life the observance lies, how closely it is connected with the equipoise and unity of the social forces. It is rarely departed from, even in an individual case; never, as far as my knowledge goes, on a wider scale. From accidental circumstances it happened that I was Secretary of State between December 1845 and July 1846, without a seat in the House of Commons. This (which did not pass wholly without challenge) is, I believe, by much the most notable instance for the last fifty years; and it is only within the last fifty years that our Constitutional system has completely settled down. Before the reform of Parliament it was always easy to find a place for a Minister excluded from his seat ; as Sir Robert Peel, for example, ejected from Oxford University, at once found refuge and repose at Tamworth. I desire to fix attention on the identification, in this country, of the Minister with the member of a House of Parliament.

It is, as to the House of Commons, especially, an inseparable and vital part of our system. The association of the Ministers with the Parliament, and through the House of ·Commons with the people, is the counterpart of their association as Ministers with the Crown and the prerogative. The decisions that they take are taken under the competing pressure of a bias this way and a bias that way, and strictly represent what is termed in mechanics the composition of forces. Upon them, thus placed, it devolves to provide that the House of Parliament shall loyally counsel and serve the Crown, and that the Crown shall act strictly in accordance with its obligations to the nation. I will not presume to say whether the adoption of the rule in America would, or would not lay the foundation of a great change in the Federal Constitution ; but I am quite sure that the abrogation of it in England would either alter the form of government, or bring about a crisis. That it conduces to the personal comfort of Ministers, I will not undertake to say. The various currents of political and social influences meet edgeways in their persons, much like the conflicting tides in St. George's Channel or the Straits of Dover ; for, while they are the ultimate regulators of the relations between the Crown on the one side, and the people through the Houses of Parliament on the other, they have no authority vested in them to coerce or censure either way. Their attitude toward the Houses must always be that of deference ;

their language that of respect, if not submission. Still more must their attitude and language toward the Sovereign be the same in principle, and yet more marked in form ; and this, though upon them lies the ultimate responsibility of deciding what shall be done in the Crown's name in every branch of administration, and every department of policy, coupled only with the alternative of ceasing to be Ministers, if what they may advisedly deem the requisite power of action be denied them.

In the ordinary administration of the government, the Sovereign personally is, so to speak, behind the scenes; performing, indeed, many personal acts by the Sign-manual, or otherwise, but, in each and all of them, covered by the counter-signature or advice of ministers, who stand between the august personage and the people. There is, accordingly, no more power, under the form of our Constitution, to assail the monarch in his personal capacity, or to assail through him, the line of succession to the Crown, than there is at chess to put the king in check. In truth, a good deal, though by no means the whole, of the philosophy of the British Constitution is represented in this central point of the wonderful game, against which the only reproach — the reproach of Lord Bacon — is that it is hardly a relaxation, but rather a serious tax upon the brain.

The Sovereign in England is the symbol of the nation's unity, and the apex of the social structure ; the maker (with advice) of the laws ; the supreme governor of the Church ; the fountain of justice ; the sole source of honor; the person to whom all military, all naval, all civil service is rendered. The Sovereign owns very large properties; receives and holds, in law, the entire revenue of the State ; appoints and dismisses Ministers ; makes treaties; pardons crime, or abates its punishment; wages war, or concludes peace; summons and dissolves the Parliament; exercises these vast powers for the most part without any specified restraint of law; and yet enjoys, in regard to these and every other function, an absolute immunity from consequences. There is no provision in the law of the United Empire, or in the machinery of the Constitution, for calling the sovereign to account; and only in one solitary and improbable, but perfectly defined, case — that of his submitting to the jurisdiction of the Pope — is he deprived by Statute of the Throne. Setting aside that peculiar exception, the offspring of a necessity still freshly felt when it was made, the Constitution might seem to be founded on the belief of a real infallibility in its head. Less, at any rate, cannot be said than this. Regal right has, since the Revolution of 1688, been expressly founded upon contract; and the breach of that contract destroys the title to the allegiance of the subject. But no provision other than the general rule of hereditary succession, is made to meet either this case, or any other form of political miscarriage or misdeed. It seems as though the Genius of the Nation would not stain its lips by so much as the mere utterance of such a word; (nor can we put this state of facts into language more justly than by saying that the Constitution would regard the default of the Monarch, with his heirs, as the chaos of the State, and would simply trust to the inherent energies of the several orders of society for its legal reconstruction.

The original authorship of the representative system is commonly accorded to the English race. More clear and indisputable is its title to the great political discovery of Constitutional

Kingship. And a very great discovery it is. Whether it is destined, in any future day, to minister in its integrity to the needs of the New World, it may be hard to say. In that important branch of its utility which is negative, it completely serves the purposes of the many strong and rising Colonies of Great Britain, and saves them all the perplexities and perils attendant upon successions to the headship of the Executive. It presents to them, as it does to us, the symbol of unity, and the object of all our political veneration, which we love to find rather in a person, than in an abstract entity, like the State.) But the Old World, at any rate, still is, and may long continue, to constitute the living centre of civilization, and to hold the primacy of the race; and of this great society the several members approximate, in a rapidly extending series, to the practice and idea of Constitutional Kingship. The chief States of Christendom, with only two exceptions, have, with more or less distinctness, adopted it. Many of them, both great and small, have thoroughly assimilated it to their system. The autocracy of Russia, and the Republic of France, each of them congenial to the present wants of the respective countries, may yet, hereafter, gravitate toward the principle, which elsewhere has developed so large an attractive power. Should the current, that has prevailed through the last half-century, maintain its direction and its strength, another fifty years may see all Europe adhering to the theory and practice of this beneficent institution, and peaceably sailing in the wake of England.

No doubt, if tried by an ideal standard, it is open to criticism. Aristotle and Plato, nay, Bacon, and perhaps Leibnitz, would have scouted it as a scientific abortion. Some men would draw disparaging comparisons between the mediæval and the modern King. In the person of the first was normally embodied the force paramount over all others in the country, and on him was laid a weight of responsibility and toil so tremendous, that his function seems always to border upon the superhuman; that his life commonly wore out before the natural term; and that an indescribable majesty, dignity, and interest surround him in his misfortunes, nay, almost in his degradation; as, for instance, amidst

> " The shrieks of death, through Berkeley's roof that ring,
> Shrieks of an agonizing King." [1]

For this concentration of power, toil, and liability, milder realities have now been substituted; and Ministerial responsibility comes between the Monarch and every public trial and necessity, like armor between the flesh and the spear that would seek to pierce it; only this is an armor itself also fleshy, at once living and impregnable. It may be said, by an adverse critic, that the Constitutional Monarch is only a depository of power, as an armory is a depository of arms; but that those who wield the arms, and those alone, constitute the true governing authority. And no doubt this is so far true, that the scheme aims at associating in the work of government with the head of the State the persons best adapted to meet the wants and wishes of the people, under the conditions that the several aspects of supreme power shall be severally allotted; dignity and visible authority shall lie wholly with the wearer of the crown, but labor mainly, and responsibility wholly, with its servants. From hence, without doubt, it follows that should differences arise,

---

1 Gray's " Bard."

it is the will of those in whose minds the work of government is elaborated, that in the last resort must prevail. From mere labor, power may be severed ; but not from labor joined with responsibility. This capital and vital consequence flows out of the principle that the political action of the Monarch shall everywhere be mediate and conditional upon the concurrence of confidential advisers. It is impossible to reconcile any, even the smallest, abatement of this doctrine, with the perfect, absolute immunity of the Sovereign from consequences. There can be in England no disloyalty more gross, as to its effects, than the superstition which affects to assign to the Sovereign a separate, and so far as separate, transcendental sphere of political action. Anonymous servility has, indeed, in these last days, hinted such a doctrine ;[1] but it is no more practicable to make it thrive in England, than to rear the jungles of Bengal on Salisbury Plain.

There is, indeed, one great and critical act, the responsibility for which falls momentarily or provisionally upon the Sovereign ; it is the dismissal of an existing Ministry, and the appointment of a new one. This act is usually performed with the aid drawn from authentic manifestations of public opinion, mostly such as are obtained through the votes or conduct of the House of Commons. Since the reign of George III there has been but one change of Ministry in which the Monarch acted without the support of these indications. It was when William IV, in 1834, dismissed the Government of Lord Melbourne, which was known to be supported, though after a lukewarm fashion, by a large majority of the existing House of Commons. But the

---

[1] *Quarterly Review*, April, 1878, Art. I.

royal responsibility was, according to the doctrine of our Constitution, completely taken over, *ex post facto*, by Sir Robert Peel, as the person who consented, on the call of the King, to take Lord Melbourne's office. Thus, though the act was rash, and hard to justify, the doctrine of personal immunity was in no way endangered. And here we may notice, that in theory an absolute personal immunity implies a correlative limitation of power, greater than is always found in practice. It can hardly be said that the King's initiative left to Sir R. Peel a freedom perfectly unimpaired. And, most certainly, it was a very real exercise of personal power. The power did not suffice for its end, which was to overset the Liberal predominance; but it very nearly sufficed. Unconditionally entitled to dismiss the Ministers, the Sovereign can, of course, choose his own opportunity. He may defy the Parliament, if he can count upon the people. William IV, in the year 1834, had neither Parliament nor people with him. His act was within the limits of the Constitution, for it was covered by the responsibility of the acceding Ministry. But it reduced the Liberal majority from a number considerably beyond three hundred to about thirty; and it constituted an exceptional but very real and large action on the politics of the country, by the direct will of the King. I speak of the immediate effects. Its eventual result may have been different, for it converted a large disjointed mass into a smaller but organized and sufficient force, which held the fortress of power for the six years 1835–41. On this view it may be said that, if the Royal intervention anticipated and averted decay from natural causes, then with all its immediate success, it defeated its own real aim.

But this power of dismissing a Ministry at will, large as it may be under given circumstances, is neither the safest nor the only power which, in the ordinary course of things, falls Constitutionally to the personal share of the wearer of the crown.' He is entitled, on all subjects coming before the Ministry, to knowledge and opportunities of discussion, unlimited save by the iron necessities of business. Though decisions must ultimately conform to the sense of those who are to be responsible for them, yet their business is to inform and persuade the Sovereign, not to overrule him. Were it possible for him, within the limits of human time and strength, to enter actively into all public transactions, he would be fully entitled to do so. What is actually submitted is supposed to be the most fruitful and important part, the cream of affairs. In the discussion of them, the Monarch has more than one advantage over his advisers. He is permanent, they are fugitive; he speaks from the vantage-ground of a station unapproachably higher; he takes a calm and leisurely survey, while they are worried with the preparatory stages, and their force is often impaired by the pressure of countless detail. He may be, therefore, a weighty factor in all deliberations of State. Every discovery of a blot, that the studies of the Sovereign in the domain of business enable him to make, strengthens his hands and enhances his authority. It is plain, then, that there is abundant scope for mental activity to be at work under the gorgeous robes of Royalty.)

This power spontaneously takes the form of influence; and the amount of it depends on a variety of circumstances; on talent, experience, tact, weight of character, steady, untiring industry, and habitual presence at the seat of government. In proportion as any of these might fail, the real and legitimate influence of the Monarch over the course of affairs would diminish; in proportion as they attain to fuller action, it would increase. It is a moral, not a coercive, influence. It operates through the will and reason of the Ministry, not over or against them. It would be an evil and a perilous day for the Monarchy, were any prospective possessor of the Crown to assume or claim for himself final, or preponderating, or even independent power, in any one department of the State. The ideas and practice of the time of George III, whose will in certain matters limited the action of the Ministers, cannot be revived, otherwise than by what would be, on their part, nothing less than a base compliance, a shameful subserviency, dangerous to the public weal, and in the highest degree disloyal to the dynasty. Because, in every free State, for every public act, some one must be responsible; and the question is, Who shall it be? The British Constitution answers: The Minister, and the Minister exclusively. That he may be responsible, all action must be fully shared by him. Sole action, for the Sovereign, would mean undefended, unprotected action; the armor of irresponsibility would not cover the whole body against sword or spear; a head would project beyond the awning, and would invite a sunstroke.

.. The reader, then, will clearly see that there is no distinction more vital to the practice of the British Constitution, or to a right judgment upon it, than the distinction between the Sovereign and the Crown. The Crown has large prerogatives, endless functions essential to the daily action, and even the life, of the State. To place them in the hands of persons who should be mere tools in a Royal will, would expose those powers to constant unsupported collision with the living forces of the nation, and to a certain and irremediable crash. They are therefore entrusted to men, who must be prepared to answer for the use they make of them. This ring of responsible Ministerial agency forms a fence around the person of the Sovereign, which has thus far proved impregnable to all assaults. The august personage, who from time to time may rest within it, and who may possess the art of turning to the best account the countless resources of the position, is no dumb and senseless idol; but, together with real and very large means of influence upon policy, enjoys the undivided reverence which a great people feels for its head; and is likewise the first and by far the weightiest among the forces, which greatly mould, by example and legitimate authority, the manners, nay the morals, of a powerful aristocracy and a wealthy and highly trained society. The social influence of a Sovereign, even if it stood alone, would be an enormous attribute. The English people are not believers in equality; they do not, with the famous Declaration of July 4, 1776, think it to be a self-evident truth that all men are born equal. They hold rather the reverse of that proposition. At any rate, in practice, they are what I may call determined inequalitarians; nay, in some cases, even without knowing it. Their natural tendency, from the very base of British society, and through all its strongly built gradations, is to look upward: they are not apt to "untune degree." The Sovereign is the highest height of the system, is, in that system, like Jupiter among the Romans gods, first without a second.

" Nec viget quicquam simile aut secundum. " [1]

---

[1] Hor. Od., I, xii, 18.

Not, like Mont Blanc, with rivals in his neighborhood; but like Ararat or Etna, towering alone and unapproachable. The step downward from the King to the second person in the realm is not like that from the second to the third: it is more even than a stride, for it traverses a gulf. It is the wisdom of the British Constitution to lodge the personality of its chief so high, that none shall under any circumstances be tempted to vie, no, nor dream of vieing, with it. The office, however, is not confused, though it is associated, with the person; and the elevation of official dignity in the Monarch of these realms has now for a testing period worked well, in conjunction with the limitation of merely personal power.

In the face of the country, the Sovereign and the Ministers are an absolute unity. The one may concede to the other; but the limit of concessions by the Sovereign is at the point where he becomes willing to try the experiment of changing his Government, and the limit of concessions by the Minister is at the point where they become unwilling to bear, what in all circumstances they must bear while they remain Ministers, the undivided responsibility of all that is done in the Crown's name. But it is not with the Sovereign only that the Ministry must be welded into identity. It has a relation to sustain to the House of Lords; which need not, however, be one of entire unity, for the House of Lords, though a great power in the State, and able to cause great embarrassment to an Administration, is not able by a vote to doom it to capital punishment. Only for fifteen years, out of the last fifty, has the Ministry of the day possessed the confidence of the House of Lords. On the confidence of the House of Commons it is immediately and vitally

dependent. This confidence it must always possess, either absolutely from identity of political color, or relatively and condi-
tionally. This last case arises when an accidental dislocation
of the majority in the Chamber has put the machine for the
moment out of gear, and the unsafe experiment of a sort of
provisional government, doomed on the one hand to be feeble,
or tempted on the other to be dishonest, is tried ; much as the
Roman Conclave has sometimes been satisfied with a provisional
Pope, deemed likely to live for the time necessary to reunite the
factions of the prevailing party.

I have said that the Cabinet is essentially the regulator of
the relations between King, Lords, and Commons; exercising
functionally the powers of the first, and incorporated, in the
persons of its members, with the second and the third. It is,
therefore, itself a great power. But let no one suppose it is the
greatest. In a balance nicely poised, a small weight may turn
the scale ; and the helm that directs the ship is not stronger than
the ship. It is a cardinal axiom of the modern British Constitution, that the House of Commons is the greatest of the powers
of the State. It might, by a base subserviency, fling itself at
the feet of a Monarch or a Minister ; it might, in a season of
exhaustion, allow the slow persistence of the Lords, ever eyeing
it as Lancelot was eyed by Modred, to invade its just province
by baffling its action at some time propitious for the purpose.
But no Constitution can anywhere keep either Sovereign, or
Assembly, or nation, true to its trust and to itself. All that can
be done has been done. The Commons are armed with ample
powers of self-defence. If they use their powers properly, they
can only be mastered by a recurrence to the people, and the way

in which the appeal can succeed is by the choice of another House of Commons more agreeable to the national temper. Thus the sole appeal from the verdict of the House is a rightful appeal to those from whom it received its commission.

This superiority in power among the great State forces was, in truth, established even before the House of Commons became what it now is, representative of the people throughout its entire area. In the early part of the century, a large part of its members virtually received their mandate from members of the Peerage, or from the Crown, or by the direct action of money on a mere handful of individuals, or, as in Scotland, for example, from constituencies whose limited numbers and upper-class sympathies usually shut out popular influences. A real supremacy belonged to the House as a whole ; but the forces of which it was compounded were not all derived from the people, and the aristocratic power had found out the secret of asserting itself within the walls of the popular chamber, in the dress and through the voices of its members. Many persons of gravity and weight saw great danger in a measure of change like the first Reform Act, which left it to the Lords to assert themselves, thereafter, by an external force, instead of through a share in the internal composition of a body so formidable. But the result proved that they were sufficiently to exercise, through the popular will and choice, the power which they had formerly put ·in action without its sanction, though within its proper precinct and with its title falsely inscribed.

The House of Commons is superior, and by far superior, in the force of its political attributes, to any other single power in the State. But it is watched ; it is criticized ; it is hemmed in and about by a multitude of other forces : the force, first of all, of the House of Lords, the force of opinion from day to day, particularly of the highly anti-popular opinion of the leisured men of the metropolis, who, seated close to the scene of action, wield an influence greatly in excess of their just claims; the force of the classes and professions; the just and useful force of the local authorities in their various orders and places. Never was the great problem more securely solved, which recognizes the necessity of a paramount power in the body politic to enable it to move, but requires for it a depository such that it shall be safe against invasion, and yet inhibited from aggression.

The old theories of a mixed government, and of the three powers, coming down from the age of Cicero, when set by the side of the living British Constitution, are cold, crude, and insufficient to a degree that makes them deceptive. Take them, for example, as represented, fairly enough, by Voltaire : the picture drawn by him is for us nothing but a puzzle : —

> " Aux murs de Vestminster on voit paraître ensemble
> Trois pouvoirs étonnés du nœud qui les rassemble,
> Les députés du peuple, les grandes, et le Roi,
> Divisés d' intérêt, réunis par la Loi." [1]

There is here lacking an amalgam, a reconciling power, what may be called a clearing-house of political forces, which shall draw into itself every thing, and shall balance and adjust every thing, and ascertaining the net result, let it pass on freely for the fulfilment of the purposes of the great social union. Like a stout buffer-spring, it receives all shocks, and within it their opposing elements neutralize one another. This is the function

---

[1] Henriade, I.

of the British Cabinet. It is perhaps the most curious formation in the political world of modern times, not for its dignity, but for its subtlety, its elasticity, and its many-sided diversity of power. It is the complement of the entire system; a system which appears to want nothing but a thorough loyalty in the persons composing its several parts, with a reasonable intelligence, to insure its bearing, without fatal damage, the wear and tear of ages yet to come.

It has taken more than a couple of centuries to bring the British Cabinet to its present accuracy and fulness of development; for the first rudiments of it may sufficiently be discerned in the reign of Charles I. Under Charles II it had fairly started from its embryo; and the name is found both in Clarendon and in the Diary of Pepys.[1] It was for a long time without a Ministerial head; the King was the head. While this arrangement subsisted, constitutional government could be but half established. Of the numerous titles of the Revolution of 1688 to respect, not the least remarkable is this, that the great families of the country, and great powers of the State, made no effort, as they might have done, in the hour of its weakness, to aggrandize themselves at the expense of the crown. Nevertheless, for various reasons, and among them because of the foreign origin, and absences from time to time, of several Sovereigns, the course of events tended to give force to the organs of Government actually on the spot, and thus to consolidate, and also to uplift, this as yet novel creation. So late, however, as the impeachment of Sir Robert Walpole, his friends thought it

---

[1] Vol. v, pp. 94, 95. Ed. London, 1877.

expedient to urge on his behalf, in the House of Lords, that he had never presumed to constitute himself a Prime-Minister. The breaking down of the great offices of State by throwing them into commission, and last among them of the Lord High Treasurership after the time of Harley, Earl of Oxford, tended, and may probably have been meant, to prevent or retard the formation of a recognized Chiefship in the Ministry; which even now we have not learned to designate by a true English word, though the use of the imported phrase "Premier" is at least as old as the poetry of Burns. Nor can anything be more curiously characteristic of the political genius of the people, than the present position of this most important official personage. Departmentally, he is no more than the first-named of five persons, by whom jointly the powers of the Lord Treasurership are taken to be exercised ; he is not their master, or, otherwise than by mere priority, their head : and he has no special function or prerogative under the formal constitution of the office. He has no official rank except that of Privy Councillor. Eight members of the Cabinet, including five Secretaries of State, and several other members of the Government, take official precedence of him. His rights and duties as head of the Administration are nowhere recorded. He is almost, if not altogether, unknown to the Statute Law.

Nor is the position of the body, over which he presides, less singular than his own. The Cabinet wields, with partial exceptions, the powers of the Privy Council, besides having a standing ground in relation to the personal will of the Sovereign, far beyond what the Privy Council ever held or claimed. Yet it has no connection with the Privy Council, except that every one, on first becoming a member of the Cabinet, is, if not belonging to it already, sworn a member of that body. There are other sections of the Privy Council, forming regular Committees for Education and for Trade. But the Cabinet has not even this degree of formal sanction, to sustain its existence. It lives and acts simply by understanding, without a single line of written law or constitution to determine its relations to the Monarch, or to the Parliament, or to the nation; or the relations of its members to one another, or to their head. It sits in the closest secrecy. There is no record of its proceedings, nor is there any one to hear them, except upon the very rare occasions when some important functionary, for the most part military or legal, is introduced, *pro hac vice*, for the purpose of giving to it necessary information.

Every one of its members acts in no less than three capacities: as administrator of a department of State; as member of a legislative chamber; and as a confidential adviser of the Crown. Two at least of them add to those three characters a fourth; for in each House of Parliament it is indispensable that one of the principal Ministers should be what is termed its Leader. This is an office the most indefinite of all, but not the least important. With very little of defined prerogative, the Leader suggests, and in a great degree fixes, the course of all principal matters of business, supervises and keeps in harmony the action of his colleagues, takes the initiative in matters of ceremonial procedure, and advises the House in every difficulty as it arises. The first of these, which would be of but secondary consequence where the assembly had time enough for all its duties, is of the utmost weight in our overcharged House of

Commons, where, notwithstanding all its energy and all its dili-
gence, for one thing of consequence that is done, five or ten are
despairingly postponed. The overweight, again, of the House
of Commons is apt, other things being equal, to bring its Leader
inconveniently near in power to a Prime-Minister who is a Peer.
He can play off the House of Commons against his chief; and
instances might be cited, though they are happily most rare,
when he has served him very ugly tricks.

The nicest of all the adjustments involved in the working of
the British Government is that which determines, without formally defining, the internal relations of the Cabinet. On the
one hand, while each Minister is an adviser of the Crown, the
Cabinet is a unity, and none of its members can advise as an
individual, without, or in opposition actual or presumed to, his
colleagues. On the other hand, the business of the State is a
hundred-fold too great in volume to allow of the actual passing
of the whole under the view of the collected Ministry. It is
therefore a prime office of discretion for each Minister to settle
what are the departmental acts in which he can presume the
concurrence of his colleagues, and in what more delicate, or
weighty, or peculiar cases, he must positively ascertain it. So
much for the relation of each Minister to the Cabinet; but here
we touch the point which involves another relation, perhaps the
least known of all, his relation to its head.

The head of the British Government is not a Grand Vizier.
He has no powers, properly so called, over his colleagues: on
the rare occasions, when a Cabinet determines its course by the
votes of its members, his vote counts only as one of theirs.
But they are appointed and dismissed by the Sovereign on his

advice. In a perfectly organized administration, such for example as was that of Sir Robert Peel in 1841–6, nothing of great
importance is matured, or would even be projected, in any
department without his personal cognizance; and any weighty
business would commonly go to him before being submitted to
the Cabinet. He reports to the Sovereign its proceedings, and
he also has many audiences of the august occupant of the
Throne. He is bound in these reports and audiences, not to
counterwork the Cabinet; not to divide it; not to undermine
the position of any of his colleagues in the Royal favor. If he
departs in any degree from strict adherence to these rules, and
uses his great opportunities to increase his own influence, or
pursue aims not shared by his colleagues, then, unless he is prepared to advise their dismissal, he not only departs from rule,
but commits an act of treachery and baseness. As the Cabinet
stands between the Sovereign and the Parliament, and is bound
to be loyal to both, so he stands between his colleagues and the
Sovereign, and is bound to be loyal to both.

As a rule, the resignation of the First Minister, as if removing
the bond of cohesion in the Cabinet, has the effect of dissolving
it. A conspicuous instance of this was furnished by Sir Robert
Peel in 1846; when the dissolution of the Administration, after it
had carried the repeal of the Corn Laws, was understood to be
due not so much to a united deliberation and decision as to his
initiative. The resignation of any other Minister only creates a
vacancy. In certain circumstances, the balance of forces may
be so delicate and susceptible that a single resignation will
break up the Government; but what is the rule in the one case
is the rare exception in the other. The Prime Minister has no

title to override any one of his colleagues in any one of the departments. So far as he governs them, unless it is done by trick, which is not to be supposed, he governs them by influence only. But upon the whole, nowhere in the wide world does so great a substance cast so small a shadow; nowhere is there a man who has so much power, with so little to show for it in the way of formal title or prerogative.

The slight record that has here been traced may convey but a faint idea of an unique creation. And, slight as it is, I believe it tells more than, except in the school of British practice, is elsewhere to be learned of a machine so subtly balanced, that it seems as though it were moved by something not less delicate and slight than the mainspring of a watch. It has not been the offspring of the thought of man. The Cabinet, and all the present relations of the Constitutional powers in this country, have grown into their present dimensions, and settled into their present places, not as the fruit of a philosophy, not in the effort to give effect to an abstract principle; but by the silent action of forces, invisible and insensible, the structure has come up into the view of all the world. It is, perhaps, the most conspicuous object on the wide political horizon; but it has thus risen, without noise, like the temple of Jerusalem.

> " No workman steel, no ponderous hammers rung;
> Like some tall palm the stately fabric sprung." [1]

When men repeat the proverb which teaches us that "marriages are made in heaven," what they mean is that, in the most

---

[1] Heber's "Palestine." The word "stately" was in later editions altered by the author to "noiseless."

fundamental of all social operations, the building up of the family, the issues involved in the nuptial contract, lie beyond the best exercise of human thought, and the unseen forces of providential government make good the defect in our imperfect capacity. Even so would it seem to have been in that curious marriage of competing influences and powers, which brings about the composite harmony of the British Constitution. More, it must be admitted, than any other, it leaves open doors which lead into blind alleys; for it presumes, more boldly than any other, the good sense and good faith of those who work it. If, unhappily, these personages meet together, on the great arena of a nation's fortunes, as jockeys meet upon a racecourse, each to urge to the uttermost, as against the others, the power of the animal he rides; or as counsel in a court, each to procure the victory of his client, without respect to any other interest or right: then this boasted Constitution of ours is neither more nor less than a heap of absurdities. The undoubted competency of each reaches even to the paralysis or destruction of the rest. The House of Commons is entitled to refuse every shilling of the supplies. That House, and also the House of Lords, is entitled to refuse its assent to every bill presented to it. The Crown is entitled to make a thousand Peers to-day and as many to-morrow: it may dissolve all and every Parliament before it proceeds to business; may pardon the most atrocious crimes; may declare war against all the world; may conclude treaties involving unlimited responsibilities, and even vast expenditure, without the consent, nay, without the knowledge, of Parliament, and this not merely in support or in development, but in reversal, of policy already known to and sanctioned by the nation.

But the assumption is that the depositaries of power will all respect one another; will evince a consciousness that they are working in a common interest for a common end; that they will be possessed, together with not less than an average intelligence, not less than an average sense of equity and of the public interest and rights. When these reasonable expectations fail, then, it must be admitted, the British Constitution will be in danger.

Apart from such contingencies, the offspring only of folly or of crime, this Constitution is peculiarly liable to subtle change. Not only in the long run, as man changes between youth and age, but also, like the human body, with a quotidian life, a periodical recurrence of ebbing and flowing tides. Its old particles daily run to waste, and give place to new. What is hoped among us is, that which has usually been found, that evils will become palpable before they have grown to be intolerable.

There cannot, for example, be much doubt among careful observers that the great conservator of liberty in all former times, namely, the confinement of the power of the purse to the popular chamber, has been lamentably weakened in its efficiency of late years; weakened in the House of Commons, and weakened by the House of Commons. It might indeed be contended that the House of Commons of the present epoch does far more to increase the aggregate of public charge than to reduce it. It might even be a question whether the public would take benefit if the House were either intrusted annually with a great part of the initiative, so as to be really responsible to the people for the spending of their money; or else were excluded from part at least of its direct action upon expenditure, intrusting to the executive the application of given sums which that executive should have no legal power to exceed.

Meantime, we of this island are not great political philosophers; and we contend with an earnest, but disproportioned, vehemence about changes which are palpable, such as the extension of the suffrage, or the redistribution of Parliamentary seats, neglecting wholly other processes of change which work beneath the surface, and in the dark, but which are even more fertile of great organic results. The modern English character reflects the English Constitution in this, that it abounds in paradox; that it possesses every strength; but holds it tainted with every weakness; that it seems alternately both to rise above and to fall below the standard of average humanity; that there is no allegation of praise or blame which, in some one of the aspects of its many-sided formation, it does not deserve; that only in the midst of much default, and much transgression, the people of this United Kingdom either have heretofore established, or will hereafter establish, their title to be reckoned among the children of men, for the eldest born of an imperial race.

In this imperfect survey, I have carefully avoided all reference to the politics of the day and to particular topics, recently opened, which may have undergone a great development even before these lines appear in print on the other side of the Atlantic. Such reference would, without any countervailing advantage, have lowered the strain of these remarks, and would have complicated with painful considerations a statement essentially impartial and general in its scope.

For the yet weightier reason of incompetency, I have avoided the topics of chief present interest in America, including that proposal to tamper with the true monetary creed which (as we should say) the Tempter lately presented to the Nation in the Silver Bill. But I will not close this paper without recording my conviction that the great acts, and the great forbearances, which immediately followed the close of the Civil War form a group which will ever be a noble object, in his political retro-spect, to the impartial historian; and that, proceeding as they did from the free choice and conviction of the people, and founded as they were on the very principles of which the multi-tude is supposed to be least tolerant, they have, in doing honor to the United States, also rendered a splendid service to the general cause of popular government throughout the world.[1]

---

[1] [In reply to the intended work of Mr. Adams on the Constitution of the United States, Mr. Livingstone, under the title of a Colonist of New Jersey, published an Examination of the British Constitution, and compared it unfavorably as it had been exhibited by Adams, and by Delolme, with the institutions of his own country. In this work, of which I have a French translation (London and Paris, 1789), there is not the smallest inkling of the action of our political mechanism, such as I have endeavored to describe it. On this subject I need hardly refer the reader to the valu-able work of Mr. Bagehot, entitled, "The English Constitution," or to the Constitu-tional History of Sir T. Erskine May. — W. E. G., December, 1878.

www.ingramcontent.com/pod-product-compliance
Lightning Source LLC
Chambersburg PA
CBHW031351290326
41932CB00044B/881